Negotiating with ETA

BOOKS IN THE BASQUE SERIES

A Book of the Basques
  by Rodney Gallop
In A Hundred Graves:
A Basque Portrait
  by Robert Laxalt
Basque Nationalism
  by Stanley G. Payne
Amerikanuak:
Basques in the New World
  *by William A. Douglass
  and Jon Bilbao*
Beltran: Basque Sheepman of
the American West
  *by Beltran Paris, as told to
  William A. Douglass*
The Basques: The Franco Years
and Beyond
  by Robert P. Clark
The Witches' Advocate:
Basque Witchcraft and the
Spanish Inquisition (1609–1614)
  by Gustav Henningsen
Navarra: The Durable Kingdom
  by Rachel Bard
The Guernica Generation:
Basque Refugee Children of the
Spanish Civil War
  by Dorothy Legarreta
Basque Sheepherders of the
American West
  *Photographs by Richard H. Lane
  Text by William A. Douglass*

A Cup of Tea in Pamplona
  by Robert Laxalt
Sweet Promised Land
  by Robert Laxalt
Traditional Basque Cooking
History and Preparation
  by José María Busca Isusi
Basque Violence:
Metaphor and Sacrament
  by Joseba Zulaika
Basque-English Dictionary
  by Gorka Aulestia
The Basque Hotel
  by Robert Laxalt
Vizcaya on the Eve of Carlism:
Politics and Society, 1800–1833
  by Renato Barahona
Contemporary Basque Fiction:
An Anthology
  by Jesús María Lasagabaster
A Time We Knew:
Images of Yesterday in the
Basque Homeland
  *Photographs by
  William Albert Allard
  Text by Robert Laxalt*
English-Basque Dictionary
  *by Gorka Aulestia and
  Linda White*
Negotiating with ETA:
Obstacles to Peace in the
Basque Country, 1975–1988
  by Robert P. Clark

The Basque Series

ROBERT P. CLARK

Negotiating with

ETA

Obstacles to Peace
in the Basque Country,
1975–1988

UNIVERSITY OF NEVADA PRESS
Reno and Las Vegas

Basque Series Editor: William A. Douglass

The paper used in this book meets the requirements of American National Standard for Information Sciences—Permanence of Paper for Printed Library Materials, ANSI Z39.48-1984. Binding materials were chosen for strength and durability.

Library of Congress Cataloging-in-Publication Data

Clark, Robert P.
Negotiating with ETA : obstacles to peace in the Basque country, 1975–1988 / Robert P. Clark.
p.   cm. — (The Basque series)
ISBN 0-87417-162-8 (alk. paper)
1. País Vasco (Spain)—Politics and government—20th century.   2. País Vasco (Spain)—History—Autonomy and independence movements.
3. ETA (Organization)   4. Terrorism—Spain—País Vasco—History—20th century.   5. Nationalism—Spain—País Vasco—History—20th century.
6. Negotiation.   I. Title.   II. Series.
DP302.B53C56   1990
946'.6—dc20   90-33577
                                                                        CIP

University of Nevada Press, Reno, Nevada 89557 USA
Copyright © University of Nevada Press 1990. All Rights Reserved
Designed by Kaelin Chappell
Printed in the United States of America

9   8   7   6   5   4   3   2   1

DEDICATION

Since 1968, hundreds of men and women have died violently in
Euskadi. Some were combatants on one side or the other of ETA's
armed struggle for Basque independence; others were simply bystanders caught in the random tragedies that such violence pro-
duces. This book is dedicated to the memory of all of these people.
It was written in hopes that it may help in some small way to bring
this bloodshed to an end.

CONTENTS

Acknowledgments   xi

INTRODUCTION
Insurgency and Negotiations   I

CHAPTER ONE
The Interested Parties and Factions   7

CHAPTER TWO
Spanish Antiterrorist Policy: 1978–1988   35

CHAPTER THREE
Early Attempts to Negotiate with ETA: 1975–1980   73

CHAPTER FOUR
"Social Reintegration" and the End of ETA (p-m):
1981–1983   93

CHAPTER FIVE
New Actors, New Initiatives, New Failures:
1982–1983   117

CHAPTER SIX
New Negotiation Initiatives and a Second Attempt
at "Social Reintegration": 1984–1986   139

CHAPTER SEVEN
The "Algerian Connection," Phase One: 1986–1987   165

CHAPTER EIGHT
The "Algerian Connection," Phase Two: 1987–1988   187

CHAPTER NINE
Obstacles to Peace   223

Notes   241
Glossary   261
Index   265

ACKNOWLEDGMENTS

It would be impossible to name here all the people who helped me in the preparation of this book. Some have asked to remain anonymous; others would no doubt dispute much of what I have included here. I want to express my great indebtedness to all of them, however, and especially to my wife and to the members of her family in Euskadi who have been of invaluable assistance in this project, as well as my two earlier books on Basque politics. I want them all to know that in the quiet self-sacrifice of their daily lives, they have been an inspiration to me. Without them and the example they have set, this book would never have been written.

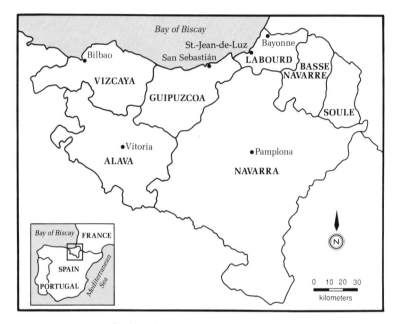

Euskadi: The seven Basque provinces.

So we, "Children of our Universal Mother,"
touch hands and go our ways in the very midst
of the horror of this war of brothers.[1]

ERSKINE CHILDERS

Insurgency and Negotiations

MOST violent insurgencies seem to end in one of two ways. One way is for the government in power to combine a vigorous policy of repression of the rebels with a judicious program of reforms, thus isolating the insurgents from their base of popular support and eventually defeating them militarily and politically. The specific outcome may be a formal settlement in which the insurgents give up the struggle (as in the Biafran rebellion), a gradual fading away of the insurgency without a formal declaration of its conclusion (as in the armed struggle of the Quebec Liberation Front), or a government-declared amnesty followed by the rebels' return to civil politics (as in Venezuela in the late 1960s). The second way is for the government's armed forces and/or police to lose either their taste for combat or their confidence in the regime, and for the government itself to lose its legitimacy with the people. The ensuing insurgent victory either sweeps away the incumbent regime (as Castro did in Cuba in 1959), or results in the separation of the insurgents from the core state (as Algeria broke away from France in the 1960s). The history of contemporary armed insurgencies suggests, then, that very few of them end as the result of a negotiated general truce or cease-fire. In fact, in the European setting, there is not a single case of an armed insurgency having been ended through negotiations since World War II.

Writers on insurgency and counterinsurgency have little to say about negotiations leading to an end to armed struggle, not only because there have been so few successful cases in recent history, but also because they believe that negotiations with insurgents are a mistake. They argue, for example, that negotiations give the insurgents respectability approximately equal to that of the government, or legitimacy by admitting that they have real grievances that are negotiable. In addition, they assert, the demands of insurgents are usually expressed in extreme and non-negotiable rhetoric, so negotiations can never have a positive or productive outcome. Finally, if cease-fire negotiations *are* successful and result in a temporary cessation of hostilities, the consequence is simply giving the insurgents time to regroup and gather strength for a new round of violence later.

This book proceeds from a contrary assumption: that there are some benefits to be gained from a negotiated settlement and some reasons why negotiations with insurgents might be a good idea. Admittedly, some insurgents might be stoutly against yielding to an illegitimate government and some insurgent demands might be couched in intransigent terms; but other insurgents and their demands may be much more flexible, and without entering into negotiations the government can never know which is which. Moreover, even though a truce is just a temporary lull in the fighting, it will still help to reduce the level of emotion and anger so common in insurgent situations, so that other steps may be taken to terminate the struggle once and for all and bring the insurgents back into civil society. A successfully negotiated truce that lasts helps build mutual trust and confidence, qualities usually in short supply in these situations. Successful negotiations strengthen the moderates on both sides of the conflict, thereby moving the system toward the conclusion of hostilities. And, after all, if the rebels are so strongly supported by their host population that the government cannot suppress them or win over the bystanders, as is the case with the Basques and ETA, then negotiations become the only realistic way out of violence.[2] In other words, negotiation may be the best solution to insurgency, not because it is such a good option, but simply because all the others are so bad.

From November 1975 to mid-1988 (the point at which this book concludes), there were between twenty and thirty serious attempts to negotiate an end to insurgent violence in the Basque provinces of Spain. The great majority of these initiatives were frustrated by a series of unfortunate—and often tragic—events that prevented the parties from even *reaching* the stage of negotiation, much less engaging in serious bargaining and compromise. These attempts have been stymied in their preliminary stages, or at best have dealt only with relatively superficial questions having to do with the fate of single individuals, not with the insurgent organization itself and its aims. What can we learn from these failures? I believe that by studying the specific case of ETA we can discover patterns in the failures, and that these patterns will help us understand better why it is so difficult to negotiate an end to armed struggles.

What exactly do we mean by "negotiations"? The events described and analyzed in this book consist of face-to-face meetings and discussions between representatives of ETA and other persons—either intermediaries or representatives of other interested parties—whose purpose was to arrive at agreements that would cause the organization to end its violent attacks or to alter its behavior in some other way. Negotiations with ETA can be classified according to four different kinds of objectives. Two of these will not be addressed in this book, except incidentally. I exclude, first of all, negotiations that were part of routine (for an insurgency) transactions, such as the payment of the "revolutionary tax" or the granting of amnesty to an individual ETA member. I also exclude negotiations connected with specific hostage situations, usually involving the payment of ransom. This book concentrates, instead, on two much more difficult kinds of negotiations: those having to do with the cessation of violence, and other issues related to law and order (e.g., general amnesty and pardon questions, human rights violations, and so forth); and "political negotiations" involving fundamental objectives of the insurgent group (e.g., the Basques' right of self-determination). While there have been numerous examples of successful negotiations of the first two types, and even a few cases where the third type of negotiation has concluded successfully, we unfortunately have no examples of successful political negotiations; and so, as of late 1989, the killing continues in the Basque Country as it has since 1968.

Some Personal Observations

By coincidence, I completed the first draft of this book on July 31, 1989, thirty years to the day after the founding of ETA. These thirty years have been filled with killings and woundings, kidnappings and ransom payments, extortion and robberies; but they have also seen torture, unjust imprisonment, human rights abuses, police surveillance and harrassment, "dirty wars," and exiles and armed forces occupation. They have been thirty years of widows, children without fathers, and mothers who have lost their sons. For nearly half that time, since late 1975, there have been numerous attempts to end all this by negotiating a settlement. At times it appeared as if the parties to the conflict had come close to an accord, only to see their hopes crushed by willful sabotage, bad luck, misunderstandings that could have been avoided, missed communications, or just plain stupidity.

When I began the research for this book in 1986, I believed (probably naively) that I might discover some secret that—once uncovered—would facilitate a resolution of this conflict. After more than fifteen years of close contact with contemporary Basque politics, through my writing and research as well as through family ties and close friendships, I wanted above all for this study to be of some value to those about whom it is written. There are some significant findings in chapter 9 that suggest some ways in which the negotiation process might be improved, but I confess they do not go much beyond what common sense and a careful reading of the historical record would yield.

Contrary to what some might believe, there is no great mystery here. ETA's insurgency continues because, for nearly everyone concerned, *the cessation of violence is not the most important thing on their political agenda.* Of course, nearly everyone wants an end to the violence; it's just that other objectives are paramount. Everyone wants the insurgency to end; they just want it to end on their terms. As long as this condition exists, neither this book nor any other will have much to offer to the parties in conflict.

Despite this pessimistic finding, I personally have not given up hope. I still believe that members of ETA will always be regarded as heroes by a large proportion of the Basque people, regardless of the outcome of their struggle. I still believe that Felipe González could go down in history as one of Spain's great leaders if he could only summon the political will necessary to strike a bargain with ETA. I still believe that a number of Basque leaders—Carlos Garai-koetxea, José Antonio Ardanza, Juan María Bandrés, and Joseba Azkarraga, to name only a few—have behaved honorably and done all that anyone could reasonably ask of them to bring the violence to a close. And I still believe that those who have given their lives in the cause of peace—Pertur, Portell, Argala, Brouard, and others—have not died in vain. History will vindicate their sacrifice if there is any justice in this world.

An earlier book of mine about ETA was criticized by some who alleged that in it I supported or advocated terrorism. The gap between that charge and reality was so great that I believed it did not deserve even acknowledgment, much less denial or rebuttal. However, I could not then, and I do not now, condemn the members of ETA for feeling themselves compelled to follow the path of armed struggle, even though I could not approve of some of their acts of indiscriminate violence. I know that in their hearts they want only what we all want, what the great Basque composer Iparaguirre wrote more than a century ago: "Bakean bizi dadin Euskaldunen yendrea"—"May the Basque people live in peace."

CHAPTER ONE

The Interested Parties
and Factions

ANALYSTS of insurgency usually begin with the assumption that insurgents employ armed struggle to secure political objectives that cannot be achieved in any other way.[1] Insurgents are seen as relatively weak partisans in an intensely felt conflict against an insurmountably stronger opponent. For various reasons, the insurgents have ruled out both conventional political tactics as well as straightforward military confrontation. Analysts further presuppose that insurgents seek three objectives: to be noticed (i.e., publicity); to be understood (i.e., for the people to see their struggle as having political aims, or, in other words, that they are not "common criminals"); and to alter the existing political situation by transforming both elite and mass attitudes. This last objective can be achieved in one of two ways. By means of "the propaganda of the deed," some insurgents have tried to mobilize the masses through example and demonstration—to overcome the conservatism or fatalism of the masses by showing them that audacious strikes against the state can be mounted successfully. Other insurgent groups have emphasized the use of violence to provoke the state into vigorous counterviolence, thereby angering the masses and mobilizing them through police repression. All of this presumes that the insurgents have as their ultimate goal some sort of revolutionary transformation of the existing situation, accompanied by large-scale violence that results in either the overthrow of the state or its surrender to the insurgents.

In ETA's early days, that is before 1974, the organization's ideology could be described by this so-called revolutionary war thesis.[2] During the mid-1970s, however, there began to emerge within ETA factions that favored a negotiated settlement that would bring about a cessation of all violence, free all ETA prisoners, leave the organization intact, and achieve a number of important intermediate goals that would lead eventually to full Basque independence. Once these objectives had been achieved, they believed, the struggle could be shifted to the parliamentary arena where mass organizations, including parties and unions, could undertake electoral and other popular strategies to achieve the profound revolutionary transformation that ETA activists sought. To understand how this transformation came about and to set the stage for the rest of the book, we need to review briefly the important stages in the early history of ETA.

ETA (Euzkadi ta Askatasuna, or Basque Homeland and Freedom) was founded on the saint's day of the patron of the Basque Country, St. Ignatius of Loyola: July 31, 1959.[3] The organization grew out of the experiences of a small group of university students in Bilbao who had begun in 1952 the arduous process of consciousness raising that must precede all revolutionary undertakings. During the mid-1950s, the more conservative Basque Nationalist Party (Partido Nacionalista Vasco, or PNV) had tried to absorb the students into the party's youth wing, but they proved too much to digest and ETA was the result.

ETA's leaders spent the organization's first decade in debates aimed at refining a coherent ideology which defined their objectives, as well as a strategy that would achieve these goals. By 1968, after much internal conflict and not a few expulsions (or resignations, depending on one's perspective), the phase of ideological debate had concluded. ETA's chosen strategy for the next few years would be that of *lucha armada* (armed struggle) and *guerra revolucionaria* (revolutionary war); and the specific tactical imperative of this strategy was known as the action-repression spiral theory.

The fundamental principle of the spiral theory was that ETA

could control the pace and the dynamic of the struggle against the Francoist state by intervening in popular causes, such as labor disturbances and, by means of carefully selected violent attacks, provoke the Spanish government into repressive acts that would land indiscriminately on ETA and non-ETA Basques alike. With each attack and repressive response, the violence would spiral upward until finally the masses would rise spontaneously in an army of national liberation and, in the conflagration of a renewed civil war, the Basques would seize the opportunity to secede from Spain. At that point, the transition to a socialist state would be a matter for Basques, and only Basques, to decide.

After a few minor experiments with the spiral theory, ETA's leaders put the theory to its first practical test in the summer of 1968. Following the death of a popular ETA activist named Xabi Etxebarrieta at a police roadblock, the organization decided to seek reprisals by assassinating their first victim, a hated police inspector named Melitón Manzanas, in August. The response from the Franco government was ferocious. The entire Basque Country lived under a state of siege for many months, and thousands of Basques were jailed, tortured, exiled, and eventually sentenced to years in prison. The period ended with the famed Burgos trial of December 1970, which resulted in long prison sentences for some fifteen ETA leaders.

The organization was nearly destroyed by the repression of the period between 1968 and 1972. Had it not been for the infusion of new members from a disaffected youth wing of the PNV, and the charismatic leadership of a young man named Eustakio Mendizabal, the organization might never have survived the period. But, of course, it did survive and went on to carry out its most audacious attack in December 1973: the assassination of the Spanish premier Luís Carrero Blanco.

More reflective ETA leaders quickly realized, however, that the action-repression spiral theory was simply not a feasible strategy. For one thing, the Francoist police state had shown itself capable of meting out much more punishment than the organization could absorb, and the Basque people had not risen up to launch the war of national liberation as the Algerians or the Vietnamese had done in the 1960s. It also became clear that the Basques could not count on any general uprising against Franco in the rest of Spain. The rapid industrialization of the country and the modernization of its social structure had drained away much of the revolutionary zeal that had contributed to the civil war in the 1930s; and it was obvious that most groups—even those in the underground—were simply biding their time until the generalissimo passed away and some sort of constitutional monarchy could be put in his place.

Against this background, there occurred in the mid-1970s a split between two factions of ETA whose leaders held conflicting views of the role of violence in the Basque struggle. Through the early 1970s, ETA had been divided into several "fronts," including a "military wing" responsible for "direct action" (armed attacks) and a "political wing" charged with so-called popular activities, such as working with labor organizations. Relations between these two wings were always somewhat fragile. The political front criticized the military front for engaging in unnecessarily risky and provocative adventures; and the military wing complained that the political wing members did not accept their fair share of the risks and hazards of the struggle. In 1974, following a dramatic cafe bombing in downtown Madrid (alleged to have been carried out by ETA, but never proved), the two factions decided to go their separate ways. The military faction became ETA-militar, or ETA (m); the political faction became known as ETA-político-militar, or ETA (p-m). Their members were known, respectively, as *milis* and *poli-milis*.

Although it was not immediately apparent that the milis and the poli-milis were as sharply divided as they were over the negotiation issue, in fact ETA's history for the next fifteen years was marked by the organization's internal struggles over this question. Even though several pro-negotiation factions arose within the organization, they were always opposed—sometimes violently— by hard-line factions that were steadfastly against any negotiated settlement. The dynamic of ETA's internal politics was frequently dominated by the conflict between these opposing groups. Nevertheless, each faction in its own way eventually came to favor some kind of negotiated end to the violence.

The pro-negotiation faction within ETA (p-m) was led by Eduardo Moreno Bergareche "Pertur," who headed the poli-milis until his disappearance in July 1976. Eventually, the anti-negotiation faction of (p-m) split away to rejoin the milis. Those who remained in (p-m) joined with other Basques not from ETA to form

several Basque socialist political parties and coalitions that contested elections in Spain after 1977. By 1982 ETA (p-m) was able
to negotiate an end to its part of the struggle in return for selective amnesty of its members still in prison or in exile. While a
few die-hard poli-milis remain in exile in Cuba, by and large the
organization ceased to exist in the early 1980s.

The military faction of ETA also underwent a certain transformation on the negotiation issue. Between 1974 and 1978 ETA (m)
moved toward what Ibarra calls the "two-stage" theory of struggle.[4] During the first stage, violent attacks would still be used
to push the Spanish government toward negotiating the terms of
what came to be called, after February 1978, the KAS Alternative.
Although the KAS Alternative was less than what ETA (m) really
wanted, its leaders figured that it was sufficient to provide a plat-
form from which to launch the second phase of the struggle, and
in any event it was probably all that could realistically be expected
at that stage of the conflict. Once the KAS Alternative had been
achieved, the second phase could concentrate on the organization's
real long-term objective: independence. Whether or not this phase
turned violent would depend on the degree of resistance in Madrid;
but the milis did not automatically assume that they would have
to resume armed struggle. Even these major concessions were not
enough, however, and in the late 1980s ETA (m) would make further compromises in their original ideological principles regarding
negotiations and violence.

The Factions and Parties Involved

Perhaps the worst mistake we can make in trying to understand
the obstacles to peace in the Basque Country is assuming that there
are only two contending parties—ETA and the Spanish state—and
that their differences of opinion crystallize neatly on opposite sides
of a clear dividing line. The reality is quite different. There are at
least *two dozen* clearly identifiable clusters of interested parties
that have a stake in the outcome of this struggle; and if we were
to subdivide them more precisely, the number might easily reach
thirty or forty (see table 1.1 and the glossary following the notes
section at the back of this book). To complicate matters further,

Table 1.1 Interested Groups and Their Objectives.

Name and Description of Group	Objectives and Interests
ETA Organizations	
ETA (militar)	KAS Alternative; eventual cease-fire, with group left intact
ETA (político-militar) (dissolved in 1982)	Independent, socialist Euskadi; eventual parliamentary strategy via parties, other groups
ETA leadership (Executive Committee) (in France)	Pursue, secure organization's goals; achieve and extend personal power; avoid punishment
KAS (Patriotic Socialist Coordinating Council)	Coordinate ETA strategy with that of parties, unions, and other groups
Exiles and deportees (in France, Algeria, Cuba, etc.)	Return home without reprisals
Rank-and-file members (in Spain, France)	Loyalty to organization and its goals; avoid capture, punishment
Prisoners (in Spain, France)	Amnesty or pardon without conditions or reprisals
Families of ETA members, prisoners, or deportees	Return home or freedom of family member
Other Basque Organizations	
Basque government: president, advisors; department of interior, autonomous police	Secure and preserve principal role of autonomous government in negotiations, law enforcement
Basque parliament	Secure and preserve principal role in defining, implementing political features of eventual settlement
Basque political parties: PNV, EA, EE	Use negotiations to press for more autonomy; preserve key role for Basque parties
Basque political parties: HB	KAS Alternative; legitimize institutions
Basque media (print): *Egin, Punto y Hora, Deia, El Diario Vasco, El Correo Español*	Report news; transmit messages to, from ETA; defend partisan point of view; survey, report Basque public opinion on negotiations
Basque media (electronic)	Radio has little role; television (ETB) is government owned, operated, and reflects government interests
Independent "free-lance" negotiators (e.g., Juan Félix Eriz)	Serve as intermediary, especially in hostage situations and ransom payments

Name and Description of Group	Objectives and Interests
Gestoras Pro-Amnistía	Committees formed to pressure for amnesty, protection of human rights
Catholic church leaders, bishops of leading diocese	Urge conciliation, end to violence, negotiated settlement
Autonomous Community of Navarra	Separate autonomous community, with its own institutions, parties, and media. Paramount objective: to prevent Navarra from being forced to integrate with Basque A.C. (Basque Autonomous Community) as part of deal with ETA

Spanish Organizations

King Juan Carlos	Bring about end to violence without jeopardizing Spanish democracy; grant collective pardons
Spanish government: president and advisors; ministries of justice (courts, prisons), interior (police, Civil Guard), defense (armed forces), foreign relations (matters involving ETA and foreign countries)	Bring about end to violence without giving in to any of ETA's "political" demands; protect institutional (i.e., ministerial) interests; preserve principal role in negotiations; protect individual police, civil guards, military from attack; preserve national unity
Spanish parliament	Preserve role in monitoring actions of government in negotiations; approve antiterrorist legislation
Spanish courts	Adjudication of individual cases involving criminal charges and punishment, amnesty, human rights violations, etc.
Spanish political parties (most of these have branches in the Basque Country as well): PSOE, UCD (disappeared after 1982), PP (formerly AP, CP), CDS, PCE, IU	All parties oppose negotiating anything that involves "political" concessions; conservative parties advocate hard-line antiterrorist policies
Spanish media (print): *El País, Diario 16, Tiempo, Cambio 16*, others	Interested principally in news reporting and defending partisan points of view; more sensationalist media used to leak government information; survey,

Table 1.1 Continued

Name and Description of Group	Objectives and Interests
	report Spanish public opinion on negotiations
Spanish media (electronic)	Radio plays little role; television is state owned, controlled
Other Groups, Principally International	
Other governments: France (and Belgium to much lesser degree)	Prevent ETA insurgency from spilling over into France; after 1984, increasingly hard-line against ETA
Other governments: Algeria	Play major role as intermediary, venue for negotiations
Other governments: Togo, Gabon, São Tomé, Cuba, Panama, Venezuela, Ecuador, Dominican Republic	Receive ETA deportees from France
International human rights organizations: Amnesty International	Monitor status of human rights in Spain, especially regarding torture, other prison abuses; report on these issues; pressure Spanish government to make reforms
International press: *New York Times*, *Le Monde*	Report news of international interest
International law enforcement and intelligence agencies: Interpol, Trevi Group	Pursuit, capture of terrorists; prevention of acts of terrorism
Members of counterinsurgent organizations: BVE, GAL, etc.	Carry out violent attacks against Basques; avoid capture and punishment
Scholars and other more or less independent researchers (Basque, Spanish, and international)	Preserve access to important information sources; publish studies about ETA

each of these groups has important interests at stake that extend beyond the relatively clear-cut issue of Basque self-determination. These interests are at times ideological and at other times personal, political, or even bureaucratic. Finally, while some groups are centrally concerned with this problem virtually all the time (e.g., ETA itself, or the families of ETA prisoners), for many others (e.g., the

Spanish Ministry of Justice or King Juan Carlos) the question of in-surgency is only one of many important problems that rise or fall in intensity depending on the circumstances of the moment. Despite these ambiguities, we shall attempt below to sketch out briefly the universe of interested parties, with some attention to the nature of each important group and of their principal objectives.

EUZKADI TA ASKATASUNA[5] The original ETA, founded in 1959, no longer exists, having split into smaller groups some half dozen times since the 1960s. Some of these schisms have resulted from clashes between members favoring a "cultural" struggle based on ethnicity and language and those favoring a "class" struggle based on Marxist ideology. Another source of division involved the relative merits of continuing armed struggle versus organizing for competition in the electoral arena. To some degree, these conflicts have persisted into the 1980s.

The total number of people killed by ETA since 1968 is be-tween 550 and 600, or about three-fourths of all people killed by terrorist acts in Spain. My own estimate is that through the end of 1988, 568 people lost their lives through ETA attacks. These casualties were inflicted in six fairly clearly defined phases: 1959–1967, a formative period free from killings; 1968–1973, a period of tentative attacks, during which killings never exceeded 3 per year; 1974–1977, a period of cautious expansion, when killings ranged between 9 and 17 annually; 1978–1980, ETA's most intense phase, when killings soared to between 67 and 88 each year; 1981–1987, marked by a reduction in operations, when killings ranged between 30 and 52; and finally a period beginning in 1988, when killings declined to the lowest levels since the mid-1970s.

Since 1974, the principal element of ETA has been ETA (mili-tar). The members of ETA (m), or milis, tend to be more intransi-gent and more committed to armed struggle; but they are also the members who define the struggle primarily in ethnic, cultural, and linguistic terms. The other branch created in 1974, ETA (político-militar) or ETA (p-m), tended to favor a Marxist or class analysis of the struggle. One faction of the poli-milis which favored a nego-tiated end to violence eventually split off and in 1982 abandoned armed struggle in return for amnesty or pardons from the Spanish government. The remnants of (p-m) declined in importance and have been reduced to a handful of leaders in exile in Cuba since the mid-1980s. There is also a small splinter faction called the Comandos Autónomos (Autonomous Cells) created in 1977, and an armed organization in the French Basque region called Iparretarrak (the Northerners) which has existed since 1973. Neither of these latter two groups is connected to ETA (m), and neither contributes much to ETA's struggle.

Until late 1987, ETA (m) had a simple organizational structure. At the head was the Executive Committee in France, composed of about a dozen people, each responsible for one of the key operating elements (e.g., recruiting, training, weapons, intelligence, finances, and so forth). In Spain, the operational elements consisted of two kinds of *comandos*, or cells. Most of these cells were made up of the *legales*, members not known to the police who could carry on a more or less normal life. These cells were only part-time elements since they conducted operations only on call, and usually at widely spaced intervals. The legales were responsible for much of the infrastructure of the organization, including intelligence and logistics. The major attacks (assassinations, kidnappings, and so forth) were conducted by comandos of *liberados*, people known to the police and therefore unable to work or carry on a normal life. There was at least one such cell in each important Basque city as well as in Madrid and Barcelona. Connecting all these elements was an elaborate network of couriers and safe houses in Spain and France. In all, ETA's rank-and-file membership may number several hundred at any given moment. Massive French police sweeps in late 1987 so disrupted this organizational structure that new and relatively unknown *etarras* (ETA members) were pressed into leadership positions, and new channels of command and communication had to be constructed. What has become clear since that time is that key leaders retain their power within the organization even if they are in jail or in exile; and important steps involving negotiations have to be cleared with them before they can be implemented.

ETA's formal organizational structure is by no means all there is to the organization's interested population. There were in the late 1980s more than five hundred etarras in Spanish prisons and about sixty in jail in France, as well as more than forty members who had been deported from France to a number of third countries in Africa and Latin America.[6] The fate of these men and women has been a subject of intense interest throughout the Basque Country; and their families have frequently become involved in public ceremonies and political movements on behalf of their freedom or safe return from exile.

The interests of this diverse group include not only more political objectives such as Basque self-determination or the withdrawal of all Spanish law enforcement authorities from Euskadi, but also a number of important personal and institutional goals as well. ETA leaders want to preserve their personal and organizational power, especially as it bears on negotiations with Madrid. Exiles and deportees want to be able to return home without facing reprisals from Spain or their former comrades; detainees want to be released from their extremely harsh prison life. And, of course, their families want to see their loved ones returned to them as quickly and as easily as possible.

OTHER BASQUE ORGANIZATIONS   The post-Franco Spanish constitution, promulgated in late December 1978, enshrined the principle of regional home rule through the institution of the autonomous community.[7] These institutions were to be based on one or more of Spain's existing fifty provinces; and they were to stand midway between the provinces and the central government in Madrid. Some observers contend that the constituent parliament elected in 1977 to draft the new constitution originally intended there to be only three such communities, corresponding to the three "historical regions" that had enjoyed some sort of autonomy before the civil war: Catalonia, Galicia, and Euskadi. Nevertheless, soon after these first three regions acquired their autonomous institutions, the leaders of Andalucia demanded and received a similar regime; and immediately thereafter all of Spain's regions petitioned for autonomous communities. By May 1983, the system of autonomous communities covered Spain's entire territory except the North African enclaves of Ceuta and Melilla.

Along with Catalonia, the Basque Autonomous Community (Comunidad Autónoma Vasca, or CAV), consisting of the three provinces of Alava, Guipúzcoa, and Vizcaya, was the first such institution to be created. The autonomy statute establishing the Basque Autonomous Community (Basque A.C.) was approved by referendum in October 1979; and the first Basque parliament was elected in March 1980. There have been subsequent elections of the parliament in February 1984 and November 1986. The first two parliaments were dominated by the Basque Nationalist Party, which enjoyed razor-thin majorities because the deputies of Herri Batasuna did not occupy their seats. In the third parliament, however, the split of the PNV made it impossible for any single party to hold a majority of seats; so the PNV entered into a coalition with the Basque wing of the Spanish socialist party, the Partido Socialista de Euskadi (PSE).

The parliament, as well as the government it elects, sits in Vitoria, the capital city of Alava. The Basque president is chosen by the newly elected parliament, and the president then selects the cabinet of department heads called "councillors." The first president, chosen in March 1980 and reaffirmed by the second parliament in 1984, was Carlos Garaikoetxea, a young and charismatic Navarrese who rose rapidly in the late 1970s from political obscurity to the leadership of the PNV and then to the presidency of the provisional "pre-autonomy" Basque government. After 1983, however, his relations with leaders of the PNV from Vizcaya worsened and his ability to govern was seriously eroded. In December 1984, therefore, he resigned the presidency and was succeeded by another PNV leader, José Antonio Ardanza, former head of the provincial government of Guipúzcoa. Ardanza's relations with the Spanish socialists were more cordial than were those of Garaikoetxea; and he (Ardanza) remained in office as president even after the PNV-PSE coalition organized the parliament in early 1987. Of the dozen or so departments that make up the Basque government cabinet, the most important as far as public order is concerned is the Department of Interior, counterpart of the Spanish Ministry of Interior. The Basque interior department supervises the Basque autonomous police force, called the Ertzainza, which began to function in October 1982. One of the chief areas of dispute between ETA and Madrid involved the responsibility for law enforcement; and the autonomous Basque police was seen by many Basques as the obvious force to replace the Spanish national police and the Civil Guard within the Basque Autonomous Community (CAV).

The system of political parties in the CAV is extremely complex and still in a state of flux after more than a decade of realigning elections and party schisms.[8] Out of a total population of slightly more than 2.5 million, between 900,000 and 1.1 million residents of the autonomous community vote regularly; of this number, between 500,000 and 700,000 typically cast their votes for one of four Basque nationalist parties, known by the Basque label *abertzale* (patriotic). Of these four parties, three generally accept the legitimacy of the institutions of the post-Franco era (the 1978 constitution, the Basque autonomy statute, and the parliaments and governments that they established).

The oldest of these three is the Basque Nationalist Party (PNV), founded in 1895 by the father of Basque nationalism, Sabino de Arana y Goiri. From the 1930s on through the civil war, World War II, and the Franco dictatorship, the PNV was the symbol of Basque resistance to centralist Spanish rule. Ideologically, the party has always reflected the conservative and Catholic urban middle-class and small-village constituencies that supported it. In the late 1950s, therefore, the impatient youths of Ekin split away from the PNV's attempt to embrace the more radical nationalist elements; and this schism continues to plague Basque politics to this day. In elections for the Basque parliament in 1980 and 1984, the PNV won about 350,000 and 450,000 votes, respectively. Although they did not win absolute majorities in the parliament either time, the absence of Herri Batasuna deputies enabled them to organize the parliament, although by very thin margins. After the split of the party in 1986, President Ardanza was forced to dissolve the parliament and call new elections because of a lack of a majority. In the ensuing elections in November, the PNV vote dropped to 270,000 (23.7 percent), and they were forced into coalition with the Basque wing of the Spanish socialist party in order to retain control of the presidency.

The second Basque nationalist party to be formed was Euzkadiko Ezkerra (EE), or Basque Left. This party was originally a coalition of smaller parties formed in 1977 by former members of the poli-mili wing of ETA. The decision of the EE coalition to contest the 1977 Spanish parliamentary elections was extremely controversial, since the more intransigent ETA (m) and its supporters had decided to boycott the vote. EE generally supports socialist economic reforms and a vision of Basque autonomy that can be accommodated within the 1979 statute. In its earlier days, EE did not accept the legitimacy of the Spanish constitution; but after ETA (p-m) dissolved itself and returned to civil politics in 1982, EE has increasingly supported the legitimacy of the existing system. EE generally wins about 10 percent of the popular vote; slightly fewer than 125,000 voters voted for them in 1986.

The 1986 split of the PNV resulted in the creation of the third abertzale party that accepts the existing system as legitimate: Eusko Alkartasuna (EA), or Basque Solidarity. Ideologically, EA stands between the center-right PNV and the socialist EE. In economic terms, it advocates a moderate form of social democracy; on the question of Basque rights, it supports the autonomy statute, but accuses the PNV of collaborating too much with Madrid. The party's principal strength is its leader, Carlos Garaikoetxea, the former Basque president, who still enjoys a powerful popular following. In the 1986 parliamentary vote, EA won about 180,000 votes, or slightly less than 16 percent.

All of the institutions and parties so far discussed have one overriding objective insofar as negotiations with ETA are concerned, and that is to defend the principle that working through democratic institutions is the proper way to accomplish Basque home rule. In 1978 and 1979 it was not easy for Basque nationalists to support Spanish constitutionalism as the road to self-determination; since that time, there have been numerous occasions when these same leaders must have been tempted to swing their support to a more radical solution. They now believe that if Madrid negotiates some sort of political arrangement with ETA, which in effect circumvents the Basques' own institutions, it would betray their risky commitment to democracy. Even though they may welcome political concessions by the Spanish government to convince ETA to lay down their arms, these more moderate Basque politicians reject decisively any steps taken by Madrid to deal only with ETA and to ignore the Basques' own parliament and government.

The one abertzale party that does not share this view, because it does not regard the existing system as legitimate, is Herri Batasuna (HB), or Popular Unity. Formed in early 1978 partly as a response to EE's participation in the 1977 elections, HB is actually a coalition of parties that defend the Basques' right of self-determination and espouse the set of demands contained in the KAS Alternative. Successful Herri Batasuna candidates do not occupy their seats in the Basque or Spanish parliaments, although occasionally they may do so in local municipal councils. HB's share of the vote rose steadily from 1979, and the coalition customarily takes between 15 and 20 percent of the vote. In the 1986 Basque parliament election, HB won slightly fewer than 200,000 votes, about 17.5 percent of the total. HB leaders have frequently been involved in efforts to get negotiations started between ETA and Madrid, especially after the "Algerian connection" was opened in 1986. If a "two-track" negotiating strategy is ever attempted, HB would be the appropriate negotiating party to represent ETA's interests. The other parties are not willing to concede such a role to HB, however, unless the party accepts its larger responsibility and begins to participate in the work of the Basque parliament.

Herri Batasuna is only one part of a broader Basque left coalition, referred to by the acronym KAS. The Koordinadora Abertzale Sozialista (Patriotic Socialist Coordinating Council) grew out of popular protests against the execution of two ETA members, Angel Otaegi and Jon Paredes Manot, in September 1975.[9] The organization was formally constituted in August 1976 to coordinate the policies and activities of several Basque socialist parties and unions: the Basque Popular Socialist Party (EHAS, later changed to HASI), the Patriotic Revolutionary Workers Party (LAIA), the Patriotic Workers Committee (LAK), and the Patriotic Workers Council (LAB). ETA (p-m) was a full member, and ETA (m), while not a formal member, gave the organization its unconditional support.

The KAS membership has been quite unstable over the years. The Basque Revolutionary Party (EIA) joined in 1976, but left the organization in 1977 because of the KAS decision to boycott the Spanish parliamentary elections that year. ETA (p-m) also quit the KAS at the same time and for the same reason. The LAB left in 1977 but returned in 1980 after an internal power struggle changed its leadership. The LAK and LAIA both disappeared in early 1980. As of 1988, the KAS was composed of ETA (m), the Basque socialist party (HASI), a youth wing called JARRAI, and another group called ASK, which mobilized popular demonstrations. Herri Batasuna is not a part of the KAS; rather, it is linked to the coalition by the political party HASI, which is a member of both groups.

It would be a mistake to see the KAS as merely a loose coalition of socialist parties and other groups. As Ibarra points out, the group has real decision-making authority, and is considered the guardian of the revolutionary purity of the left wing of the Basque struggle for independence. The presence of ETA (m) in the organization assures that the KAS adheres to the correct ideological and programmatic principles of the struggle.

Public institutions and political parties are not, of course, the only Basque organizations with a stake in negotiations with ETA. The media of mass communications are an essential part of the negotiating process, especially as a conduit of information and messages back and forth between parties that are not in direct contact with one another. The principal newspapers in the Basque Country are *El Correo Español* (Bilbao) with daily sales of 80,000 to 90,000; *El Diario Vasco* (San Sebastián), about 60,000; *Deia* (Bilbao), about 50,000; and *Egin* (San Sebastián), 40,000 to 50,000.[10] *Egin*, as well as the weekly newsmagazine *Punto y Hora* are generally considered to be supportive of ETA; and they both have suffered serious repression through the 1980s because of this. However, without *Egin* available to publish ETA messages and communiqués, it is hard to envision how the negotiation process could be initiated. The other newspapers also represent well-defined points of view. *Deia*, for example, has close ties to the PNV, and usually reflects the party's position on important issues.

Table 1.1 also lists several other groups in the private sector that have been involved in issues connected with ETA over the years. For example, a number of individuals have served as intermediaries between ETA and other groups, even when to do so has meant extreme personal danger to them. The history of failed negotiation attempts is marked by attacks against persons who tried, as intermediaries, to initiate these talks. Others have performed valuable services to the families of ETA kidnap victims in delivering ransom payments and securing the freedom of the hostages. The best known of these is a Vizcayan named Juan Félix Eriz, who was involved in some of the most famous hostage cases, as well as the failed 1978 negotiations which led to the death of José María Portell.[11] Another group active in the area of human rights has been the Pro-Amnesty Committees (Gestoras Pro-Amnistía), formed in the Basque Country in 1977 and the primary defender of prisoners' rights ever since. The list should also include Catholic church leaders, who enjoy much popular support in the still strongly Catholic Basque population. These men have generally confined their role to issuing public pronouncements urging conciliation and an end to violence; but on occasion they have worked behind the scenes to bring about talks between ETA and the government.

The list of Basques interested in negotiations would not be complete without reference to the autonomous community of Navarra. The relationship of the province of Navarra to the rest of the Basque people is extremely complicated, a full discussion of which would take us far beyond our subject. While many Basque nationalists see Navarra as the cradle of their ethno-nation, the fact is that Basque nationalism has never enjoyed much support in Navarra. The Basque language has virtually disappeared south of Pamplona; and Basque political parties have traditionally done poorly throughout the southern half of the province. Most natives of the province probably see themselves as "Navarrese" rather than "Basque" or "Spanish." As the Spanish constitution was being drafted in late 1977, Basque nationalist leaders sought to have Navarra included in the Basque General Council, the provisional pre-autonomy regime set up by Madrid to ease the transition to regional autonomy. Pressure from conservative Navarrese, especially from the ruling Spanish party, the UCD, was successful in blocking the inclusion of Navarra; and the Basque Autonomous Community was created with only the other three provinces. The separate Navarrese autonomous community came into existence in August 1982. Nevertheless, ETA and many other Basque groups have never ceased calling for the integration of the four provinces into a single autonomous community; and as we shall see, this issue proved to be one of the most contentious in negotiations with ETA in the late 1980s.

The Navarrese autonomous community is endowed with its own political institutions, parliament, and government, as well as a set of Basque, Spanish, and Navarrese political parties. In the 1987 parliamentary elections, the leading party was the Spanish socialists with more than 78,000 votes (27 percent), while second place went to the conservative Navarrese party Unión del Pueblo Navarro (UPN) with more than 69,000 votes (24 percent). Of the Basque parties, the leaders were Herri Batasuna with 38,000 votes

(13 percent) and Eusko Alkartasuna with nearly 19,000 votes (7 percent). About two-thirds of the total vote went to parties opposed to the merger of the two autonomous communities. The chief objective of these groups is to prevent their province from being forced to integrate itself with the Basque Autonomous Community as a part of any political arrangement with ETA.

SPANISH ORGANIZATIONS The Spanish constitution combines a democratically elected parliament with a constitutional monarch as the head of state.[12] While the naming of Juan Carlos to the throne was not a surprise (he had been designated to succeed General Franco as head of state upon the general's death), the young king's vigorous defense of democracy was unexpected. His most dramatic moment came in February 1981 when he successfully faced down a group of military and Civil Guard plotters who were trying to overthrow the constitutional regime. However, in countless other ways Juan Carlos quietly and without fanfare gave Spaniards (and even many Basque nationalists) faith and confidence in the stability and continuity of the regime, and so is quite rightly regarded as one of the principal reasons why democracy succeeded in Spain. As far as the issue of ETA's insurgency was concerned, Juan Carlos was primarily a very interested bystander whose principal role, as the symbol of a united Spain, lay in convincing the more conservative elements in the country that there would be no betrayal of the principle of national unity. The king could also have been involved in the question of amnesty for convicted ETA members, since the constitution gave him sole authority to grant collective amnesty. Since the Spanish government's approach after 1977 favored selective amnesty, however, this potential role for the monarch never emerged as significant.

Below the king as head of state, the constitution established a parliament made up of two chambers, a senate of relatively minor significance and a 350-member Congress of Deputies, where the real legislative power rests. Not counting the 1977 vote for a constituent assembly, there were three elections for parliament during the period covered by this book: in March 1979, October 1982, and June 1986. The first of these three was won by the center-right party, the Unión del Centro Democrático (UCD), which despite falling narrowly short of an absolute majority in the Congress of

Deputies nevertheless managed to govern alone for some three and a half years. In October 1982, however, the UCD was buried in an electoral landslide by the Partido Socialista Obrero Español (PSOE), or Spanish Socialist Workers' Party. The UCD quickly disappeared after this election; and the PSOE's hold on the parliament was reaffirmed (although with a reduced majority) in the June 1986 vote.

The role of the Congress of Deputies in the insurgency issue is threefold. Its principal function is to approve all legislation bearing on public order, including antiterrorist laws as well as bills dealing with courts, prisons, law enforcement, and so forth. The parliament has also tried to retain a significant role in monitoring government actions and policies in several key areas, including alleged human rights violations and negotiations with ETA. This role is accomplished by means of questioning government ministers, and occasionally the president himself, on the floor of the parliament. However, on really sensitive issues, particularly those having to do with ongoing negotiations, the government has usually bypassed the congress and dealt directly with representatives of political parties. Finally, the congress provides minority parties with the opportunity to criticize government policies and a forum that guarantees them access to the media when they do so. While Herri Batasuna deputies have never availed themselves of this forum, other Basque parties have spoken out in the parliament, although with what impact it is difficult to judge.

A primary function of the Congress of Deputies is to elect the prime minister, known formally as the president of the government. For practically the entire period between Franco's death and the 1979 parliamentary elections, the prime minister's post was held by Adolfo Suárez, the leader of the UCD. Suárez was elected president by the 1979 congress, and held that post until February 1981, when he resigned under criticism by his own party. It was during the election of his successor that the Guardia Civil staged its abortive coup attempt mentioned above. Following Suárez as president until October 1982 was another UCD leader, Leopoldo Calvo Sotelo. When the PSOE won control of the parliament, it elected to the presidency its leader, Felipe González, who was re-elected following the 1986 vote and again in October 1989.

In the president's cabinet, the key department as far as the insurgency question is concerned is the Ministry of Interior, which houses both the national police and the Civil Guard.[13] The first UCD interior minister was Rodolfo Martín Villa, who was replaced in May 1980 by Juan José Rosón. Rosón was replaced in 1982 by socialist José Barrionuevo, who remained in the office for the remainder of the period covered by this study. Barrionuevo was replaced in mid-1988 by José Luís Corcuera. Directly beneath the minister is the director of state security, a position held during the early part of the socialist government by Julián Sancristobal, but occupied for most of the time by Rafael Vera. Below the state security office are the director of national police, the director of the Civil Guard, and the various intelligence agencies. Both the police and the Civil Guard are directly involved in antiterrorist operations, which are coordinated by an office known as the Special Operations Cabinet, which reports directly to the state security director. This office has existed since administrative changes were made in 1981 aimed at centralizing antiterrorist operations and improving coordination. The intelligence services operate in support of all of these agencies. Since they acquire much of their information about ETA through interrogation of prisoners and suspects, these agencies have a very unsavory reputation among Basques; and some of their leaders, including Jesús Martínez Torres, the controversial head of police intelligence, have been accused by Spanish news media of torture.[14]

Interior is only one of several cabinet-level departments with direct interests in the insurgency issue. The Ministry of Justice, for example, in charge of courts and prisons, is directly involved in questions having to do with amnesty and pardon of specific etarras, as well as with charges of mistreatment or torture in prison. The Ministry of Defense represents the interests of the armed forces in antiterrorist questions. While Spain has used regular army and navy personnel against insurgents only very rarely, the country's armed forces are supremely sensitive to two ETA-related issues. First, senior military commanders have been favorite targets of ETA attacks; and second, the military, probably more than any other agency of government, perceives itself as the guardian of national unity and opposes any attempt to negotiate with ETA the question of Basque self-determination. Finally, the Ministry of Foreign Relations has a stake in any matters involving ETA and foreign countries, an extremely important question as far as Spain's relations with France, Algeria, and several other countries are concerned.

The paramount interest of all of these executive departments, as well as of the president himself, has been to bring about an end to ETA's violence without appearing to give in to any of ETA's "political" demands, such as self-determination for the Basque Country. While they have been willing to discuss amnesty for specific ETA prisoners or exiles, that is usually as far as they have been disposed to go in order to bring the insurgency to a close. Beyond this general objective, each ministry tries to protect its own institutional status and prerogatives, and to maintain some influence over the conduct of negotiations. As a group, they believe that it is they (i.e., the Spanish state), and not the Basque parliament and government, that should be negotiating with ETA. The agencies that have borne the brunt of ETA attacks—the national police, the Guardia Civil, and the armed forces—also insist on measures to provide maximum personal security to their members in the Basque Country and in large cities like Madrid and Barcelona.[15] Finally, while all of these agencies hold Spanish national unity as the supreme value, the armed forces see themselves as the primary protector of that value and so oppose any separation of the Basque Country, which they view as the beginning of an unacceptable dismembering of the Spanish nation.

Spain's national court system, while not as powerful as the other branches of government, has become increasingly important in issues related to ETA and the administration of justice. For example, in 1982 and 1983 the government pursued a policy called "reinserción social," or "social reintegration." This program granted amnesty or pardons on a selective, case-by-case basis to convicted or exiled etarras. The courts were the key agency for hearing each case and deciding on the appropriateness of selective amnesty for each prisoner. Courts have also been active in hearing accusations of torture, mistreatment, or other alleged human rights violations in prison. In addition, in the late 1980s several judges in Madrid began investigations into the complicity of Spanish government agencies in the covert counterterrorist war waged against ETA in southern France. Finally, Spain's ultimate judicial authority, the Constitutional Tribunal, declared portions of the government's 1984 antiterrorist law unconstitutional, although the case dragged on so long that most of the law's provisions had already lapsed or been repealed by the time the verdict was handed down.

Spain's political parties span the entire ideological spectrum.[16] The dominant party in the congress since 1982 is the socialist party, PSOE. Originally a fairly radical Marxist party, the PSOE renounced its Marxist-Leninist heritage before the 1982 election and has carried out rather conservative economic and social policies since coming to power. Many Basques believe that this socialist shift to the right, carried out in order to placate Spain's rightist voters and other neo-Francoist forces, caused the PSOE to betray the commitments they had made to promote regional home rule.[17] In the 1986 Spanish parliamentary vote, the PSOE won about 44 percent of the popular vote and 184 seats in the 350-member Congress of Deputies. In both cases, these figures represent a slight decline from their 1982 levels. Like most Spanish parties, the PSOE maintains a branch in the Basque Autonomous Community, where the party campaigns under the label of the Partido Socialista de Euskadi (PSE). In the 1986 Basque parliament elections, the PSE won slightly more than 250,000 votes (about 22 percent), second to the PNV's 270,000. However, aided by the peculiar vote-counting system, the socialists actually won one more seat in the regional parliament than did the PNV. In early 1987, a coalition of PNV and PSE agreed to organize the parliament and elected José Antonio Ardanza of the PNV to the presidency for a second time. One of the strongest reasons Ardanza gave for entering into a coalition with the socialists was that they would be able to guarantee support in Madrid for Basque government initiatives since they were allied with the ruling Spanish party.

The second strongest party in Spain is the conservative Partido Popular (PP), formerly known as the Alianza Popular and subsequently as the Coalición Popular (the label under which the party contested the 1986 elections). The leader of PP during the period of this study, Manuel Fraga, was a cabinet minister in several governments under General Franco and remains committed to many of the operating principles of Spanish politics that were dominant in that era. Foremost among these are the absolute non-negotiable nature of Spanish national unity, and a firm stand against terrorism. On several occasions, Fraga has called for making pro-ETA parties illegal or for declaring a state of emergency and a suspension of constitutional guarantees in the Basque Country. Throughout the various negotiation attempts, PP leaders have strongly opposed any deal that might yield on the question of Basque self-determination. In 1986, Fraga's party won 26 percent of the vote and 105 seats in the Spanish Congress of Deputies. As one might suspect, the Basque branch of PP does not fare well at the polls; in the November 1986 Basque parliament vote, its candidates received less than 5 percent of the vote.

The only other significant Spanish parties are the centrist Centro Democrático Social (CDS), a social democratic party founded by Adolfo Suárez after his return to politics, and two wings of the communist movement: Izquierda Unida (IU), or United Left, and the Partido Comunista de España (PCE). The CDS in 1986 won about 9 percent of the popular vote and 19 seats in the Spanish parliament, but only 3.5 percent of the vote in the Basque elections later in the year. Adolfo Suárez retains considerable personal influence, however, because of his reputation as a key figure in the country's democratic transition in the late 1970s and early 1980s. Indeed, in the Basque Country Suárez is one of the few Spanish politicians to retain any sort of personal popularity, due primarily to the strides made toward Basque home rule during his tenure as president in 1979 and 1980. The two communist parties together won about 6 percent of the vote in Spanish elections in June 1986, but only a bit more than 1 percent in Basque parliament elections in November.

While these parties may disagree with one another over just about every aspect of politics, they show fundamental unity on issues relating to insurgency and ETA. They are unanimously opposed to negotiating away anything that might be considered "political," including especially the Basque right of self-determination. There are some differences on the question of amnesty, however, where Suárez has been known to favor a more liberal amnesty policy, perhaps to include ETA prisoners convicted of so-called *delitos de sangre,* or blood crimes. The other parties, especially PP, strongly oppose amnesty for any etarra convicted of murder. In

November 1987, all Spanish parties joined in a statement of common policy toward ETA which guided government actions through the 1988 and 1989 negotiation attempts.

In contrast to the Basque Country, where newspapers play a key role in the insurgency question, in Spain as a whole the mass media are of little relative importance. Spain generally is not a country of newspaper readers; only one Spaniard in ten buys a daily newspaper, and the only European countries with a lower newspaper circulation are Greece and Portugal. Two Madrid dailies provide significant coverage and occasionally publish lengthy interpretive articles about ETA or negotiations. These are *El País*, the country's most influential daily with a circulation of about 348,000, and *Diario 16* with a circulation of 130,000. Several weekly newsmagazines also provide coverage, although they lean somewhat more toward sensationalism. The foremost of these are *Cambio 16* with a circulation of 170,000, and *Tiempo*. These media are interested primarily in simply reporting the news and defending their own respective partisan points of view. They also contribute to the discussion of related issues by surveying Spanish public opinion on ETA, negotiations, etc., and reporting the results in their publications. Some of the more sensationalist media, such as *Tiempo*, are used occasionally to leak government information to the public. The electronic media are of little significance in this issue; radio has little role to play, and television is state owned and operated.

INTERNATIONAL GROUPS Compared with other insurgent groups, ETA has not had extensive international connections, nor has the Basque insurgency attracted much attention abroad.[18] However, table 1.1 lists a few foreign governments and other international agencies that have become involved to varying degrees in the ETA question.

In the case of two foreign governments, the ETA issue has come to occupy an important place on their respective national political agendas. The first case is France, which has the potential makings of a "Basque problem" in its own southwest where more than 200,000 Basques live. From the early 1960s, ETA maintained its headquarters and some support facilities on the French side of the border, mostly in the small mountain towns and fishing villages of the French Basque region. For the 1960s and most of the

1970s, Paris tolerated ETA's presence in France so long as the organization committed no crimes there and refrained from whipping up nationalist sentiment among French Basques. This unspoken arrangement was more or less faithfully observed until democracy returned to Spain in the late 1970s, at which time the French government began to harrass Spanish Basques living in France. French policy toward ETA became steadily more repressive through the 1980s. After a decade of increasingly hard-line policies, however, there is now virtually nothing that Spain might wish the French to do against ETA that the French government is not willing to undertake.

France's chief interest in the whole affair is to prevent the insurgency from spilling over onto French territory. There are several ways in which this might occur. One way would be for ETA to shift its violent attacks north of the border; another would be for the organization to stimulate pro-ETA sentiments among fellow Basques in France. In fact, these things have not happened to any great degree. What *did* occur, however, was an extension of the violence by the Spanish police who followed ETA across the border in "hot pursuit," and by the several covert counterterrorist groups that have assassinated Basques on French soil. It was primarily as an attempt to stem this tide of cross-border violence that Paris agreed in early 1984 to begin to expel ETA members from its territory, first by deporting them to third countries, then by formally extraditing them to Spain to stand trial, and then finally by simply expelling them to Spain without even an extradition procedure.

The other foreign government very much interested in the ETA matter was that of Algeria. In 1986, the leader of ETA, Txomin Iturbe, was expelled from France and eventually came to live in exile in Algeria. The Algerian government quickly took advantage of his presence to propose that their country be the venue for negotiations. They offered to serve as the intermediaries to get the talks started, and they even proposed to guarantee the outcome of the negotiations. This "Algerian connection" remained operational for nearly three years until April 1989 when the third phase of talks broke down, ETA resumed its violent attacks, and Algiers began to expel etarras to other countries.

It has been alleged that Algeria once served as the training base for a number of etarras in the mid-1970s; but that connection seems far too remote to justify all the costs that Algiers has incurred in order to pursue this role in the ETA affair. There are other much more rational interests that Algeria has at stake. For one thing, Algeria has prided itself on its special role in resolving a number of difficult international disputes, chief among which was the release of the American hostages in Iran; and it is possible that they were seeking to add another success to their list. There are also some fairly concrete things that the Algerians wanted from Spain, including the expulsion of a group of anti-government Algerians who were using Madrid as a base of operations, and help from Spain in resolving the conflict in the Western Sahara. The presence of ETA leaders in Algiers gave them an important card to play in their dealings with Spain; and in the long run, that mattered much more to them than anything specific about the Basque struggle.

Several other governments have also been drawn into this issue by virtue of receiving ETA deportees from France. At one time or another since 1984, etarras have been deported to Togo, Gabon, and São Tomé in Africa; and Cuba, Panama, Venezuela, Ecuador, and the Dominican Republic in Latin America. The arrangements by which these countries agreed to receive these deportees have not been made public; but presumably the host countries were able to bargain for something of value to compensate them for the trouble and expense associated with receiving the ETA members. It is known that the costs of their presence are borne by the Spanish government; but no doubt other inducements, such as trade or other financial concessions, have been necessary to bring the deals to conclusion.

Finally, a number of international organizations or agencies have demonstrated either direct or indirect interests in resolving the Basque insurgency. Some of these organizations are the international media of communication, including such global newspapers as the *New York Times* or *Le Monde*; some are part of the international network of academic research institutions that sponsor investigations (more or less unconnected to government policy) into the insurgency. Another important international player has been Amnesty International, the global human rights monitoring agency. Amnesty has been deeply interested in the precarious state of human rights protections in Spain for many years. It sent special investigation teams to Spain on three occasions (1975, 1979, and

1983) to look into allegations of torture and other abuses; and in every one of its annual reports in this decade, its section on Spain has expressed great concern over these practices. The results of these efforts have been negligible. International law enforcement agencies such as Interpol have become much more deeply involved in antiterrorist programs through the latter half of the 1980s, especially as the international narcotics trade has become so profoundly enmeshed in political insurgencies. Spain has also worked to get the ETA problem onto the agenda of the Trevi Group, the regular meetings of the ministers of interior of all the member countries of the European Community, thus expanding ETA from a Spanish or a Spanish-French problem to a European one. And last, but certainly not least, we should include the members of the so-called *guerra sucia*, the "dirty war" of assassination and counterterror that has been carried on in southern France by covert groups like the Spanish-Basque Battalion (BVE) and the Antiterrorist Liberation Groups (GAL). As we shall soon see, these groups played a major role in expanding the fight against ETA to French soil.

CHAPTER TWO

Spanish Antiterrorist Policy:
1978–1988

ATTEMPTS to negotiate with ETA between 1978 and 1988 did not take place in a vacuum; on the contrary, these negotiations were usually part of more general Spanish policies aimed at defeating the group's violent insurgency. For a full understanding of the dynamics of the negotiation process, then, we must review the development of Spanish antiterrorist policy over the eleven-year period.

Our analysis focuses primarily on four dimensions of this policy.[1] First, the basic principles of these policies were set forth in acts of the Spanish parliament that defined terrorism and related crimes, and that established the legal status and rights of persons suspected of terrorist acts. These laws also defined the illegality of various levels of association with proscribed groups, including giving them aid or assistance, meeting with them for any purpose, acting as intermediary to resolve hostage situations, or writing or saying things in public that could be construed as a defense of, or an apologia for, terrorism. These last provisions also affected media coverage of insurgent and counterinsurgent activities. Since television in Spain is government owned, control over electronic media coverage was never very controversial; but the printed media—

newspapers and magazines—were on occasion suppressed because of what the government considered destabilizing stories about ETA and antiterrorist measures.

Next, we consider the treatment afforded to arrested suspects and convicted insurgents while in prison or otherwise under police control. We are interested here in the government's detention policies, how suspects were treated before being brought to trial, how convicted insurgents were treated while in prison, and the general conditions of imprisonment, paying particular attention to allegations of the use of torture against both suspects and convicted persons. The several hundred accused and convicted ETA members were often the focal point of the negotiations; and whether or not to offer them amnesty or a pardon was a central question in discussions between Madrid and the insurgents.

A third important dimension involves the level of law enforcement activity as well as the organizational changes introduced to improve the government's antiterrorist efforts. Of special importance here would be the development of specialized counterinsurgent organizations, and the use of military or paramilitary force (counterterrorist groups) against the insurgents, their families, or their communities.

Finally, an especially crucial policy dimension in the ETA case has been Spain's ability to secure international cooperation against the insurgents. Because of what the Spanish government perceived as an ETA "sanctuary" on the French side of the border, French collaboration became an important key to the success of the effort to reduce ETA's violent attacks. While Paris was initially quite reluctant to become involved in the anti-ETA effort, as time went on French policies became increasingly repressive, leading eventually to widespread arrests, deportation, and extradition of suspected ETA members and even of some of their family members.

After a brief review of the status of government antiterrorist policies as of early 1978, this chapter discusses five phases in the development of those policies. The first two phases cover the last four and a half years of the center-right government of the Unión del Centro Democrático (UCD), first under President Adolfo Suárez and then under Leopoldo Calvo Sotelo. The first phase, from July 1978 to the spring of 1981, was marked by increasingly repressive policies following the killing of Bilbao journalist José María Portell.

The second phase, from the spring of 1981 to November 1982, was dominated by the massive military buildup in the Basque Country after the abortive Guardia Civil coup attempt in February 1981.

The latter three phases in counterinsurgent policy span the years since November 1982, when the Spanish Socialist Workers' Party (PSOE) government of Felipe González was in office. The period from November 1982 to November 1984, the first two years of the PSOE regime, witnessed a steady expansion of government power accompanied by vigorous attempts to persuade the French government to cooperate in the anti-ETA effort. The period from November 1984 to January 1987 brought antiterrorist policy to its most coercive level since Franco's death. Between early 1987 and mid-1988, there was a slight relaxation of Spanish government policy in a few areas, particularly as that policy was defined by acts of the Spanish parliament. However, French policies toward Basques became increasingly stringent during this period.

Thus, while Spanish antiterrorist policies could be described as fairly moderate at the beginning of the period, they became steadily more repressive and coercive throughout the decade regardless of whether the party in power was conservative or socialist. Indeed, the leftist PSOE government was clearly much more strongly anti-ETA, especially between late 1984 and early 1987, than its rightist predecessors. After early 1987, however, government policy tended to relax somewhat, although at the end of the 1980s it remained significantly more coercive and "harsh" than it had been at the end of the 1970s.

Antiterrorist Policy in Early 1978

By February 1978, when ETA published the first list of its demands, the KAS Alternative, Spanish antiterrorist policy had reached a crucial turning point. After nearly two years of steady liberalization following Franco's death, Madrid found itself under increasing pressure to meet rising terrorist violence with harsh countermeasures. During the late winter and early spring of 1978, these measures began to crystallize into a concrete set of policies aimed at stemming the tide of ETA's insurgency.

Shortly before his death, General Franco had decreed an extremely harsh Law on the Prevention of Terrorism, which King Juan Carlos and Premier Carlos Arias Navarro abrogated in February 1976.[2] By the end of that same year, the king had signed a decree formally abolishing the special courts that Franco had established to try accused terrorists. A number of special public security measures were reinstated on an emergency basis in early 1977 following two sensational kidnappings and more than a half dozen politically related deaths; but these measures were withdrawn quickly after the threat subsided. Thus, by early 1978, Spain had no permanent antiterrorist legislation. Accused terrorists were treated as common criminals, to be tried in the same courts under the same rules and detained in prison along with nonpolitical criminals. ETA was still defined as illegal, and it was a crime to be a member of the organization; but the crime that made it different from other Spanish groups was not its violence but its advocacy of Basque separatism from Spain.

A similar trend could be seen in the numbers of Basques in prison accused of politically related crimes against the state. (This circumlocution is necessary because of the heated disagreement over the guilt or innocence of these persons, as well as over the correct label to attach to their alleged misdeeds. In other words, we may not assume that every Basque in prison is a killer, or even that they are all ETA members; but, by the same token, we should not presume that they are all "prisoners of conscience," in jail simply because of their beliefs, as Amnesty International might describe them. Of course, it is also somewhat incorrect to refer to them all as simply "Basques," since there are some who are not even that—but that is another issue altogether.) Before 1975, this figure oscillated between 100 and 250; but in Franco's last days, it soared to nearly 750. Between November 1975 and March 1976, the Spanish government issued three amnesty decrees aimed at clearing prisons of most of these people by the June 1977 parliamentary elections. Finally in October 1977, the parliament approved a general amnesty law for all political prisoners, and the last Basque to be affected by this legislation was freed on December 9. As of early 1978, then, the number of Basques in prison for politically related crimes was between 5 and 10. Because the number of prisoners had been so reduced during this period, there was correspondingly less interest in the problems of torture, mistreatment, and human rights violations. This relative silence meant not that conditions in Spanish prisons had improved, but only that for a brief time relatively few Basques experienced them directly.

In the area of law enforcement level and organization, the picture was mixed. In these early days, before the Basque autonomous government existed, the law enforcement function was performed entirely by Spanish agencies, principally the national police and the paramilitary Guardia Civil. To assert that there was tension between these forces and the general public would be an understatement. For example, after analyzing a large volume of data on Spanish public order policies in the Basque Country in the late 1970s and early 1980s, Miguel Castells found that during the last six months of 1977 police charged into and broke up some 30 demonstrations, killing 3 and wounding 87.[3]

Much of the violence done against Basques in the interest of suppressing threats to public order was inflicted by groups of vigilantes or mercenaries that operated with relative impunity outside the law. When this violence was directed against large groups of ordinary citizens, it usually stemmed from urban riots unleashed by so-called *incontrolados*, mobs of rightists who would attack Basques on the streets, in public transportation, in other gathering places (bars, restaurants), or during demonstrations. According to Castells, during the last half of 1977 these mobs committed more than 20 such attacks, leaving 1 dead and 24 wounded. There were also attacks directed against individual Basques either in Spain or in France among the refugee population. The perpetrators of these crimes were organized into shadowy right-wing antiterrorist death squads acting under the orders of unknown sponsors. These groups had existed as far back as April 1975. The best-known group, which was responsible for most of the attacks, was the Batallón Vasco-Español, or BVE. In all, between 1975 and 1977 this underground war, known as the dirty war, or guerra sucia, accounted for 5 killed, 34 wounded, and 2 kidnappings.[4]

French government policy toward Basques and ETA in particular was also mixed.[5] While Franco was alive, Paris tended to see the problem of ETA as one entirely for the Spanish to solve. Beginning in 1976, however, the French began to increase the pressure against known or alleged ETA members, as well as against ordinary Basque citizens. Work and residence permits became much harder to obtain; official refugee status was increasingly denied to Basques; police surveillance of refugees increased; Basques had their homes broken into and searched without warrants; and police detained Basques for routine interrogation in rising numbers. Preventive detention came to be much more widely used, and increasing numbers of suspected ETA members were sent to prison islands where they were confined for months at a time without having even been charged with criminal acts, much less tried and convicted. The one thing Paris would not do, however, was extradite alleged ETA members to Spain; so from Madrid's point of view, ETA continued to enjoy its French sanctuary.

In sum, in February 1978, the antiterrorist policies faced by ETA could be generally described as less harsh than those that prevailed during the Franco era. On the other hand, it was clear that not only had the worst elements of Franco's police state survived the transition to democracy in Spain, but the trend during the last half of 1977 and the first half of 1978 was in the direction of more coercion and more punishment, not only for ETA itself but for the community that supported it.

The Hardening of Spain's Antiterrorist Policy: July 1978–Spring 1981

On June 28, 1978, Bilbao journalist José María Portell was shot to death in front of his home, presumably by members of ETA. His assassination, which caused the collapse of the first serious attempt to negotiate with ETA, also provoked the return to the harsh antiterrorist policies reminiscent of the Franco years.[6]

Actually, the new antiterrorist law that the government pushed through parliament in response to the Portell assassination had been under consideration for several months, ever since the pace of ETA killings quickened in late winter and early spring.[7] The draft law had appeared in early May, and was introduced into the parliament for debate on June 8, where it was being discussed at the time of the Portell shooting. In the aftermath of Portell's death, the pressure for tough antiterrorist measures was irresistible. The Spanish minister of interior, Rodolfo Martín Villa, called for the immediate enactment of the government's draft law; and on June 29 the

Council of Ministers approved the bill as a decree-law. The practical effect of this step was to make the bill law without waiting for parliament to act. Once approved by the parliament's Committee on Legislative Urgency, the law took effect on July 1.

The new law, known as Law 21/1978, gave police new powers of arrest and detention with which to apprehend suspected terrorists. Suspects could be held without charges filed against them for more than seventy-two hours if police first notified the courts. Judges had the authority to halt the detention, but in practice this check was almost never applied. Police were also granted the right to intercept mail and telephone messages received by suspected terrorists. Amnesty and pardons were ruled out for any crime dealt with in the law; and courts were not allowed to release prisoners on bond before their trial.

Law 21/1978 remained Spain's basic antiterrorist law for about eighteen months. It was supplemented by a second piece of emergency legislation, Law 56/1978, known as Special Measures toward Crimes of Terrorism Committed by Armed Groups, approved by parliament on December 4, 1978. This law approved the detention of persons for up to ten days with the permission of a court, as well as the holding of suspects incommunicado—that is, without notifying family or attorney—for the duration of their detention.[8]

In addition to these two decree-laws, King Juan Carlos promulgated a third measure on January 26, 1979, a decree-law entitled On the Protection of Citizen Security. Among other provisions, this law introduced criminal penalties for "apologia for terrorism," or printing or saying anything that could be construed as the defense of terrorist acts or groups. The law also increased the penalties for terrorist crimes, placed the national police in charge of maximum security prisons, and restricted the rights of accused to seek and be given provisional release from prison. Under the terms of this law, the vice president of the provincial parliament of Navarra was kept in jail for forty-five days without ever being charged with a crime. He was eventually released and cleared of all charges, as were most of the persons arrested under this and other antiterrorist laws.

The net effect of these three laws was to place in the hands of police extraordinary powers with which to attack ETA. However, since the laws had been enacted under emergency provisions, they were vulnerable to criticism from the government's opponents as leaving the way open for unconstitutional abuses of human rights. In response, in late 1979 the government prepared a new draft anti-terrorist law, called the Organic Law on Citizen Security. This law was formally approved as Organic Law 11/1980 by the Spanish Congress of Deputies on October 29, 1980. Of the 350 members of the chamber, only 2 voted against, while 7 Basque nationalist deputies abstained.[9]

The 1980 law replaced and codified the provisions of the preceding laws, and remained Spain's basic antiterrorist legislation for about four years. It suspended fundamental constitutional rights for persons suspected of a wide range of terrorist acts, including apologia for terrorism or for those persons suspected of such crimes. Preventive detention and holding suspects incommunicado were authorized, as were telephone taps, mail interception, and police invasion of private homes without court order.

Armed with these new laws, Spain's police and Guardia Civil launched a vigorous assault on ETA and its supporters. In September 1978, Minister of Interior Martín Villa consulted with terrorism experts in Germany and returned with a fifteen-point program intended to blunt the sharp edge of ETA's attacks. Shortly thereafter, a new antiterrorist police unit of about 50 men was created in Bilbao under the leadership of Roberto Conesa. In addition to much more aggressive search and detention activities, this new unit attempted to infiltrate ETA with spies and to reward informers for information about ETA members and operations. From September through December 1978, Conesa's group made more than 180 arrests of suspected ETA members. In February 1979, they launched a sweep to capture 36 of ETA's most wanted leaders; while they did not locate any of the 36, they did manage to arrest more than 50 other members during the first ten days of February. Conesa's group was joined in February 1980 by Spain's first elite counterterrorist police units: the 120-man Special Operations Group (GEO), trained for dealing with urban terrorism; and the 450-man Guardia Civil detachment, called Rural Antiterrorist Groups (GAR). Along with some 12,000 regular Guardia Civil troops and 6,000 national police (plus assorted provincial and municipal police units), these special antiterrorist units constituted a formidable force. The police buildup was reflected almost immediately in arrest statistics. Monthly average arrest rates doubled from fewer than 25 in early 1978 to nearly 50 by the end of the year, and doubled again to 100 or more by the end of 1980. (See table 2.1 and figure 2.1.)

The number of Basques in prison also climbed sharply during this period. From fewer than 10 in early 1978, the number of detainees rose to about 100 at the end of the year and to nearly 300 by the beginning of 1981. (See table 2.2 and figure 2.1.) Concern for their treatment while in prison rose at the same pace. In October 1979, Amnesty International (AI) sent an investigative team to Spain to look into charges of torture in prison. Their report, issued in November 1980, found persuasive evidence that "maltreatment amounting to torture has occurred in police stations in Madrid, Barcelona and Bilbao between September 1978 and June 1979."[10] The Spanish government formally replied to the charges in February 1982, rejecting the accusations and claiming that the testimony gathered by the AI team was false. The special mission report, plus the AI annual report covering the period from May 1980 to April 1981, found that the laws approved since mid-1978 had so weakened the protection of human rights that suspected terrorists were now routinely held incommunicado for up to ten days, during which time they were subjected to torture and other abuses. Also of great concern was the government's policy of transferring ETA prisoners from one prison to another without informing their families or attorneys.

Torture in prison was not the only cause for concern about the erosion of human rights protections in the Basque Country. Violent attacks against Basques in both Spain and France reached new highs during this time. According to Miguel Castells, during the three-year period from 1978 through 1980 police used force to break up demonstrations or meetings on 591 occasions, leading to 41 deaths and some 670 injuries. The so-called incontrolados were responsible for 35 deaths and 132 injuries during the same period.[11] The clandestine "dirty war" in France had also heated up after the Portell killing. In the same three-year period, there were 36 killings of Basques by right-wing assassination squads, including the dramatic bombing of the car of ETA leader José Miguel Beñarán Ordeñana in December 1978. Some 115 Basques were wounded by these attacks, including two assaults on ETA chief Txomin Iturbe in May 1979 and February 1980.

Table 2.1 Antiterrorist Arrests in the Basque Country, 1978–1988.

Month/Year	Numbers Arrested (Monthly Average)	Notes and Sources
1-78/1-79	287 (23.9)	*Euskadi 1988* (San Sebastián: Anuario EGIN, 1988), p. 163
9-78/12-78	184 (46.0)	Estimate, based on *Cambio 16*, no. 370, 1-7-79
1-79/12-79	468 (42.5)	*Deia*, 12-6-79
1-79/1-80	561 (46.8)	*Euskadi 1988*, p. 163
1-80/4-80	132 (44.0)	*Deia*, 4-2-80
1-80/7-80	329 (54.8)	*Deia*, 7-19-80
1-80/1-81	2,140 (178.3)	*Euskadi 1988*, p. 163
12-80/3-81	296 (74)	*Deia*, 4-2-81
12-80/5-81	499 (99.8)	*Deia*, 5-22-81
4-81	44 in one week (176)	*Deia*, 4-5-81
6-81/10-81	71 (14.2)	*El País*, 10-30-81
1-81/10-81	410 (41.0)	*Deia*, 12-30-81
1-81/10-81	394 (39.4)	*Cambio 16*, 11-9-81
1-81/1-82	1,300 (108.3)	*Euskadi 1988*, p. 163
1-80/11-82	2,374 (67.8)	*Deia*, 11-25-82
1-81/6-82	572 (95.3)	*Deia*, 12-16-82
1-82/1-83	1,261 (105.1)	*Euskadi 1988*, p. 163
12-80/3-83	1,776 (63.4)	Gestoras Pro-Amnistía
1-83/4-83	78 (26.0)	*Deia*, 4-17-83
1-83/1-84	1,157 (96.4)	*Euskadi 1988*, p. 163
1-84/1-85	1,879 (156.6)	*Euskadi 1988*, p. 163. 337 arrested under Anti-Terrorist Law. *Deia*, 1-4-85, 1-22-85
1-85/4-85	115 (28.8)	*Deia*, 5-8-85
1-85/1-86	1,181 (98.4)	*Euskadi 1988*, p. 163. 940 arrests under Anti-Terrorist Law
12-82/2-86	2,004 (51.4)	Gestoras Pro-Amnistía
1-86/1-87	990 (82.5)	*Euskadi 1988*, p. 163. Arrests up 34 percent from 85. *El País*, 1-6-87
1-87/12-87	194 (17.6)	*Deia*, 3-26-88. Refers only to alleged ETA members
1-87/1-88	601 (50.1)	*Euskadi 1988*, p. 163
11-87/10-88	181 (15.1)	*Euskadi 1988*, pp. 166–8. Arrests were made under Anti-Terrorist Law

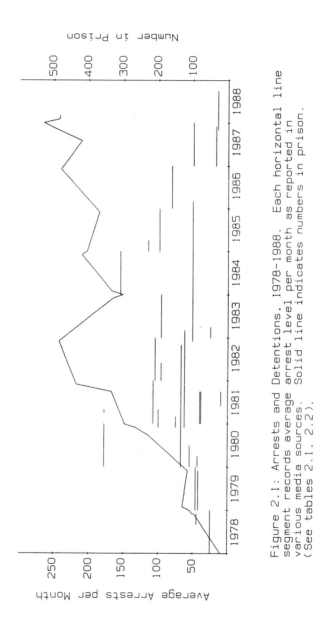

Figure 2.1: Arrests and Detentions. 1978-1988. Each horizontal line segment records average arrest level per month as reported in various media sources. Solid line indicates numbers in prison. (See tables 2.1, 2.2).

Table 2.2 Imprisonment of Alleged and/or Convicted ETA Members, 1978–1988.

Month/ Year	Number in Prison	Notes and Sources
12-78	97	This is a minimum number, those transferred to Soria prison in late 1978. *Diario Vasco,* 12-28-78
12-78	102	*Euskadi 1988* (San Sebastián: Anuario EGIN, 1988), p. 173
1-79	111	*Diario Vasco,* 1-4-79
2-79	130	*Deia,* 2-7-79
12-79	117	*Euskadi 1988,* p. 173
10-80	231	*Deia,* 10-22-80
12-80	265	*Euskadi 1988,* p. 173
1-81	298	*Deia,* 1-14-81
10-81	335	Gestoras Pro-Amnistía
12-81	435	*Euskadi 1988,* p. 173
12-82	485	*Euskadi 1988,* p. 173
12-83	331	*Euskadi 1988,* p. 173
1-84	305	*Deia,* 1-8-84
2-84	337	Gestoras Pro-Amnistía
12-84	419	*Euskadi 1988,* p. 173
1-85	402	*Deia,* 1-4-85
12-85	369	*Euskadi 1988,* p. 173
12-86	477	*Euskadi 1988,* p. 173
8-87	418	*Deia,* 8-5-87
12-87	504	*Euskadi 1988,* p. 173
1-88	530	*Deia,* 3-3-88
2-88	485	*Deia,* 3-3-88
3-88	484	*Deia,* 3-13-88

There were also changes in French policies toward the Basques and toward ETA. On June 30, 1978, French president Valéry Giscard d'Estaing announced that Basques living in France would no longer be considered political refugees and that the government would no longer issue them political refugee cards. After a meeting of the Spanish and French foreign ministers in January 1979, this decision was formally put into effect. No new cards were issued, and those already issued were allowed to expire. Also in January and February 1979, the French government launched a vigorous policy of detention and forced relocation of dozens of Basque refugees; and throughout 1979 and 1980, Basques were subject to harassment, intimidation, arrest, interrogation, and even violent attacks on the streets, at their workplaces, and in their homes. In one important respect, however, French policy did not change: extradition. From 1977 through mid-1981, Madrid lodged 29 requests for extradition of suspected ETA members; the French did not grant a single request. There were instances, however, of French police unofficially detaining suspected ETA members and delivering them into the hands of Spanish police at the border.[12]

Antiterrorist Policy During the Last Months of the UCD Government: Spring 1981–November 1982

During the first three months of 1981, the still-young Spanish democracy was subjected to a series of attacks that it just barely managed to survive. ETA's violent attacks continued at a high level, and included several extremely provocative murders. The kidnapping and murder of a young engineer, José María Ryan, construction manager of the Lemoiz nuclear plant, was especially inflammatory of public sentiment. It was violence from the political right, however, that nearly brought the government to its knees. On February 23, more than 100 Guardia Civil troops, under the command of a lieutenant colonel, invaded the parliament building in Madrid and took hostage the entire membership of the Congress of Deputies. This dramatic attack was part of a broader military plot to seize the government and terminate Spain's experiment in democracy. Thanks to the valor of the country's democratic leadership, especially of the king, the coup attempt failed in a matter of hours. On the other hand, the government's reaction to the attempted coup, and to the other acts of violence of the period, was felt for more than eighteen months.

The government's initial response was to "fill in the gaps" in the existing antiterrorist legislation. In March 1981, the government introduced a new draft law called the Law for the Defense of the Constitution.[13] For one thing, the new law defined terrorism as embracing any attack on the integrity of the Spanish nation or any effort to secure the independence of any part of its territory, even if nonviolent. Thus, virtually any expression of separatism could have been tried under the terms of this legislation. Activities in support of a terrorist organization, including especially intelligence gathering (ETA's so-called comandos de información), were now explicitly included under the terms of the law. Perhaps most disturbing were the measures introduced against the press. The government now sought the power to close and to occupy physically any newspaper, magazine, or book publisher or distributor, or any radio or television transmitter if the information published or broadcast by these organizations were deemed to be an apologia for terrorism. The Congress of Deputies approved the law on April 1, with only three votes against, although most Basque nationalist deputies were absent from the chamber when the vote was taken. The law formally took effect on May 4.

The second step taken by the government was to press for immediate parliamentary approval of a draft law that had been before the parliament since September 1979: the Law on the States of Alarm, Exception and Siege.[14] The "state of alarm," which could be declared by the Council of Ministers without parliamentary approval, was to be applied in cases when public order and citizen security were imperiled, and could not be restored through normal procedures. The extraordinary powers granted to the government under these provisions would include the right to control the movement of persons and vehicles, to ration essential consumer goods, and to inspect private property without prior approval. The "state of exception" required parliamentary approval and could be invoked only for thirty days, after which a renewal of authority had to be granted by the legislature. These provisions, to be invoked when public order was severely threatened, permitted the government to arrest and imprison virtually anyone without cause, to invade private property without court approval, and to control the movement of persons, even to the point of forcing the relocation of individual domiciles. The final level of crisis management, the "state of siege," could be requested by the government and approved by parliament when the internal security of the state was in extreme danger. This step would be the equivalent of martial law, and most state functions would be assumed by the armed forces. The law establishing these three extraordinary sets of powers was approved by parliament and formally took effect on May 20, 1981. To my knowledge, none of these three measures was ever invoked, either during this period or at any time afterward. However, the extreme nature of their provisions and the speed with which they were approved by parliament suggest something of the climate of fear in Spain during the first half of 1981.

Police actions against suspected ETA members and supporters continued to run at a fairly high rate. Monthly arrests averaged between 50 and 100. However, as a consequence of more stringent detention policies, fewer of these arrested individuals were freed after their ten-day interrogation; thus, the number of Basques in prison for politically related crimes soared. In early 1981, there were about 300 Basques in prison; by the end of this period, in December 1982, this figure had climbed to 485 (see tables 2.1 and 2.2, and figure 2.1).

During this period there was renewed concern over the torture of suspects and prisoners. The most inflammatory case was that of accused ETA member Joseba Arregi, who died on February 13, 1981, while undergoing interrogation at the Madrid headquarters of the Directorate for State Security, a division of the Spanish Ministry of Interior.[15] Prison conditions had worsened to such a degree that imprisoned ETA members went on hunger strikes and otherwise injured themselves in order to be sent to the prison hospital. On June 19, 1981, Juan José Crespo died in the hospital of Carabanchel prison near Madrid after sixty-six days on a hunger strike. He was the first ETA member to die in a Spanish prison.[16]

Throughout the period, Amnesty International continued to express their great concern for the state of human rights in Spanish prisons. The organization's report for 1980–1981, published in October 1981, called attention to the arrest, detention, and interrogation provisions of the recent antiterrorist laws and to the opportunities they afforded to law enforcement authorities to mistreat and torture suspects with impunity.[17] On October 23, AI representatives met with Interior Minister Rosón to place before him their concerns regarding torture.[18] In February 1982, the government finally got around to answering the AI report of November 1980 (based, it will be recalled, on an investigative mission to Spain in October 1979). The government rejected all the charges of torture, alleging that the sources of AI's information were all convicted terrorists who, therefore, could not be believed.[19] Finally, the AI report for 1981–1982, published in October 1982, repeated the organization's concern that changes in Spain's antiterrorist laws had done nothing to eliminate the conditions under which torture could take place: ten days of preventive detention with the prisoner held incommunicado.[20]

There were also significant changes in the organizational structure of the government's antiterrorist efforts. On March 23, 1981, in the wake of renewed ETA attacks that included the assassination of two army colonels the preceding weekend, President Leopoldo Calvo Sotelo met with his key cabinet ministers to develop a series of countermeasures. In addition to asking the Congress of Deputies for urgent action on the two bills before the parliament, the government took four important steps to meet the crisis. First, major reinforcements of police and Guardia Civil troops were ordered into the Basque Country from their regular assignments in other regions of Spain. Second, controls over vehicle traffic were intensified, especially at the French border. Third, a unified command was established within the Ministry of Interior to coordinate all of the various elements of the antiterrorist struggle. Finally, units of the regular army and navy were ordered into the Basque Country, primarily to control the French border and to patrol the Bay of Biscay coastline.[21]

By March 25, the intensified armed forces presence began to be felt in the Basque Country. Seven ships of the Spanish navy arrived to assume their patrol duties along the coast between Santander and the Basque port of Pasajes. A company of "special operations" troops trained for mountain duty was deployed from Burgos to the French border in the Pyrenees; and armored cars and other troops were observed moving through Pamplona on their way to the border. By the end of March, four companies of infantry had been sent to patrol the border; they were withdrawn and replaced by the Guardia Civil near the end of September. Spokesmen for the armed forces emphasized that these units were being sent to reinforce and support the regular law enforcement authorities, who would retain overall responsibility for carrying on the struggle against ETA. Among other assignments, regular army units were responsible for the protection of the Lemoiz nuclear plant, the three major airports in the Basque Country, and the headquarters of the civil and military government offices in the three Basque provinces. In all, some 2,000 regular army troops saw duty in the Basque Country during this operation, which lasted approximately ten months.[22]

Within a matter of days, the unified antiterrorist command, the MULC, had been constituted under the leadership of the minister of interior, Juan José Rosón. Also named to the command were the directors of the National Police and of the Guardia Civil; the director of the CESID, Spain's military intelligence service; the director of State Security of the Interior Ministry; and the director of the Intelligence Service for the National Police. This latter member, a veteran police administrator named Manuel Ballesteros, was given responsibility for the daily operational control of the MULC. The command's responsibilities included the logistics, intelligence, and personnel aspects of the antiterrorist fight, the movement of troops, and the analysis of intelligence information.[23]

In April 1982, the armed forces were again involved in the fight against ETA after an upsurge of armed attacks, including the bombing of the country's central telephone exchange in Madrid. At an emergency meeting of the president's cabinet on April 18, new measures were adopted to coordinate the armed forces and the law enforcement agencies. These measures were kept a strict secret, but it was learned that the army had been placed under a "general alert" throughout Spain. All military leaves were cancelled, and all personnel were directed to return to their duty stations. Once again, army units were sent to the Pyrenees to seal off the French border. Meanwhile, the MULC issued an offer of up to 10 million pesetas for information leading to the capture of suspected terrorists.[24]

Despite the election of socialist François Mitterrand to the presidency in France in May 1981, there was little change in French policy toward ETA during this period.[25] When Mitterrand took office, there were about 35 suspected ETA members in French prisons and a dozen pending Spanish requests for extradition. Less than a month after assuming office, Mitterrand reversed a French court ruling that would have authorized extradition of accused ETA member Tomás Linaza; and during this period there were no more extraditions authorized. In July 1981, Calvo Sotelo visited Paris to press for stronger action against ETA; and there were some important steps taken in Paris to cooperate with Spain, especially in the military operations undertaken during 1981 to seal off the French-Spanish border. Harassment of Basques in France continued and even intensified; in June 1982, just before Mitterrand was to go to Madrid, French police cracked down hard on suspected ETA leaders, arresting a number including Txomin Iturbe. Mitterrand's visit produced few concrete changes in policy, although the French leader did promise better control of the border. In October 1982, on the eve of elections in Spain, a French government spokesman reiterated that French extradition policy was based on their belief that the Basque problem was essentially one for Spain to solve and there could be no consideration of extraditions until there was a fundamental change in Spanish policy toward the Basques. Such changes would include greater regional autonomy for Basques as well as an improvement in Spain's record regarding human rights and treatment of prisoners.

Antiterrorist Policy Under the New Socialist Government: November 1982–November 1984

On October 28, 1982, the Spanish Socialist Workers Party, led by Felipe González, won a smashing victory in elections for the nation's parliament. For the next two years antiterrorist policy grew steadily tougher and more coercive as the socialists tried to answer right-wing critics who believed them to be "soft on terrorism." In addition to introducing a new antiterrorist law and formulating a new security plan for the Basque Country, the González government finally succeeded in obtaining active French cooperation to eliminate ETA's sanctuary on French soil. Another important element in antiterrorist policy was the return to the clandestine "dirty war" in France. Following the assassination of popular Basque political figure Santiago Brouard in November 1984, this initial phase of socialist antiterrorist policy gave way to an even more stringent set of measures that was to last more than two years.

Within a month of taking office, the González government was already actively reviewing the antiterrorist policy it had inherited from its predecessors, with a view toward making it stronger and eliminating the few remaining loopholes that could be used to block vigorous government pursuit and punishment of suspected terrorists. On December 15, the new minister of interior, José Barrionuevo, announced that he was conducting a thorough review of existing antiterrorist policies and organizational arrangements;

and the following month it was revealed that the government intended to pursue and punish anyone whose conduct might be interpreted as "assisting" terrorists. In early 1983, the government introduced two new draft laws intended to regulate the right of accused to legal assistance and the use of habeas corpus in legal proceedings.[26] These two laws were finally approved by the Congress of Deputies in December 1983 (as Organic Law 14/1983) and March 1984 (as Organic Law 6/1984), respectively. About the latter law, Basque deputy Juan María Bandrés said that it was "useless and a practical joke."[27]

In October 1983, a wave of ETA killings, including the kidnapping and assassination of army captain Alberto Martín Barrios, led to the introduction of yet another antiterrorist law. The presentation of the bill to the Congress of Deputies by the government was preceded by a meeting between President González and the leader of the conservative opposition, Manuel Fraga, who emerged from the meeting saying he was basically satisfied with González's proposals, although he personally would have preferred the declaration of a "state of exception" in the Basque provinces.[28] According to Basque nationalist deputy Marcos Vizcaya, the proposed legislation would indeed have the effect of creating a "semipermanent state of exception in the Basque country."[29] Despite the government's request that the parliament approve the draft law immediately under emergency legislative procedures, there were delays. The bill was not approved by the Congress of Deputies until September 1984, and by the senate until November 21, and so did not become law until December.[30] Therefore, the impact of the law was not felt until the next phase of antiterrorist policy.

One of the immediate consequences of this shift to a tougher antiterrorist policy was felt in the mass media. While many newspapers and magazines suffered government harassment or worse, the Spanish government reserved its strongest measures for the two publications most closely associated with ETA—the San Sebastián newspaper *Egin* and the Basque magazine *Punto y Hora*.

In late 1982, Javier Sanchez Erauskin, former editor of *Punto y Hora* and a columnist for *Egin*, was arrested, charged with publishing articles that insulted the Spanish government and the king, and subsequently convicted. After an appeal in January 1983, the conviction was upheld and Sanchez Erauskin was sentenced to eighteen months in prison. He entered prison in April amid much protest from the Basque population.[31] Mass demonstrations were mounted in Bilbao as well as outside the Nanclares de Oca prison where he was confined; and the Basque parliament passed a resolution asking that he be pardoned. Several days after entering prison, Sanchez Erauskin began a hunger strike to force the prison to classify him as a "political prisoner" instead of a common criminal, a battle he eventually won. In January 1984, Sanchez Erauskin was released after serving nearly three-fourths of his sentence.

The Sanchez Erauskin case was only one of a number of measures taken by Madrid to try to silence *Egin* and *Punto y Hora*. The editor of *Egin*, José Félix Azurmendi, was on trial almost continuously for two years defending himself against a series of accusations of apologia for terrorism, charges that stemmed primarily from the publication of ETA communiqués or of columns attacking the government's antiterrorist policies. In each case, either the charges were dropped or Azurmendi was found innocent of the accusations. A director of *Punto y Hora*, Mertxe Aizpurua, was sentenced to a year in jail in October 1984 for offenses against the state. The heads of the *Egin* offices in Bilbao and Madrid were both charged with having written articles that were disrespectful of government authority; and in the former case, the editor was convicted and sentenced to three months in jail. Several reporters for the newspaper were charged with having written articles critical of the government, as were columnists for *Egin*, such as sociologist Justo de la Cueva and Herri Batasuna leader Miguel Castells. Even people who were interviewed for the publications could be prosecuted for things they said, as was shown by the case of the Spanish Air Force captain who was tried (and acquitted) in September 1983 for comments made in an interview for *Punto y Hora*. Leaders of Herri Batasuna were also in court frequently during this period to defend themselves against charges of apologia for terrorism for remarks made in press conferences that were reported by *Egin*. On several occasions, editions of the newspaper and the magazine were confiscated or removed from kiosks, or had offending pages removed before being authorized for sale.

When the socialists took office, there were about 485 Basques in prison for various crimes against the state or public order (see table 2.2). As the policy of "social reintegration" or selective amnesty, undertaken by the previous government, began to take effect and members of ETA (p-m) were slowly released from prison, the number dropped to slightly more than 300 by January 1984. However, the tougher antiterrorist stance of the socialists reversed the trend. In 1983, arrest rates averaged slightly below 100 per month; during 1984, they soared to more than 150 per month (see table 2.1). As a consequence, by December 1984 the number of Basque political prisoners had climbed again to well over 400. In the spring of 1983, the government began to transfer ETA prisoners from prisons all over Spain to several maximum security prisons, especially Herrera de la Mancha. Here they were guarded by a special detachment of Civil Guards and subject to extensive periods in punishment cells or solitary confinement. In December 1983, more than twenty ETA prisoners were being held in solitary confinement in Herrera de la Mancha. By the following September, these and other prisoners had been subjected to more than two hundred days of continuous punishment by this means.

Despite claims by both Interior Minister Barrionuevo and the new director of state security, Rafael Vera, that mistreatment and torture of prisoners were not going to be allowed under the socialist government, the abuse of human rights in Spanish prisons remained a serious concern through González's first two years in office.

The evidence of continued torture in prisons came from several sources. In February 1983, Basque nationalist senator Joseba Azkarraga charged that torture in local police stations was continuing under the new government.[32] In April 1983, the Madrid magazine *Tiempo* published documentation of some 160 cases of torture since the socialists took office.[33] In July 1984, the Pro-Human Rights Association of the Basque Country conducted a month-long public review of the torture issue, complete with photographic displays of recent victims. In a press conference at the conclusion, association spokesmen, including two judges and an attorney, asserted that the loss of human rights in the Basque Country constituted a "scandalous situation."[34] In August 1984, the Pro-Amnesty Committees of the Basque Country presented a detailed study of some three thousand cases of torture over the preceding three and one half years, or since the beginning of 1981. In November, *Tiempo* returned to the issue with an article claiming that more than twenty police and Civil Guards accused of torture had recently received decorations or awards from Interior Minister Barrionuevo.[35]

Amnesty International also continued its close scrutiny of the condition of prisoners and accused suspects under police interrogation. In its annual reports for 1982, 1983, and 1984, the human rights organization repeated its charges that torture and mistreatment of prisoners were still problems in the Spanish penal system.[36] In April 1984, AI published its special report on torture around the world in the 1980s; its section on Spain alleged that "torture and mistreatment of arrested persons were continuous" from 1980 through 1983.[37]

In May and June 1983, a special Amnesty International team visited Spain to investigate charges of torture—the third time the organization had sent a team to the country since 1975. The report of the mission was discussed with both the ministers of justice and interior, as well as with President González himself in meetings held in October 1984. The final report, which was not published until 1985, concluded that "the infliction of torture and ill-treatment on detainees continued in Spain throughout 1983," and that "the major rights for the protection of detainees enshrined in the 1978 constitution were of only limited value in preventing abuses."[38] Minister of Interior Barrionuevo responded to these charges in a lengthy memorandum dated November 29, 1984. After dismissing most of the evidence of torture as being false or the product of self-injury, the minister went on to defend the system of safeguards contained in the Spanish legal system as being "entirely acceptable in the most demanding of European democracies." If there were occasional abuses and harsh practices, he wrote, these "are ultimately justified by the grave threat that is posed by terrorism to the lives and security of citizens and the survival of the democratic way of life."[39]

The new socialist government extended its review of antiterrorist policy into the organizational area as well, and the result was a tough new plan to restore public order to the Basque Country. In February 1983, Interior Minister Barrionuevo launched a series of meetings to discuss his new plan for citizen security. By early March, the minister began to reveal parts of his plan to the press and to other political leaders. In May, state security director Rafael

Vera announced the plan formally, and in June Barrionuevo went to the parliament for their approval. The plan went into effect in September. It was officially labeled "Plan ZEN," for "Zona Especial del Norte," or "Special Northern Zone."[40]

Plan ZEN was contained in a lengthy document drafted in Rafael Vera's state security bureau in the interior ministry.[41] The plan covered the entire range of actions envisioned in a coordinated attack on terrorism. In the political realm, the plan stressed the isolation of ETA by obtaining the full cooperation of the more moderate Basque political parties as well as of the Basque autonomous government. In the social field, the plan called for a public relations effort designed to change the popular images of both ETA and the police and Civil Guard, so that the general public would come to support the latter and turn their backs on the former. The plan also recognized a need to tighten the country's antiterrorist legislation, a dimension of policy we have already discussed; and it was also proposed that Spain emulate the Italian model by offering amnesty to convicted or exiled terrorists who would agree to collaborate with the government's antiterrorist struggle. Improved police methods were not overlooked in Plan ZEN, and the document spelled out numerous ways in which law enforcement could be improved, especially through better coordination, better intelligence, and better training for police and paramilitary units. The plan even called openly for the planting of false information in the news media to confuse ETA or to reduce popular support for the group. To pay for all these measures, the plan presented a two-year budget of some 14.6 billion pesetas, more than $97 million at current exchange rates. By May 1983, the Ministry of Interior had already allocated more than $17 million to the plan.[42]

Despite the efforts of Barrionuevo and Vera to explain the plan to the Basques, Plan ZEN never received the much-needed support from the Basque political community. In June and July, numerous municipal governments in the Basque Country passed resolutions stating their opposition to, and refusal to cooperate with, Plan ZEN; and in October, the Basque parliament passed a resolution that stated in part: "citizen security must be achieved through the fulfillment of the Basque Autonomy Statute. In this sense, the Basque parliament considers the so-called Plan ZEN to be inopportune."[43] Very little was heard from Madrid again about Plan ZEN.

Following the Martín Barrios killing in October 1983, the Spanish government took a number of additional police measures to try to meet this provocative challenge. More than forty ETA prisoners were transferred immediately from Nanclares de Oca prison to one of several maximum security prisons outside the Basque Country, where they would be guarded by Civil Guards and National Police instead of regular prison authorities.[44] Extra detachments of Guardia Civil forces and police were dispatched to the Basque Country to strengthen the protection afforded to political leaders and government buildings. There were also discussions about how the government could prosecute leaders of radical Basque parties, especially Herri Batasuna, to punish them for what was alleged to be apologia in defense of terrorism.

Meanwhile in Madrid, a new government agency, the Police Intelligence Council, was created to study problems related to police intelligence and terrorist activity, to propose special measures that were needed, and to advise the minister of interior on the coordination of antiterrorist measures.[45] In addition to the heads of the Guardia Civil and the National Police, and of their respective intelligence services, this agency also gave new responsibilities to several key leaders of antiterrorist policy under the former Suárez government. The most important of these was Manuel Ballesteros, who had been removed from his position as the operational head of the Unified Counterterrorist Command after the socialist electoral victory and given an insignificant job far removed from the antiterrorist field.

But of all the new measures undertaken during this period to suppress terrorist violence, by far the most troublesome was the reappearance of the clandestine "dirty war" of the right-wing assassination squads in France. It will be recalled that the last attack of the Basque-Spanish Battalion (BVE) had taken place in December 1980, after which an uneasy calm had settled over the Basque community in southern France. On October 16, 1983, about ten days after Martín Barrios was kidnapped by ETA, two Basque refugees living in France, José Antonio Lasa and José Ignacio Zabala, disappeared, apparently kidnapped. Their bodies were never discovered and they were presumed killed. That crime was never solved and its perpetrators never claimed responsibility. However, most observers believe that the Lasa-Zabala kidnapping was the first in a long series of attacks launched against Basques by a group known as the Grupos Antiterroristas de Liberación (GAL).[46]

From the very beginning of the GAL attacks, Basque leaders alleged that Spanish law enforcement agencies were involved. On December 30, 1983, just two days after the GAL had claimed its second victim, PNV leader Xabier Arzalluz said in a public meeting, "I am personally persuaded, although I cannot prove it, that the GAL and that 'dirty war' have ties to government measures in Madrid."[47] In March 1984, leaders of Herri Batasuna charged at a press conference that there was "connivance between the GAL and the apparatus of the [Spanish] state."[48] As early as April 1984, there was evidence that a Civil Guard had acted as intermediary to set up a GAL assassination the preceding month.[49]

The first attack for which the GAL claimed responsibility was the kidnapping of Segundo Marey, a Spanish citizen living in France, on December 4, 1983. Marey was subsequently released unharmed near the French-Spanish border; but on December 19 the GAL assassinated a Basque refugee named Ramón Onederra in a bar in Bayonne.[50] From that point on, until November 1984, the GAL was responsible for killing a total of thirteen victims (including Lasa and Zabala), wounding five, and kidnapping one (Marey). Among the persons killed during this period were Javier Pérez Arenaza, brother-in-law of ETA leader Txomin Iturbe, and Tomás Pérez Revilla, one of the "historic" leaders of ETA. The most serious attack of the GAL was the assassination of Santiago Brouard in his Bilbao office on November 20, 1984. Not only was this attack inflammatory of public opinion, but it also doomed to failure an attempt by Brouard and others to get negotiations started between ETA and Madrid. For these and other reasons, the Brouard killing brought to a close the initial attempts at antiterrorist policy by the González government.

Of all the changes that were introduced in Spain's antiterrorist policies during the first two years of the PSOE government, the most significant involved obtaining French cooperation in the fight against ETA. At first, despite the transfer of power in Spain to a fellow socialist regime, the French gave little evidence of wanting to change their policies. Shortly after the Spanish parliamentary elections, the French government issued a statement of the criteria it would use in the future to decide extradition cases: the nature of the judicial system in the state requesting extradition, the political motivation in the request, the risks faced by the person to be extradited, and the political character of the alleged crime.[51] While these criteria simply restated France's long-standing policy, the statement added one new criterion: "When criminal acts . . . have been committed in a state respectful of basic rights and liberties, and these acts are of such a nature that the alleged political end cannot justify unacceptable means, the infraction will not be considered of a political nature, and in principle extradition will be granted." This statement, which applied only to crimes committed after November 11, 1982, was widely interpreted as signaling a change in French policy to facilitate extradition. However, it could also have been taken as a warning that France would be looking for improvements in Spain's human rights record before considering extraditing accused ETA members. This latter interpretation was reinforced by the new French ambassador to Spain, who, on January 13, 1983, was quoted in the press as saying "France does not flee from its responsibilities in the case of Basque terrorism, but what we are discussing is a totally Spanish problem."[52]

In addition to these ambiguous verbal indications coming out of the French government, French actions also sent unclear signals to Madrid. On November 6, 1982, French police arrested two important ETA leaders, Pello Ansola "Peio el viejo," and Carlos Ibarguren "Nervios." The head of ETA, Txomin Iturbe, was already in jail in France, having been arrested the preceding June for violating French firearm possession laws. Within eight months, all three were back on the street, however. Iturbe and Ansola were released in March 1983, and Ibarguren was freed in June.

Despite these ambiguities in French policy, or perhaps heartened by them, Spain's new socialist leaders launched an aggressive campaign to persuade its northern neighbor to reverse its historic policy toward ETA and deny the use of its territory to the Basque insurgents. This important mission was headed by the leader of the socialist party in the Basque Country, Txiki Benegas.[53]

Efforts to alter French policy began even before the 1982 Spanish elections. In June 1982, at a meeting of the Socialist International in Rome called to discuss terrorism, Spanish socialists succeeded in persuading the French delegates to support a vigorous antiterrorist policy, including a commitment that no socialist government would allow terrorists from democratic countries to operate from their soil. Shortly after the Spanish elections, at a meeting of the Union of Socialist Parties in Paris in November, French socialists formally committed themselves to the agreements voted on in Rome in June. It was during this meeting that the French government issued the statement on extraditions referred to earlier. The November meeting was also useful in establishing numerous personal ties between officials from the interior ministries of the two countries who were actively involved in antiterrorist activities.

During 1983 and 1984, contacts between Spain and France over the subject of terrorism both increased in frequency and warmed in spirit. In January 1983, Spanish foreign minister Fernando Moran visited his French counterpart, Claude Cheysson, to discuss a number of outstanding issues between their two countries, including antiterrorist collaboration. At the close of the meetings, Moran declared that a "new stage" in French-Spanish relations was about to unfold.[54] Later that same month, Felipe González visited Paris to meet with French president Mitterrand, who returned the visit to Madrid in late June.[55] The two interior ministers, José Barrionuevo and Gaston Deferre, held a number of meetings during the two-year period, as well. In April 1983, Spain sent to Paris a permanent representative to coordinate the flow of information between the two countries' interior ministries on issues related to terrorism. Lastly, the Spanish director of state security, Rafael Vera, organized three meetings between Spanish and French officials who dealt with terrorism at the working level: in March–April and October–November 1983, and February–March 1984.[56]

In the course of many of these meetings, the Spanish concentrated on trying to change the French perception of the insurgency problem. Their strategy focused on persuading Paris that democracy in Spain was genuine, that Basques had no legitimate reason to resort to violence to gain their aims, and that alleged ETA members who were returned to Spain for trial would be fairly treated. In addition, Madrid pressed the French to take stronger action against specific targets, alleged ETA members, especially key leaders, and other Basque refugees living in France. In late October, following the Martín Barrios killing, Barrionuevo delivered to the French ambassador in Madrid a list of about thirty ETA members, including five "most wanted" leaders. The Spanish government insisted that Paris increase its surveillance of these men, and arrest them whenever possible.[57] Finally, the Spanish government pressed strongly on the extradition issue, the last remaining element in their case against French tolerance of ETA.

When the French failed to respond immediately to these demands, Spain launched a policy of direct Spanish intervention against ETA on French soil. The return to the "dirty war" of the GAL shortly after the Martín Barrios killing was one of the most dramatic aspects of this policy. The GAL was not the only anti-ETA force acting in France, however. In mid-1983, Spanish police in plain clothes began operating across the border. These operations were kept secret until October, when four Spanish police were arrested in the French Basque town of Hendaye after they had kidnapped and severely beaten an alleged ETA member, José María Larretxea.[58] The official Spanish version of this incident was that the four police officers had been sent to France to try to negotiate the release of Martín Barrios and that they had not been involved in the kidnap attempt of Larretxea. Nevertheless, Madrid was forced to call a halt to this policy of "hot pursuit" across the French border.[59]

By early 1984, the Spanish efforts began to pay dividends.[60] In January, French police conducted a major sweep of Basque towns, arresting more than forty alleged ETA members. Such police actions were not especially new; what signaled the major change in French policy was the immediate deportation of six of those arrested, first to the island of Guadeloupe and then to Panama. In March, these six were joined by a seventh deportee, and in May all seven were moved from Panama to Cuba. Included in the list were Pello Ansola and Carlos Ibarguren, arrested in November 1982 and released in March and June 1983, respectively, and José María Larretxea, the victim of the Spanish police kidnapping the preceding October.

The arrests and deportations continued throughout 1984. In April and May, six ETA members were sent to Venezuela; in June and September, five were deported to Panama; and in September, four were sent to the African state of Togo. The real prize was key ETA leader Eugenio Etxebeste "Antxon," arrested on July 31 in the French Basque town of Anglet and deported to the Dominican Republic on August 10.

In all, in 1984 the French deported some twenty-three members of ETA, including several who had held important leadership posts. In most instances those deported had not violated any French law and resided in France legally. While many of these were at least given a court hearing before deportation, some were not afforded even this minimum protection; and in later years, deportations would be carried out in large numbers without judicial hearings. The simple fact is that the French wished to be rid of what had become a major irritant to them, and seized upon the weapon of deportation as the easiest method of dealing with the problem.

These deportations were only the prelude to the really significant change in French policy toward ETA that took place in late summer of 1984. The stage was set on July 14, when Belgium became the first country ever to extradite alleged ETA members, sending Joseba Artexte and Josu Ormaza back to Spain to await trial. (Ironically, both were eventually freed by Spanish courts.) In late July and early August, a number of suspected ETA members were taken into custody by the French; and Madrid initiated extradition requests for seven of these. On August 8, the seven began a hunger strike that eventually forced the French to move them to a prison hospital. Across the Basque Country there were major demonstrations against the pending extraditions. In late August, a French court decided that the seven should be extradited. The issue then went to the French government, where it was determined on September 23 to extradite only three of the accused—Juan Carlos García Ramírez, José Manuel Martínez Beiztegi, and Francisco Lujambio.[61] The other four were instead deported to Togo, as mentioned earlier. By the end of 1984, five ETA members in all had been returned to Spain for trial.

Within two years, the tougher French policy on deportations and extraditions had significantly weakened ETA's infrastructure in France. Indeed, many Spanish observers would later claim that it was the change in French attitudes and policies that brought about the decline in terrorist violence in the Basque Country by 1988, and that forced ETA to negotiate from a position of relative weakness in the late 1980s. The real French objective was probably more accurately expressed by the anonymous government sources who were quoted by France Press on September 25, 1984, as expressing their "hope that the González government would put an end to the GAL activities as a counterpart to the extraditions."[62]

Antiterrorist Policy at Its Most Severe: November 1984–January 1987

Following the assassination of Santiago Brouard in November 1984, Spanish antiterrorist policy reached new severity with measures that some observers compared with the worst years of the Franco dictatorship. The antiterrorist law introduced in 1983 was approved and in effect for more than two years. The "dirty war" of the GAL continued for another eighteen months, and Basques were detained in Spanish prisons in near record numbers. The French government also increased its pursuit of ETA members and leaders, deporting some to third countries and expelling others directly to Spain without benefit of an extradition hearing.

The González government reacted to the Martín Barrios killing in October 1983 by proposing new antiterrorist legislation. The bill remained in the congress for about a year, and was finally approved by the parliament on December 21, 1984. The measure was officially promulgated by King Juan Carlos on December 26 as Organic Law 8/1984, and published in the Official State Bulletin on January 3, 1985.[63]

The 1984 antiterrorist law reaffirmed the extraordinary police powers contained in earlier laws, including those dealing with preventive detention, holding detainees incommunicado, and authority to tap telephones and enter and search homes without a warrant. The new law went far beyond existing legislation in many other areas, however.[64] Under the law, judges were authorized to ban political parties and other groups led by convicted terrorists, to close down newspapers and magazines that supported terrorist aims, and to order the detention without trial of suspected terrorists for periods of up to two and a half years. Penalties for terrorist acts were sharply increased, and a new category of crime—attacks against members of the armed forces—was created. People who incited, supported, or engaged in apologia for terrorist acts were to be punished with the same penalties as those who actually committed

the acts. Henceforth it would be a crime for any elected public official to criticize the Spanish nation, its symbols, or its flag. The law
also amended Spain's existing criminal code to make it possible
to prosecute Spanish citizens for crimes they committed in other
countries, such as extortion or kidnapping. Provincial governors
were instructed to ensure that public demonstrations would not
be used to support terrorist aims or to defend terrorists or their
actions. Finally, the law called on the French government to observe the provision of the Geneva Convention of 1951 that denied
refugee status to persons who had committed serious crimes outside the country of refuge.

Basque political leaders across the spectrum attacked the law
as unnecessary and repressive, saying that it would just make more
difficult the maintenance of public order in the Basque Country. HB
leader Miguel Castells called it a "Nazi law more regressive than
the Francoists in many aspects," and Juan María Bandrés labeled
the law "a licence to torture." On January 5, 1985, the Basque parliament officially asked Spain's highest court, the Constitutional
Tribunal, to declare unconstitutional 10 of the law's 22 articles;
and in May, the court agreed to hear the case.[65] While the court
eventually found that 4 of the law's provisions were indeed unconstitutional, by the time it reached its verdict—December 1987—
parts of the law had already lapsed automatically, and the government had requested repeal of the remainder.[66]

Armed with these tough new laws, Spain's law enforcement
authorities stepped up the pace of detentions in the Basque Country. According to the Basque Pro-Amnesty Committees, there were
940 arrests under the antiterrorist law in 1985 (out of more than
1,100 total detentions), a number that increased to 990 in 1986.[67]
Between December 1984 and September 1986, 1,026 persons were
held incommunicado in the Basque provinces. While the number of
Basques in prison dropped from 419 in December 1984 to 369 one
year later, by December 1986 the number had risen again to 477,
the highest level since the socialists came to power (see table 2.2).

For those detained in local police stations or in prison, conditions remained harsh. In March 1985, 182 ETA prisoners went on a
hunger strike to protest their mistreatment, and there were reports
of ETA prisoners deliberately injuring themselves to be sent to the
prison hospitals. In June 1985, the body of José Ramón Goikoetxea

was discovered in the showers of Alcala-Meco prison, an apparent suicide. Two other ETA prisoners died because of illnesses that could be traced to mistreatment while in prison during the period.[68] Amnesty International reports for both 1985 and 1986 began with expressions of concern over the torture and ill-treatment of detainees being held incommunicado under the provisions of the antiterrorist law. The most inflammatory incident during this period occurred in December 1985, when a Basque youth named Mikel Zabalza disappeared after having been taken into custody by the Guardia Civil. His body was retrieved several days later from the Bidasoa River, his hands still cuffed behind his back. Civil Guard officials maintained that he had escaped and jumped in the river to elude his pursuers, but an autopsy showed that he died before entering the river. In response, there were massive protests, culminating in a general strike across the Basque Country.

Following the Brouard killing in November 1984, the GAL continued its wave of attacks against alleged ETA members, ordinary Basque refugees, and even French citizens living in the Basque region. The attacks lasted until mid-June 1986, although there was one more killing, apparently in error since the victim had no known links to ETA, in July 1987.[69] The bloodiest GAL attack came on September 25, 1985, when four alleged ETA members were shot to death in a bar in Bayonne. Exact numbers of victims are difficult to prove, but most sources agree that the GAL was responsible for twenty-seven or twenty-eight killings in its history.

As one might expect with a clandestine group like the GAL, there were many vivid and imaginative speculations about its origins, its sources of funding and of assassins, and its ties to the Spanish government. Most stories about the GAL traced it back at least to the Spanish-Basque Battalion (BVE), and some back as far as the Franco period; but all agree that the GAL surpassed any such group that had come before in its expertise, the quality of its intelligence, and the ferocity with which it pursued Basques in France. The group apparently recruited its assassins from a number of different sources: Italian neo-fascists, Portuguese mercenaries, former members of the French army in Algeria, Spanish undercover agents, professional killers from Marseilles, and so forth.[70] One of the earliest clues to the nature of the GAL came in March 1984, when an Algerian *pied noir*, Jean Pierre Cherid, was killed accidentally while trying to plant a bomb in Biarritz. It was later discovered that Cherid, a former member of the French secret army, the OAS, had been working for Spanish police agencies since 1970.[71]

Early in the group's history, there was active speculation that the GAL was financed by a small circle of wealthy Basque business-men from Guipúzcoa who used the counterterrorist group to force ETA to stop trying to extort the "revolutionary tax" from them.[72] Business groups denied these accusations, but the public remarks of outspoken industrialist Luis Olarra, who defended the GAL as being a "soft response to ETA," added fuel to these speculations.[73] At other times, press reports claimed that the GAL was financed by international crime syndicates such as the Mafia that wanted to dissuade ETA from attacking the tourist resorts of southern Spain, where these syndicates had built casinos and hotels. But eventually the evidence became clear that at least some of the money used to hire GAL assassins had come from secret accounts maintained by officials of the Spanish interior ministry.

As late as November 1989, the most serious cases involving the GAL, including the Brouard assassination, were still being pro-cessed through the Spanish court system. Thus, even at this dis-tance from the attacks themselves, we are unable to say defini-tively to what degree the Spanish government was involved. What is clear, however, is that at least two key Spanish police officials, José Amedo and Michel Domínguez, were identified by confessed GAL killers as being their contact point with the Madrid gov-ernment; that Amedo and Domínguez traveled frequently to the French and Spanish regions of the Basque Country, as well as to Lisbon, using false names and fake credit cards and spending huge sums of money; and that these two men had access to secret funds allocated to the Spanish Ministry of Interior, for which they have never been asked to account. Amedo had been sought by French courts since November 1987 to stand trial for GAL attacks, and both he and Domínguez went on trial in Spain in January 1989, in a sensational case the Spanish press referred to as "GALgate."[74] Despite the refusal of the Spanish interior ministry to reveal to the judge how much money Amedo and Domínguez received, who authorized its expenditure, or for what it was spent, there seems to be incontrovertible evidence that Spanish government officials were connected to the GAL, probably from its very beginning, and supported the organization with substantial sums of money, intelligence information, and in other ways. A 1987 opinion poll carried out by the Madrid magazine *Tiempo* showed that 52 percent of the respondents believed that some agency of the Spanish government was responsible for creating and financing the GAL. Almost the same proportion, 51 percent, approved of the GAL's killing of ETA members in order to halt, or at least to impede, the terrorists.[75]

What brought the wave of GAL killings to a close? Most speculation suggests that the attacks were ended after the French government changed its policy regarding the expulsion of accused ETA members to Spain. On March 16, 1986, voters in France elected as prime minister the conservative Jacques Chirac, whose approach to dealing with ETA and with terrorists in general differed considerably from his predecessors. In early April, France was hit by a wave of terrorist attacks, mostly by Middle East groups. The resulting heightened antiterrorist sentiment toughened the French position against terrorist violence in general, and particularly in the area of international cooperation.[76]

While President François Mitterrand was willing to arrest and deport several dozen ETA members in 1984 and 1985, he was still reluctant to extradite them to Spain for trial. In fact, only five had been extradited since France's change in policy in September 1984. On July 19, 1986, however, four months after Chirac's election, the French government, using a 1945 law allowing such measures for reasons of "urgent procedures," expelled a Basque refugee—Txema Lopez—to Spain. One week later, the French foreign minister assured that there would be others similarly returned. Except for the (presumably erroneous) killing in July of the next year, there were no more GAL killings after this date.[77] In all, a total of seventy Basques were expelled to Spain in the first twelve months after this new policy went into effect. Of these, twenty-eight were eventually freed.[78]

These expulsions of alleged ETA members to Spain were not the only sign of increased French pressure against the organization. In November 1986, while Felipe González was meeting with Chirac in Madrid, French police carried out one of the most significant raids against ETA headquarters in France. The target was Sokoa, a Basque-owned furniture and office equipment import-export firm in Hendaye. For some months previously, French police had had the firm under surveillance on suspicion that its accounting system was being used to launder funds for ETA. The police raid turned up huge quantities of documents that proved invaluable in guiding the French in subsequent waves of arrests of ETA members.[79]

The French policy of deportation to third countries continued, although at a slightly reduced pace from 1984. In 1985 France deported one ETA member to the Dominican Republic, one to the African island country of São Tomé, and three to Cape Verde.[80] These deportations, plus one more (to Cape Verde) in 1986, brought to twenty-nine the number of ETA members expelled to third countries since mid-1984.

During the 1985–1986 period, French police arrested a number of top ETA leaders, including the organization's "number two" leader, Juan Lorenzo Santiago Lasa Mitxelena "Txikierdi," in January 1985; ETA's logistics chief, Isidoro Maria Garalde "Mamarru," in February 1985; and the group's propaganda head, Juan Ramón Aramburu Garmendia "Juanra," in December 1985.[81] The decisive blow, however, was the arrest of ETA's top leader, Txomin Iturbe, in April 1986. These arrests, plus that of Antxon Etxebeste in 1984, effectively dismembered the ETA leadership in France and forced a new generation of leaders to assume control of the organization.

Antiterrorist Policy Relaxes Slightly:
January 1987–February 1988

For the last year of the period covered by this study, Spanish antiterrorist policy relaxed slightly, especially in the area of legislation. Except for one apparently isolated killing in mid-1987, the GAL all but disappeared, although court cases against its alleged members and leaders continued to inflame Basque public opinion. In most other areas, however, including detention levels, police activity, and mistreatment of prisoners, the pursuit of ETA continued unabated. And in the all-important area of French cooperation, there was even a new element of antiterrorist policy introduced—the widespread detention and deportation to Spain of Basques, including family members as well as suspected terrorists.

In January 1987, six of the twenty-two articles of the 1984 antiterrorist law lapsed automatically, as provided for in the Final

Disposition of the law's text.[82] Some of these provisions had little effect on the actual implementation of the law, but a few were of great significance, including the article that had permitted judges to close down associations led by persons who had been convicted of terrorist acts. In February, during his "state of the nation" address, President González announced his intention to ask the congress to repeal the entire law since it was no longer necessary. Later that same year, in November, all the Spanish political parties and all the Basque parties except Eusko Alkartasuna and Herri Batasuna signed an antiterrorist pact that called for the early repeal of the law. The government introduced legislation in late November to repeal Organic Law 8/1984 and transfer most of its provisions to the country's regular penal code.[83] Detention incommunicado was reduced from ten days to five, and pro-ETA apologists would not be punished as long as they refrained from actual attacks themselves.[84] By May 1988, the parliament had approved the repeal legislation, and Spain was without special antiterrorist legislation for the first time in more than a decade.[85]

After 1986, arrest rates declined noticeably, to as low as fifteen per month and as high as fifty (see table 2.1). Detention levels continued to rise, however, reflecting the fact that the government's selective amnesty program, "social reintegration," had in effect ceased to function by this time, and few if any ETA prisoners were being returned to the streets. By December 1987, there were more than five hundred Basques in prison for alleged political crimes, the highest number since the last days of the Franco regime (see table 2.2). There was, however, a slight decline in that number in early 1988.

For those who remained in prison, these proved to be trying times. ETA continued to insist on loyalty to the organization and solidarity with other prisoners; so most ETA members in jail refused even to consider appealing for selective amnesty. As time passed, however, and the opportunity for a negotiated cease-fire with a general amnesty grew less likely, there were indications that the prisoners were becoming desperate. A few even started to look for more dramatic release from their captivity. On March 2, 1988, the body of Mikel Lopetegi was discovered in his cell in Herrera de la Mancha prison, apparently a victim of suicide from hanging. In

June 1988, a second ETA prisoner, Juan Carlos Alberdi Martiarena was discovered dead of causes not announced.[86]

The principal development on the French side of the border came on September 30, 1987, when French police, in two separate actions, arrested the leader of ETA's armed attack cells, Santiago Arrospide "Santi Potros," and a second important ETA member, José Ignacio Pikabea.[87] When arrested, Arrospide had in his possession more than 30 pounds of documents with important information about ETA's organizational structure and membership. These documents, together with the information gathered in the Sokoa raid the preceding year, enabled French and Spanish authorities to carry out the most massive series of arrests ETA had ever experienced.

Since the raids on ETA's infrastructure went on for several months, it became difficult to keep track of the exact numbers of Basques detained, tried, and convicted. Of the 104 persons arrested in Spain because of the materials seized in the Arrospide raid, 23 eventually were sent to prison, 28 were held in police stations or other facilities for a limited time and then released, and the remaining 55 were freed almost immediately after their detention.[88] Numbers from the French side were more ambiguous. Initial reports suggested that the total number arrested would be about 150, with some 50 expelled to Spain; and these were the figures reported in the foreign press. However, by late October a total of 148 Basques had been expelled to Spain, and by mid-November the number had risen to between 160 and 164; so the total number arrested could have been as high as 300.[89] By June 1988, a total of 192 Basques had been expelled to Spain, as well as more than a dozen to third countries, including Algeria, under France's "urgent procedure" law.[90] It is true that some of those expelled were threats to Spanish public order; but the French indiscriminate use of detentions and expulsions also caught up a number of innocent persons, including wives and even children of accused ETA members. Of the first 147 persons expelled to Spain, only 88 eventually wound up in prison; the remaining 59 were released without charges, the coincidental victims of French and Spanish cooperation in the war against ETA.[91]

CHAPTER THREE

Early Attempts to Negotiate with ETA: 1975–1980

FOLLOWING an agonizing and lengthy illness, the body of General Francisco Franco was laid to rest on November 23, 1975. Within hours of the dictator's burial, an emissary of the newly crowned Spanish king, Juan Carlos, arrived in the French Basque region to try to begin "conversations" with ETA. The day of Franco's funeral, the emissary paid a visit to the Nafarroa bookstore in downtown Biarritz.[1] The bookstore, run by two Basque refugees, Fermin Elizari and Eusebio Iriarte, was known as a place where a person interested in talking with ETA could establish initial contacts. The visitor inquired how he could meet with ETA, and the owners described for him how to make such arrangements.

Several hours later, at another location on the French Basque coast near Biarritz, the visitor held the first of two meetings with ETA representatives. He emphasized first the need for confidentiality. He told the Basques that the presence of Juan Carlos on the Spanish throne would mean the liberalization of the regime, and that even organizations like ETA would benefit from the impending changes. In return, he asked ETA to observe a "political truce" for the immediate future to give the new king time to carry out his proposed changes. In fact, the king was about ready to announce his first package of reforms, including pardons for a large number of political prisoners, many of whom were Basque.

ETA's immediate reaction to the visitor's proposal was profound skepticism and caution. After all, the emissary had not even identified himself, and they had no reason to believe in his sincerity or in his ability to fulfill his promises. After the second meeting, the visitor returned to Spain uncertain of what he had accomplished. His identity, or even the fact of his mission, would not be revealed for a decade. The emissary was Marcelino Oreja, a Guipuzcoan who had already distinguished himself in Spain's Ministry of Foreign Affairs and in the Spanish embassy in London. Through family ties, he was linked to some of the most powerful industrial and banking interests in Spain. Through personal friendships, he was also closely associated with the new king himself. He would later go on to become Spain's foreign minister in Adolfo Suárez's second cabinet. There seems little doubt that he acted with the complete knowledge and authority of Spain's new head of state. In fact, before the year was out, Oreja would successfully negotiate for the return from France of some four hundred Basque refugees against whom there were no charges pending in Spanish courts.[2] But on this occasion his mission was a failure.

The next day, November 24, ETA assassinated the mayor of the Basque town of Oyarzun, Antonio Echevarria, on the grounds, as they later claimed, that he was a Francoist spy. In a communiqué published shortly after the killing, ETA made it clear that "the waiting period is over. Every mayor, the good ones as well as the bad, runs the risk of being executed." Several days later, ETA published a long pamphlet entitled "ETA against Juancarlismo" which set forth the organization's response to the post-Franco reforms: "We cannot postpone the struggle because liberal democracy is nothing more for us than a tactical objective. . . . Pacifist organizations are worthless for us; instead we have to create struggle organizations capable of winning over the power of the oligarchy, just as much if this power is exercised under dictatorial forms as if it is done under liberal forms . . ." Less than a month later, on December 21, a plastic explosive destroyed the car of Eusebio Iriarte, the bookstore owner who had been the intermediary between the Oreja and ETA. French police attributed the attack to Spanish secret agents operating across the border as part of the clandestine counterterrorist activities aimed at weakening ETA's support structures in France. In any case, the first attempt to negotiate with ETA ended just as numerous subsequent efforts to negotiate an end to insurgent violence in the Basque Country have ended— in failure.

Pertur's Legacy: 1976–1977

Between 1967 and General Franco's death in November 1975, ETA underwent a series of internal splits that produced several competing factions.[3] While Franco was alive and the dictatorship was intact, these factions disagreed over (among other things) the relative merits of violent armed struggle by a small vanguard group versus the slow and careful mobilization of the working-class population into radical Basque nationalist unions and political parties. In the early months of 1976, these factions began to argue over whether ETA should continue armed struggle or leave the violence behind and begin to organize the masses for electoral competition and union organizing. Clearly, the latter strategy would have required some sort of negotiated settlement between ETA and the Spanish government.

In early 1976, three factions struggled for control of ETA. The most militant and intransigent force of the three, ETA (militar), was led by a young man from the Vizcayan town of Arrigorriaga named José Miguel Beñarán Ordeñana, whose nom de guerre in the organization was "Argala." Argala at that time enjoyed great prestige within ETA because of his putative role in the assassination of Carrero Blanco in 1973. His chief competition came from ETA (político-militar), which, in turn, was divided into two camps. The leader of the more activist faction of (p-m), known as the Berezi Comandos, was Miguel Angel Apalategui "Apala," from the tiny Guipuzcoan village of Ataun. Apala was a typical product of the Goierri region of Guipúzcoa, a remote, Basque-speaking, highlands area that has produced a large proportion of ETA members over the years. The leader of the opposing group and the architect of ETA's "political strategy" was Eduardo Moreno Bergareche "Pertur." Pertur's social origins (he was from a well-to-do, Spanish-speaking family in the sophisticated city of San Sebastián) set him apart from the more rustic Apala. While the two ETA (p-m) leaders disagreed with one another over many things, including their relative power in the organization, the debate over the utility or possibility of a negotiated settlement was a major part of the struggle between Pertur and Apala.

Pertur had joined ETA relatively late, entering only after the Burgos trial in late 1970. Nevertheless, the repression inflicted upon the organization left many vacancies in its leadership, and Pertur, on the strength of his formidable intelligence, rose rapidly within ETA. By 1974 or 1975, he had already begun to formulate a vision of the future without Franco.[4] He foresaw that Spain after Franco would be a formal democracy in which armed struggle would be senseless. Therefore, ETA (p-m) would have to convert itself into a political party and compete in the electoral arena. Apala, on the other hand, rejected such a strategy, believing that armed struggle would have to continue into the era of democracy if ETA were to achieve its goals.

During the first half of 1976, the two ETA (p-m) leaders moved steadily toward direct confrontation. While Pertur continued to work to form a conventional political party, Apala solidified his control over the military wing of ETA (p-m). In January, a comando (cell) from ETA (p-m) kidnapped the son of a Basque industrialist named Arrasate. At first, the group demanded the payment of a ransom of $1.6 million; but in February the young man was released unharmed, apparently without the ransom having been delivered. In April, a (p-m) comando kidnapped and killed a Basque industrialist named Berazadi, apparently under direct other sources of friction as well. In April, a massive jailbreak of ETA prisoners organized by Apala failed miserably, and nearly all the escapees were either caught or killed. The Pertur faction began to accuse the Apala group of deliberately launching provocative actions like the Berazadi killing in order to undermine their political strategy. The Apala group responded by kidnapping Pertur in April on the grounds that he had breached the security of the organization. He was released only after the other (p-m) leaders protested and demanded that he be freed.[5]
and demanded that he be freed.[5]

On July 23, 1976, Apala and Pertur met in the French Basque town of St.-Jean-de-Luz to attempt to reconcile their differences.

Against the urging of his bodyguards, Pertur accompanied Apala on a drive out of town, and was never seen again. Apala returned soon after to assume even greater control over the military operations of ETA (p-m). Later, he was to transfer his allegiance to ETA (m). Accounts differ about the identity of Pertur's killers. His family and closest associates blamed Apala and the Berezi Comandos; the Berezi group claimed that they had been infiltrated and betrayed by a Spanish police spy. Another source, a close friend of Pertur, would admit only that he had been killed by "several comrades" who opposed the idea of a negotiated settlement.[6] Years later, in January 1982, a Spanish right-wing counterterror organization, the Apostolic Anticommunist Alliance (AAA), sent a communiqué to a Bilbao newspaper claiming responsibility for the deaths of some twenty Basques, including Pertur.

It is doubtful that we will ever know for sure who killed Pertur. What we do know is that his death came at a crucial moment in the history of ETA. In the same month that Pertur disappeared, Adolfo Suárez took office as the Spanish president and, with King Juan Carlos's support, began to bring about the Spanish democratic transformation. Elements within ETA (p-m) clearly wanted to end the violence and participate in the emerging democratic political arena. Pertur's disappearance robbed this element of its essential leader.

In September and October 1976, at the first half of its Seventh Assembly, ETA (p-m) debated and agreed upon what was called "el desdoblamiento" (literally, "the opening up"), or its intention to abandon armed struggle. The result was the creation of a new political party, called Euskal Iraultzale Alderdia (EIA), or Basque Revolutionary Party. The party was formed, as one founder recalls, by "the 'poli-milis' and their lawyers."[7] EIA held its first public rally in April 1977, and shortly thereafter became a part of a Basque socialist electoral coalition known as Euzkadiko Ezkerra (EE), or Basque Left.

It was in this context, then, that the next serious attempt to negotiate with ETA took place.[8] This contact occurred in December 1976, shortly after the referendum in which the Spanish people voted to authorize Adolfo Suárez to proceed with the democratic transformation. A short time before the referendum, the civil governor of Guipúzcoa, José María Belloch, had met with organizers of the provincial Pro-Amnesty Committee to discuss the legalization of the committee. At that meeting, Belloch, who had already declared himself in favor of amnesty, sounded out the committee's lawyers about the possibility of a dialogue between ETA and Madrid. Their positive response was reported to a member of Suárez's inner circle, José Manual Otero Novas, who carried the message to Suárez and got his approval to move ahead with the contacts.

There were two meetings between ETA and Spanish government representatives, both in Geneva. The first was held in late December 1976. ETA was represented by two poli-milis, Javier Garayalde, who was closely associated with Pertur, and Jesús Mari Munoa. The Spanish representative was not identified, but apparently was someone from the armed forces general staff. At this first meeting, the terms of any eventual agreement were clearly spelled out: the acceptance of a truce by ETA; amnesty and the legalization of all political parties by Madrid. It was agreed that there should be a second meeting, at which a representative of ETA (m) should be present. That second meeting took place in early 1977. All the earlier participants were present, as well as a third poli-mili, José Luís Echegaray, two representatives of the milis (allegedly, one of them was José Manuel Pagoaga Gallastegui "Peixoto"), and two more military officers. The second meeting produced no tangible result. The poli-milis, thinking no doubt of the rebellious Apala faction, recognized their inability to guarantee the complete compliance of their comandos with a cease-fire. The representatives of ETA (m) refused to commit themselves, but they did leave open the possibility of further negotiations in which the Basque socialist parties would be invited to participate.

In the first half of 1977, Spain moved ahead steadily with the post-Franco transition. Political parties and labor unions were legalized, restrictions on the press were lifted, and Suárez called for elections in June of a new parliament that would draft a democratic constitution. Whether or not the emerging Basque socialist parties should participate in these elections became a major source of conflict within the Basque Left coalition, known as the KAS. In late 1976 and early 1977, this coalition was a shaky union of both factions of the Basque Left: those who advocated a continuation of armed struggle, such as the Basque Popular Socialist Party (EHAS, later HASI), and ETA (militar); and those, including EIA, that supported Pertur's approach of a negotiated settlement and electoral competition.

In February 1977, two hooded etarras, representatives of the Pertur faction of ETA (p-m), were interviewed in the Spanish magazine *La Actualidad Española*.[9] The poli-milis explained to the interviewer that they were moving to create their new political party because "we believe that the new formulas that the Suárez government is trying to push make new, legalized methods viable that in an earlier era would have only been repressed." The interviewer pressed the (p-m) representatives about Madrid's willingness to legalize a party that advocated Basque independence, to which they replied, "If we decide finally to go through the legalization steps, we don't think we will have problems. To begin with, if they let us move about in the light of day, we will abandon violence totally, and that must interest the government."

The June 1977 elections provoked sharp conflict between the competing ETA factions over the wisdom of a negotiated end to the violence. The (p-m) wing declared a cease-fire through the period of the campaign so long as their prisoners were amnestied. EIA declared its intention to contest the elections; and an EE leader, lawyer Juan María Bandrés, succeeded in negotiating with Otero and Suárez the release of a number of important prisoners, including Mario Onaindia, Teo Uriarte, Jokin Gorostidi, and Itziar Aizpurua.[10] The Apala faction, however, condemned that decision to participate in the elections. In May, Apala's group formally split from ETA (p-m) and announced their wish to align themselves with the milis. They then kidnapped a prominent Bilbao industrialist named Javier Ybarra and killed him in June when the family failed to deliver the huge ransom they had demanded. ETA (m) likewise rejected electoral participation, and the split between milis and poli-milis widened still further.

The KAS Alternative: February 1978

Despite the failure to begin negotiations with ETA during the first years of the democratic transition, by early 1978 conditions seemed ripe on both sides to try once more. During the first six months of the year, several key intermediaries made significant progress in bringing the warring parties together. Just when these efforts seemed about to bear fruit, one of the intermediaries, José María Portell, was assassinated. His death, followed by armed attacks on two ETA leaders, ended for several years all attempts to negotiate a cease-fire. However, the 1978 negotiation attempt set the agenda for all future negotiators and established a model that others would follow in later years.

Since the 1978 negotiations revolved around a set of ETA demands known subsequently as the KAS Alternative, and since all future negotiations would return to this list of demands as ETA's sine qua non for a cease-fire, we should examine briefly the KAS vision of Basque independence and its strategy for achieving that goal.

In November 1976, KAS revealed its *"prográma máximo"* in an internal ETA publication called *Zutik*. This set of ultimate objectives included the following: "the complete independence of Euskadi, that is, the full capacity of the Basque people to decide their own destiny, which means the achievement of an independent and reunified Basque state"; "the achievement of the socialist revolution, which must mean the installation of that Basque state as a popular and democratic socialist republic, headed by the workers, in which the constitutional forms will guarantee the full and direct participation of the people in the total management of Basque society"; "the *euskerización* [restoring Euskera as a working language of the Basque Country] and full normalization of Euskera based on a situation of bilingualism"; and "the destruction of the capitalist and imperialist structures that exploit and oppress our people."[11]

The KAS leadership recognized that its programa máximo was too ambitious to provide much guidance for the short term, so they also formulated a set of intermediate goals known as the KAS Alternative. As they saw it, the struggle for Basque independence would unfold in two stages. The first stage would come to a close with the achievement of the KAS Alternative; but ETA would not cease its struggle until the end of the second stage, at which time Euskadi would be a free and independent sovereign state within a "Europe of the Peoples." Even into the spring and summer of 1977, the still-tentative nature of the democratic transition made it seem possible that ETA could achieve the KAS Alternative without offering Madrid anything in return—that is, without a cease-fire. The March–April 1977 issue of the Basque magazine *Punto y Hora*, for example, contained a declaration from ETA that "with peace [i.e., after securing the KAS Alternative], ETA will not practice armed activity, but it will not remain inactive; on the contrary, it will seek to expand by forming cells and obtaining provisions; at the moment that there is the slightest aggression against our people, ETA will enter into action." And the July 1977 issue of *Zutik* pledged that "ETA will continue to develop armed struggle until conquering for Euskadi the minimal democratic phase contained in the KAS Alternative, and subsequently it will maintain and develop its organization to sustain that conquest . . . until the achievement of independence and socialism for Euskadi."

Early in 1978, the leader of ETA (m), Argala, convened his lieutenants in France to reconsider their strategy in light of the events of the preceding six months.[12] Apparently, he had determined that ETA had reached a critical period in its revolutionary timetable. The 1977 Spanish parliamentary elections crystallized a number of problems that had been gradually taking form since Franco's death. The withdrawal of ETA (p-m) and EIA from the KAS, and their participation in the elections, showed that ETA's solidarity had been broken on tactical issues even if the various branches of the organization remained united on long-term strategic goals. At the same time, the relatively weak showing of Basque parties in general (their combined vote was less than 40 percent of the total) and of Euzkadiko Ezkerra in particular (which won only 64,000 votes) suggested that there was not at that time strong support for a radical pro-independence program. Therefore, ETA began to reconsider the two-stage theory. To achieve the KAS Alternative might require them to offer Madrid something Adolfo Suárez badly wanted: a cease-fire.

A negotiated settlement with Madrid, if it was to be achieved at all, would have to come in 1978; once the new Spanish constitution was in place and democratization was completed, the government would have little incentive to negotiate and would be strongly positioned to suppress insurgent threats to the new democracy. At the same time, Argala concluded that the parliamentary and electoral pressures from Basque nationalists, both moderate and radical, would not suffice to push Madrid to the bargaining table. The KAS had boycotted the 1977 elections without effect; EIA had failed to secure complete amnesty for Basque prisoners; and the center-right PNV was unable to force through any significant changes in early drafts of the constitution. The solution, apparently, lay in pursuing a strategy of increased violence and hard-line communiqués matched by renewed efforts to negotiate a cease-fire with Madrid.

On February 1, 1978, Basque newspapers published a communiqué from ETA (m) announcing its wish to discuss a cease-fire and naming five basic points as the minimum needed to get discussion under way.[13] This was the first time ETA (m) had published an official set of demands for discussion and the first time the organization had publicly offered a cease-fire. The five points, known as the KAS Alternative, remained through the 1980s as the official bargaining position of the organization, although they have undergone some modification. The demands were as follows:

1. "Total amnesty."

2. "Legalization of all political parties, including those whose program includes the creation of an independent Basque state without having to reduce their statutes."

3. "Expulsion from Euskadi of the Guardia Civil, the Policia Armada and the General Police Corps."

4. "Improvement of the living and working conditions for the popular classes and especially for the working class, satisfaction of their immediate social and economic aspirations as expressed by their representative associations."

5. "An autonomy statute that, as a minimum, recognizes the national sovereignty of Euskadi, authorizes Euskera as the principal official language of the country, provides for Basque government control over all law enforcement authorities and all military units garrisoned in the Basque country, and endows the Basque people with adequate power to adopt whatever political, economic or social structures they deem appropriate for their own progress and welfare."

From other ETA internal documents circulated at about the same time, it was clear that the KAS Alternative was only an interim set of demands that would lead to the organization's prográma máximo in later years.[14] As one of these documents put it, "Once the KAS Alternative has been achieved, there will be many goals, national as well as class, that can be achieved through legal means, and we will have to exhaust these before we can proceed again to armed action against the state apparatus. The KAS Alternative will yield a Basque state, but federal, not independent. Evidently it would be a state in large measure of the bourgeoisie, and therefore with many contradictions with the masses; but these contradictions would take a long time to appear and in that time we cannot do great things. For example, it is evident that we could not attack the Basque police the day after it is created; but we could as soon as it appeared before the people as an agency similar to the Spanish police but in Basque. And that's the way with everything. Thus, the cease-fire is indeterminate, it might last years or days, the time it takes for the emergence of new contradictions that call for the initiation of armed struggle. . . . There will always be contradictions, because there always have been, and armed actions as well; what there probably will not be for some time will be reasons for an armed struggle of open confrontation against the state that we have today."

The Deaths of Portell and Argala:
March–December 1978

The public response from Madrid to the KAS Alternative was contradictory. A few days after the communiqué was published, Interior Minister Rodolfo Martín Villa discarded the five points as completely unacceptable and asserted that "the government has never had contacts with ETA and there never will be any."[15] In March, however, Bilbao's new police chief, José Sainz González, Martín Villa's handpicked man in charge of law enforcement in the Basque provinces, was quoted in the press as saying "I am ready to take the first step to enter into a dialogue with ETA."[16]

Notwithstanding these ambiguities, below the level of public pronouncements channels of communication to ETA were being opened. More than ten years later, the events of early 1978 were confusing and complex, partly because many of the people involved are either dead or reluctant to discuss their roles, but also because there were actually two sets of intermediaries working more or less at the same time trying to bring about direct talks between ETA and the Spanish government.

One line of communication led from Martín Villa through prominent Bilbao journalist José María Portell who had written several well-known books about ETA[17] and apparently was on good terms with ETA leaders.[18] Portell had been helpful in establishing contacts with ETA the preceding year when he acted as an intermediary between a Spanish armed forces officer and the former leader of ETA's military front, Jon Etxabe.[19] He was also reputed to have been a key figure in negotiating the pre-election cease-fire of ETA (p-m) in 1977. While there is no question of Portell's important role in contacts between ETA and Madrid, some observers doubt that he really was an intermediary. Instead, they see Portell as a rather naive person who let himself be used as a messenger more than anything else. At times, Portell communicated directly with ETA representatives; at other times, he worked indirectly through Juan Félix Eriz, a person already well known for his mediations in several publicized kidnap cases. Their principal contact on the other side was Jon Etxabe, an important leader of the mili wing of ETA, who had organized the 1970 kidnapping of the German consul in San Sebastián, Eugen Beihl. Etxabe, in turn, reported directly to the leader of ETA (m), Argala.

The second channel ran from Martín Villa to the leader of the Basque wing of the Spanish socialist party, Txiki Benegas. As head of the Department of Interior of the Basque General Council (CGV), the provisional pre-autonomy regime established in early 1978, Benegas was Martín Villa's counterpart in the Basque Country. According to one observer, Benegas was so heavily involved with ETA contacts during these months that he was concerned for his own safety and slept in a different location each night as a security precaution. Some sources claim that Benegas's contact with ETA ran to an unidentified newspaper reporter loosely affiliated with Herri Batasuna; others say that his contact was with a member of the Basque socialist party, HASI. In either case, both channels led eventually to ETA (m) leader Argala.[20]

If Argala was the final authority on the ETA end of these communications channels, on the other end these contacts would never have been carried very far without the express approval of the

Spanish president, Adolfo Suárez. In entering into these contacts, Suárez demonstrated considerable political courage, for conservative parties strongly opposed any negotiated deal with ETA. Nevertheless, according to one close observer, Suárez saw himself as the person chosen by circumstances to resolve the ETA problem, and he took a very close personal interest in the progress of the talks. (Suárez's personal involvement in the question resurfaced in early 1988 when he attempted to contact ETA leaders in Algeria to get talks started there again after they had broken down.)

The first attempt at negotiations came to light in late 1977 or early 1978 when Suárez revealed his plan to a group of Basque leaders visiting him in the Moncloa Palace in Madrid. The plan called for Martín Villa to schedule a trip to Panama but to go instead to an unspecified location (revealed later to be Geneva) where he would meet personally with ETA leaders. As the months passed without reaching agreement on this proposed meeting, Martín Villa sought to take advantage of another event to cover his trip to Geneva. On May 8, the new president of Costa Rica, Rodrigo Carazo, was to be inaugurated. Martín Villa was designated to represent the Spanish government at the ceremony, and it was proposed that he return via Geneva to enable him to meet with ETA. The stop in Geneva never occurred because ETA insisted that the meetings be made public, while Madrid refused—at least until there was some positive news to report. ETA also insisted that the meeting be conducted as if it were between two equal entities, a state and a "para-state," as some might call the organization; but Madrid likewise refused to consider this proposal. On the other side, Argala was also being pressured to take an uncompromising position by the hard-line poli-mili faction, led by Apala, that had joined ETA (m) less than a year earlier. Thus Martín Villa's trip to Costa Rica ended without the Geneva meeting.[21]

Meanwhile, Portell continued his efforts to get negotiations under way. On June 8, according to Juan Félix Eriz, Portell contacted him to get his assistance in carrying messages to ETA, and in particular to Jon Etxabe. It is not known how far these contacts proceeded, but they certainly had not gotten far enough to advance a specific proposal to Martín Villa. On June 28, at about 8:15 A.M., José María Portell was shot to death in front of his home in the Bilbao suburb of Portugalete as he was leaving to go to work.[22] ETA

(m) claimed responsibility for the killing, but the killers were never identified or captured. At first, ETA's responsibility was in doubt since the communiqué following the attack differed in some important respects from the organization's customary messages. Later, however, ETA leaders confirmed their organization's complicity in the assassination.

What could have motivated ETA to kill José María Portell? Speculations abound, but conclusive evidence is nonexistent. Portell received telephone threats against his life almost daily, sometimes several times a day. Eriz claimed in his book that Portell had been set up by Spanish police agents who planted a paper containing his name, address, and telephone number on a suspected Portuguese mercenary and then had him arrested in France in such a way as to make Portell look like a double agent. Then ETA would have him shot as a spy. Another version is that Portell had published in his newspaper excerpts from what was purported to be the diary of ETA (m) leader Argala, who had him shot in reprisal.[23] Other explanations place direct blame on the members of Apala's Berezi group that had split off from ETA (p-m).

Less than a week after the Portell killing, on July 3, ETA (m) leader Jon Etxabe and his wife were shot in their car in the French Basque town of St.-Jean-de-Luz. While his wife died instantly, Etxabe narrowly escaped death, although he remained in a coma for a month. Etxabe had furiously denounced ETA in public for the Portell killing, and there was speculation that the attack against him was in reprisal for his remarks. ETA (m) leader Txomin Iturbe personally assured Etxabe, however, that such was not the case. The other possible explanation is that the Etxabes were shot, perhaps by Spanish rightists or by disgruntled ETA hard-liners, because of Jon Etxabe's role as an intermediary over the preceding months. Again, the truth will probably never be known.

All the time that Portell, Eriz, and Etxabe were working unsuccessfully to bring about ETA-Madrid negotiations, Txiki Benegas was likewise meeting failure in his efforts. In May, Benegas received word that Argala wanted to start negotiations, and he duly informed Martín Villa and Suárez, as well as the leader of his party, Felipe González.[24] At about this time, Benegas began to discuss these matters with representatives of the Basque revolutionary party, HASI; and the HASI leaders carried the message back to the KAS where the issue was debated over several meetings. At the June 10 meeting of the KAS, the decision was made to demand that the Spanish government "admit publicly that it is ready to negotiate with ETA on the basis of the five points of the KAS Alternative." Nine days later, on June 19, the KAS held another meeting to discuss further talks between Benegas and HASI. At this meeting, it was suggested that the KAS could meet with representatives of the Basque provisional government without compromising ETA, and still receive favorable publicity from being treated as an equal with the CGV. Within days, Spanish leaders had even accepted the possibility of direct talks with parties from the KAS, especially HASI, without committing themselves to anything with ETA. Such an option was discussed openly in the Madrid press on the very day Portell was shot, and at a meeting of the KAS the next day, June 29.[25]

In the aftermath of the Portell and Etxabe attacks and the ensuing wave of antiterrorism in Spain, the prospects for bringing together ETA and the Spanish government were dimmed. Benegas continued to work toward negotiations until December 21, 1978, when the leader of ETA (m), Argala, was killed by a bomb placed in his car in the French Basque town of Anglet.[26]

Just as in the cases of Portell and Etxabe six months earlier, responsibility for Argala's death remained a mystery. Persons within KAS claimed that Argala had been killed by Spanish secret police working on the French side of the border, or by Spanish rightists; but the version reported most frequently in the Spanish media was that he was killed by ETA members opposed to negotiation. One close observer consulted in the preparation of this book doubted that Argala was killed by other ETA members since he had great prestige within the organization. Years after the attack, Italian neofascists claimed that Argala had been killed by "ultras" (extreme rightists) from their country who had been recruited by Spanish secret police.[27]

About the aftermath of the Portell and Argala killings, all we know for certain is that yet another opportunity was lost for a peaceful settlement between ETA and Madrid. At the time of the attack, the Spanish government was already preparing an aggressive antiterrorist policy; and in the hours after Portell's death they moved quickly to implement these measures. Despite Benegas's continued efforts until Argala's death in December, Suárez and Martín Villa had little interest in renewing discussions with ETA.

For years afterwards, both ETA and the Spanish government would deny virtually everything described in the preceding pages. Immediately after the Portell killing, Martín Villa denied that Portell had been carrying messages back and forth between the interior minister and ETA.[28] Likewise, ETA (m) denied that Argala was trying to establish contacts with the Basque or Spanish governments when he was killed.[29] The continued frustrations of attempts to bring the two parties together were beginning to wear away the spirit of agreement that had supported the government's antiterrorist policy during the early years of the transition. And repeated failures at negotiations played into the hands of those within ETA who favored a violent solution to their problems.

The angry exchange between Suárez and socialist leader Felipe González during the parliamentary debate on a censure motion against Suárez's government in May 1980 reflected the frustrations and tensions that had built up over this issue. After UCD Interior Minister José Rosón's hard-line remarks about how to combat terrorism, Basque socialist deputy Carlos Solchaga asserted that when Txiki Benegas had attempted to negotiate with ETA in 1978, President Suárez had agreed with these efforts. Whereupon Suárez took the floor to challenge Solchaga's remark: "I must say that I have never been in agreement with any negotiation of the government with ETA. At no time." At that, Felipe González rose to take issue with Suárez in what he said would be "his word against mine, since he and I have talked personally about the subject of negotiation with ETA. And I must remind him that there was a trip by the interior minister to Costa Rica after which there was going to be a meeting with ETA." And Suárez replied: "The government at no time has been ready to negotiate with ETA, and we have said this whenever we have had the chance before Spanish public opinion, and in any place." González would not back down: "I just wanted to remind everyone that we are talking about something that happened some time ago. . . . The only thing that prevented that negotiation was that ETA demanded publicity from the first, and the government wanted to have results, as would be logical, before there was publicity." But Suárez was adamant: "I repeat what I said before, that ETA has tried on many occasions to negotiate the KAS Alternative with the government. The government has always said that it does not negotiate with ETA, and I repeat what I said before. That's all."[30]

Negotiations with the Second UCD Government: 1979–1980

Following the Portell and Argala killings in 1978 and the narrow victory of Adolfo Suárez and the UCD in Spanish parliamentary elections in March 1979, efforts to negotiate a cease-fire with ETA did not resume immediately. After the Portell assassination, Suárez directed Interior Minister Martín Villa to pursue a policy of police suppression of ETA, including a strong antiterrorist law, increased preventive detentions, right-wing counterterror assassination squads operating in France, and increased cooperation with the French government. Despite these pressures, ETA-inflicted deaths rose during the period, from sixty-seven in 1978 to seventy-two in 1979, and eighty-eight in 1980.

There were voices raised in defense of negotiations, particularly in the Basque Country, but they were ignored in Madrid. During the 1979 parliamentary election campaign, the leading candidate of the PNV, Xabier Arzalluz, called on the government to meet with ETA and explore the true extent of their desire to negotiate. "When a group sets forth some conditions," he said in a newspaper interview, "in this case the KAS Alternative, it means that they are ready to talk and to reach an agreement. The government's position, that it is useless to negotiate, is gratuitous. We have to know what ETA is asking, and once these things have been said, then we can know the truth."[31] Apparently the voters in the Basque provinces agreed, since the vote of the anti-Madrid parties rose from the 36 percent they won in 1977 to 50 percent. Basque nationalist parties won 11 of 21 parliamentary seats, including 6 of 10 in Vizcaya (HB won 2; PNV, 4) and 4 of 7 in Guipúzcoa (PNV, 2; HB and EE, 1 each). The anti-Madrid vote has never dropped below 50 percent since these 1979 elections.[32]

Despite these signs of support for negotiations, the government hardened its public position against talks with ETA, to a large degree because of the deteriorating electoral position of the governing party, the UCD. In the March 1979 elections, Suárez's party fell nine seats short of a majority in the Congress of Deputies, which imperiled his efforts to maintain a one-party government throughout the period. Moreover, in March 1980 the UCD suffered serious defeats in the regional parliamentary elections in the Basque Autonomous Community and in Catalonia; and in less than a year Suárez himself would be forced to resign as president of the Spanish government. Consequently, in an effort to shore up his crumbling political position, Suárez swung back toward the right on a number of issues, chief of which was the emotional question of negotiations with "terrorists and assassins." Until the end of his tenure as president, Suárez vigorously denied that his government was involved in negotiations with ETA, or, indeed, that it had ever done so, as we saw in the tense parliamentary exchange with Felipe González in 1980.

The absence of general cease-fire negotiations does not mean that ETA had no contacts with Madrid at all, quite the contrary. Working mostly through intermediaries, ETA and Spanish government representatives exchanged views and information to resolve several issues much more narrowly defined than a general cease-fire, and occasionally these talks met with partial success. In the summer of 1979, for example, ETA (p-m) launched a campaign of bombings in Madrid and along Spain's tourist-filled resort beaches in an attempt to secure the return of more than one hundred Basque prisoners who had been moved the preceding December out of local prisons to a maximum security prison at Soria. During the first weeks in July, talks between (p-m) and Madrid met with some success. The Spanish government agreed to begin discussing the return of some prisoners to the Basque Country, and ETA (p-m) suspended the bombings. Then on July 29, in a rare departure from normal procedure, ETA (p-m) placed bombs in two of Madrid's crowded train stations and the Barajas airport, killing six and wounding dozens. The government broke off talks following this attack, but they were resumed within days. On August 2, ETA (p-m) held a clandestine press conference to announce that they were halting the bombings. Several days later, the Spanish government announced that it was returning the first group of ETA prisoners to the Basque Country, although they stressed that the move had been planned long in advance and that it had not been negotiated with ETA. The government later denied that there had been any negotiations with ETA; but in October, Basque deputy Juan María Bandrés claimed that "the government negotiated with ETA (p-m) in August. In principle, the government acceded to some of the requests of ETA (p-m) and began the movement of prisoners, but later the government failed to fulfill the agreement, and ETA (p-m) got nervous and there were the regrettable explosions [in Madrid]. But later the government returned to hold negotiations, and it has fulfilled all of the commitments they agreed to with ETA (p-m)."[33]

Later that same year, on November 13, ETA (p-m) kidnapped an important deputy of the UCD, Javier Rupérez, and held him hostage for a series of demands that included the release of a number of ETA prisoners, the return of the rest of the prisoners from Soria, and the withdrawal of Spanish law enforcement authorities from the Basque Country. This time, both sides denied that there were negotiations, but on December 12 Rupérez was freed, followed shortly by the announcement that twenty-six Basques would soon be released from prison and the Spanish parliament would create a special commission to investigate charges of torture and mistreatment of Basques in prison. The government denied any connection between these measures and the release of Rupérez.[34]

After these limited successes in 1979, the most significant development in 1980 was the publication by ETA (p-m) of several different lists of demands that could be regarded as alternatives to the five-point KAS proposal. Following an attack by rockets against the Moncloa Palace in Madrid in February, ETA (p-m) issued a communiqué with four demands: (1) that the Basque autonomy statute be expressly exempt from any contradictory or conflicting legislation passed by the Spanish parliament; (2) that there be a referendum held in Navarra to ascertain the preferences of the Navarrese people regarding integration into the Basque Autonomous Community; (3) that all ETA prisoners be returned immediately to Euskadi, and that there be a general amnesty when the Basque autonomy statute went into effect; and (4) that all special police measures in the Basque Country be halted, and the law enforcement power be transferred to an autonomous Basque police force. The Spanish government rejected any negotiations about these demands.[35] In

July, another ETA (p-m) communiqué suggested that their cooperation in a cease-fire could be achieved by meeting three demands:
(1) total amnesty for all Basque political prisoners; (2) withdrawal of
all Spanish law enforcement authorities from Euskadi (presumably
to be replaced by Basque government police); and (3) integration of
Navarra into Euskadi (the communiqué was silent as to the degree
of consultation with the Navarrese people on this question).[36]

Paradoxically, 1980 was both the year of maximum ETA violence (eighty-eight killed, a figure never exceeded before or since)
and the year when interest in negotiations reached an all-time
low. The PNV said that the Basque government would not become involved in negotiations since ETA's demands were directed
at Madrid, and only the Spanish government could satisfy them.
The Spanish government rejected any possibility of negotiations,
even during the 1980 summer bombing campaign; and the opposition socialists affirmed their belief that "you can't negotiate with
ETA."[37] In the entire country, the only people who believed in
negotiations were the leaders of Euzkadiko Ezkerra, Mario Onaindia and Juan María Bandrés; and they were not able even to obtain
an interview with Interior Minister Rosón in July to discuss the
matter.[38] In 1981 and 1982, however, these men were to become
key figures in the next stage of negotiations with ETA.

CHAPTER FOUR

"Social Reintegration" and the End of ETA (p-m): 1981–1983

Aftेर the abortive Guardia Civil and army coup attempt of February 23, 1981, the Spanish government, under its new president, Leopoldo Calvo Sotelo, found itself in a perilous position with elements in the military as well as with rightist politicians like Manuel Fraga. The government responded to this pressure by stepping up its efforts to suppress ETA's insurgency. In addition to the antiterrorist measures already in place, regular Spanish army and navy units were deployed to the Basque provinces for the first time, and a new unified antiterrorist military and police command was established. On the other side, despite a slight decline in ETA attacks in 1981, there remained little doubt that the organization could strike violently and repeatedly when it chose to do so. During the final two years of the UCD government, then, the prospects for a negotiated settlement with ETA seemed extremely remote. Despite these discouraging signs, there were three important accomplishments in the period between 1981 and 1983: the cease-fire declared unilaterally by ETA (p-m) in February 1981, which held intact for almost a year; the self-dissolution of the Pertur faction of (p-m) in September 1982; and the policy of selective amnesty, referred to as *reinserción social*, or "social reintegration," negotiated by the leaders of Euzkadiko Ezkerra, Juan María Bandrés and Mario Onaindia.

The ETA (p-m) Cease-Fire: February 1981–February 1982

Between 1980 and 1982, the policies that had been championed by Pertur—a negotiated cease-fire, the abandonment of armed struggle, and the shift to an electoral strategy—became once again the subject of an intensified debate within ETA (p-m), as well as between the poli-milis and the Basque Revolutionary Party, EIA. For many members of both groups, the events of the late 1970s and early 1980s—the 1977 parliamentary elections, the 1978 debate over the new constitution, the 1979 Basque autonomy statute, and the 1980 Basque elections—showed that public dissent and opposition to official positions would be tolerated, and that nonviolent struggle could even on occasions be successful.[1] Nevertheless, the continued resort to violence by ETA (p-m) put political figures like Bandrés and Onaindia in a precarious position. It was difficult to argue before the court of public opinion that ETA's violence was still justified when EIA and the electoral coalition of which it was a part, Euzkadiko Ezkerra, were electing deputies to both the Spanish and Basque parliaments. Bandrés's position as a member of the Spanish Congress of Deputies was especially awkward when, for example, he was forced to abstain on a vote condemning ETA (p-m)'s attacks. Moreover, EIA members were on occasion subject to arrest on the grounds that they were encouraging ETA (p-m) to continue armed struggle. It was becoming clearer that the combination of armed struggle and electoral competition was more and more untenable as democracy solidified its hold in Spain.[2]

These issues came sharply to a head during the three-month period from September through November 1980, one of the most violent in the history of ETA. In all, thirty-six people died at the hands of ETA during these three months, nearly half of those who were killed during the entire year. The victims included a national police captain, two army lieutenant colonels, thirteen members of the Guardia Civil, five policemen, and the chief of police of San Sebastián. But the killings that provoked the greatest public outcry were those of three important leaders of the Basque wing of the Spanish governing party, UCD: one in Alava province in September, and two in Guipúzcoa province in October. On November 2, leaders of the PNV, PSOE, and UCD were joined by representatives from across the Basque political spectrum in a massive demonstration in San Sebastián to condemn terrorism. The crowd was estimated by the press at 20,000.[3]

It began to appear to the less radical Basque nationalists who still enjoyed cordial relations with ETA, like Bandrés and Onaindia, that the organization was in danger of losing the one thing insurgents cannot do without: support from their host population. In December 1980, therefore, leaders of EIA and EE began to discuss the possibility of a truce that would interrupt the spiral of violence that threatened to grow out of control.[4]

When consulted about this plan, Spanish leaders at first were reluctant to authorize negotiations. Adolfo Suárez, presented with the proposal during a trip to the Basque provinces in December, was already in his final days as president and could not give the idea his full support. In May 1980, Rodolfo Martín Villa had been replaced as interior minister by Juan José Rosón, who was on record as a staunch defender of the Spanish constitution, the national unity of Spain, and the irrevocable nature of the compact among all of the minority peoples that made up the Spanish nation-state.[5] For other much more limited stakes, Rosón perhaps could have entered into negotiations that resulted in the dissolution of ETA (p-m); but the organization was not about to offer that as a possible negotiating point, at least not yet. Thus, while Rosón was willing to let the Basque leaders try to get a cease-fire declared, it was still far from certain that Madrid would be willing or able to give anything of substance in return.

The events of January and February 1981 were among the most turbulent in recent Basque history; and only the most audacious outside observer would speculate about the connections between one dramatic development and another. On January 29 ETA (m) kidnapped José María Ryan, the chief engineer of the Lemoiz nuclear plant then under construction near Bilbao, and threatened to kill him if the construction of the plant was not halted. On February 3 King Juan Carlos arrived for his first official visit to the Basque Country amid massive protests. The next day, when the king attempted to speak in the historic parliament building in Guernica, he was shouted down by demonstrators from Herri Batasuna, who were ejected from the hall by police. On February 6, Ryan was killed by his captors, an attack that elicited mass protests against ETA across the Basque Country. On February 13, an accused ETA member named Joseba Arregi died in Madrid's Carabanchel prison after having been savagely tortured in the headquarters of the State Security Directorate; and public sentiment swung back in favor of ETA and against the Spanish government.

It was in this context, on the weekend of February 14–15, that a special assembly of EIA issued a call to both wings of ETA to suspend armed attacks.[6] Referring to ETA's continuation of violence as "destabilizing" and "favoring the position of the right," the party declared itself against ETA (m)'s current strategy, and claimed that the organization was mistaken in thinking that armed struggle by itself could achieve what mass or popular struggle was incapable of obtaining. If ETA would agree to a cease-fire as soon as possible, "as a step that facilitates a negotiation among the Basque political forces, for a solution of all the problems, EIA commits itself to doing everything possible to achieve the success of the negotiations." ETA (p-m) responded on February 20 by kidnapping three consuls (from Austria, El Salvador, and Uruguay) in Bilbao and Pamplona. Finally, the entire dynamic was shifted to a new level of intensity by the coup attempt launched in Madrid on February 23 and brought to a close in the early hours of the following day.

Some observers claimed that ETA (p-m) intended to announce their cease-fire somewhat later; but the pressures of the preceding weeks made them advance their timetable. In a February 28 communiqué timed to coincide with the release of the three unharmed consuls, ETA (p-m) announced their intention to suspend violent attacks, but not necessarily kidnappings or other actions aimed at securing funds.[7] The announcement, which included a call to ETA (m) to join in the cessation of violence, came at a clandestine news conference conducted by three hooded ETA members. According to the announcement, ETA (p-m) had been studying the possibility of a cease-fire for about four months, but the coup attempt had forced them to move up the announcement. It was clear from the events of February 23 that neither ETA nor the Basque people in general would be able to defend themselves against a military take-over of the Spanish government; and so (p-m) would pull back from the brink to avoid what might be a fatal provocation of the armed forces.

According to the poli-milis, the organization was calling the cease-fire at that time in order to give the parties of the Basque Left a chance to increase the measure of home rule that Basques could enjoy through the still relatively undeveloped autonomy statute, as well as to resolve the issues that "distort its [the statute's] functioning." These issues were "amnesty for prisoners and exiles, the integration of Navarra, the referendum on Lemoiz, the repeal of the antiterrorist law, and the purification of fascist elements [from the police and the army]." The cease-fire was not set for any specific length of time, and it was not clear what criteria ETA (p-m) would use to maintain or end it. The important thing was that the truce period should be used to discuss these key issues and resolve them if possible.

The issues cited in the press conference as being open for negotiation were also presented in a slightly modified form to a representative of Interior Minister Rosón at about the same time the cease-fire was announced.[8] There were four key issues on the ETA (p-m) agenda: that the separation between Navarra and the other Basque provinces should not be permitted to widen, and as a minimum, Navarra should not be given separate status as a one-province autonomous community within the regional autonomy system then emerging in Spain; that the Basque people should be allowed to decide in a referendum whether or not the nuclear plant at Lemoiz should be completed and put into operation; that amnesty for all ETA (p-m) members should be granted by the Spanish government according to a schedule to be negotiated at that time; and that the Spanish government should commit itself to a timetable for the eventual transfer to the Basque government of all powers envisioned in the Basque autonomy statute. (While this last demand sounded relatively harmless, Spanish leaders knew well that the autonomy statute provided for the eventual transfer to the Basque government of all powers related to the administration of justice, including courts, police, and prisons; so this demand was about the same as the traditional ETA demand that Madrid withdraw all of its law enforcement authorities.) The Madrid representative replied that he was not empowered to discuss any of these matters, since they were issues that in a democracy had to be resolved by the political parties in power.

The response to the (p-m) cease-fire from the other wing of ETA was negative and, at least in Bandrés's opinion, delivered "in an insulting tone." The general secretary of HASI, the principal party in the HB coalition, Txomin Ziluaga, said that "the cease-fire of ETA (p-m) is neither a surprise nor a solution. We have known for months that there was a negotiation project between EE and the Spanish government to get ETA (p-m) to abandon armed struggle in return for nothing more than amnesty for their prisoners. But the cease-fire solves nothing because it does not deal with the outstanding issues today in Euskadi."[9] Within twenty-four hours of the (p-m) cease-fire announcement, ETA (m) exploded a bomb near two police cars on patrol in a suburb of Bilbao, wounding three policemen, one seriously.

The cease-fire held more or less effectively for nearly a year. While ETA (m) continued its attacks, (p-m) observed its commitments and practiced considerable self-restraint, although the organization maintained its command structure and continued to engage in fund-raising activities such as the "revolutionary taxes" and robberies. The selective amnesty program was a modified success; but progress was agonizingly slow. As late as January 1983, Bandrés was still negotiating for the release of six former members of ETA (p-m) and for the return from exile of some fifty more,[10] even though the branch of ETA to which they had belonged had voluntarily dissolved itself in 1982. Nothing was ever accomplished on any of the other demands: Navarra achieved its own separate autonomy statute on August 16, 1982; Lemoiz continued under construction; there was no general amnesty; and the transfer of additional powers to the Basque government was halted. Not surprisingly, then, at the beginning of 1982 ETA (p-m) leaders questioned whether the cease-fire had been a good idea and whether it should be terminated.

Arzalluz and the Cease-Fire:
March–September 1981

In late August 1985, the leader of the PNV, Xabier Arzalluz, and EE leader Juan María Bandrés engaged in a bitter exchange of accusations and personal recriminations that reached far beyond the issue of negotiations with ETA. In the course of this verbal battle, however, a story emerged of contacts between Arzalluz and leaders of ETA (p-m) during the period when the cease-fire was in effect, specifically during the spring and summer of 1981. This fascinating story gives us valuable insights into the complex interplay between ETA negotiations and Basque politics in general; and it also helps us understand better why the cease-fire collapsed five months later.

The affair began in early August 1985 when a PNV publication, *Euzkadi*, reported on Bandrés's attempts the preceding May to act as an intermediary to get negotiations started between ETA (m) and the Spanish government.[11] There were indications that the PNV resented Bandrés's efforts and was jealous of any attempt at mediation that did not include the leading Basque nationalist party. Bandrés responded in an interview with the Madrid magazine *Tiempo*, where he accused the PNV of stifling dissent. "It is completely impossible for me to believe," he said, "that I could even breathe in the atmosphere of the PNV." On August 18, Arzalluz replied in his customary Sunday column in the Bilbao newspaper, *Deia*. "Mr. Bandrés," he wrote, "until recently could breathe radical and violent air; and he also took deep breaths in the atmosphere of Eurocommunism." He went on to challenge Bandrés's credentials as a nationalist because, among other things, he preferred to send his children to a French academy rather than to a Basque-language school.[12]

Bandrés answered these accusations on August 19 with a charge of his own in a letter to the Spanish national news agency, EFE. In the letter, Bandrés claimed that in 1981 Arzalluz "traveled to Iparralde [the French Basque region] to persuade the members of ETA (p-m) not to give up the use of arms and abandon violence in order to obtain the transfer of several more areas of authority for the [Basque] government of the PNV. At that time, we had already been working for a long time negotiating a dignified peace that would conclude the violence and return the prisoners and exiles to their homes."[13]

The next day, August 20, Arzalluz gave a partial response to the charge in a radio interview, preferring to wait until his next Sunday newspaper column to give a full reply. He claimed that he went to France twice in February 1981 before the coup attempt, that he was accompanied by two other members of the PNV governing council, and that he met with ETA (p-m) leaders at their request. "At no time," he said, "did we ask ETA to continue its armed actions. On the contrary, we made them understand that our party was not going to stand for any more extortions or kidnappings. It is absurd to say that we went there to encourage ETA to continue the shooting." Bandrés, also in a radio interview the same day, altered the charge slightly, saying that "Arzalluz knows perfectly well who went to St.-Jean-de-Luz to tell the poli-milis to continue the struggle. If it is necessary, those who will have the last word will be the leaders of the poli-milis who were in St.-Jean-de-Luz, who received the visit, and who now live peacefully in Euskadi."[14]

On August 21, ETA (p-m) members and ex-members began to join the battle. The anti-truce faction of (p-m), known as the *octavos* because of their origins in the group's VIII Assembly, accused both sides of instigating a "street brawl" and charged EE with "collaborating with the Spanish police." Former members of the pro-truce faction, the so-called *séptimos* that had self-dissolved in 1982, who had been involved in the meetings with Arzalluz said that they would wait until his column appeared on Sunday before they would have any public comment. However, an ex-poli-mili told the press (anonymously) that "Bandrés is not lying," while another told *El País* that Bandrés's accusations against Arzalluz were "unjust, or at least exaggerated."[15]

Other PNV leaders, who claimed to have accompanied Arzalluz to France to meet with ETA (p-m), were heard from on August 22 and 23. Andoni Monforte, who participated in one of the meetings, called Bandrés's accusations "calumny," and said that EE explain its earlier relations with ETA (p-m). Koldo Amezketa, another participant in the meetings, claimed that "the attitude and the intention of the [PNV representatives] were not what Bandrés said." PNV spokesman Xabier Aguirre charged that Bandrés's affirmations "made a mockery of [Basque] parliament agreements on violence." Another PNV participant, Antton Jaime, also claimed that Bandrés's charges were "absolutely false."[16]

On Sunday, August 25, while Arzalluz was defending himself in his weekly column in *Deia*, the Madrid daily *El País* was carrying an interview with an ex-poli-mili living in France who confirmed in general outline the substance of Bandrés's charges. From these and other sources, we can piece together this picture. Aside from the two February meetings, which were never mentioned again after he cited them, Arzalluz met three times in 1981 with ETA (p-m) leaders. The first time was on March 16, only three weeks or so after the abortive Madrid coup attempt, and it took place at the request of ETA. In addition to Arzalluz, the PNV delegation included Antton Jaime and Koldo Amezketa. ETA (p-m) was represented by two members of the anti-truce faction, Txutxo Abrisketa (subsequently a leader of the octavos faction, and deported by France to Cuba) and Astorkiza (later a member of ETA (m)); and by two pro-truce leaders, Juan Miguel Goiburu "Goiherri" and Fernando López Castillo "Peque" (both members of the self-dissolved séptimos faction and living in Spain under the amnesty program). The second meeting took place on August 20. Arzalluz was accompanied only by Jaime; ETA (p-m) was represented only by the anti-truce faction: Abrisketa and Astorkiza. (It later turned out that pro-truce members were not even aware of this second meeting.) There was also a third meeting, in September, at which Arzalluz and Andoni Monforte met with several members who were not known to them and who did not give their names.

What exactly transpired at these meetings, and could Arzalluz's words and actions be taken as an encouragement to ETA (p-m) to break the cease-fire and return to violence? Arzalluz claimed that all he did was review the very dismal record of minimal achievements in Basque home rule through mid-1981. After the initial euphoria of autonomy in 1980, the reversal of policy in Madrid in 1981 had made moderate Basque nationalist leaders extremely pessimistic about the willingness of the Spanish government to fulfill what they regarded as a solemn commitment to grant the Basques full self-government. While the general attitude after the February 23 coup attempt had turned sour, the specific policy measure that worried the Basques most was the so-called LOAPA, the Organic Law for the Harmonization of the Autonomy Process, then being debated in the Spanish parliament. Arzalluz, like many other Basques, feared that the LOAPA would be used by the government to reverse many of the gains made in autonomy in 1979 and 1980. These opinions, he later said, were nothing that an ETA member could not read in any newspaper in the Basque Country. However, in a phrase that would be much quoted later on, Arzalluz apparently remarked at the August 20 meeting that "we are going to confront the LOAPA, then it will be your turn."

And what was the effect of Arzalluz's remarks on the commitment of (p-m) to the cease-fire? One participant, the séptimo leader Juan Miguel Goiburu, later said that "neither directly nor indirectly could one deduce from that meeting that Arzalluz's attitude was favorable to breaking the truce that we had agreed upon." However, unknown to the PNV visitors, ETA (p-m) was at that moment engaged in a serious internal struggle over the validity of the cease-fire; and the anti-truce faction—Abrisketa and Astorkiza—used Arzalluz's own words and arguments to attack the truce and the group that favored it. "I never would have imagined," wrote Arzalluz later, somewhat ironically, "that I would have such influence over that type of person."

In the context of the split of ETA (p-m) into pro- and anti-truce factions, arguments like those attributed to Arzalluz were indeed important in determining the outcome of the debate. But the role of Arzalluz in this affair seems best summed up by Patxo Unzueta: "If this hypothesis [the use by the anti-truce faction of Arzalluz's words to attack the cease-fire] is correct, the error of Arzalluz was not, as Bandrés thinks, an insufficient capacity to adapt to the language of his listeners, but rather an excessive capacity to adapt. To better convince them of the suitability of laying down their arms, he risked a language too close to what his listeners in that [August] meeting were anxious to hear."[17]

The End of the Pertur Faction Within ETA (p-m): February 1982–September 1982

According to Patxo Unzueta, the February 1981 cease-fire declared by ETA (p-m) was, from the very beginning, seen differently by two factions within the organization.[18] Even though the vote in favor of the cease-fire had been nearly unanimous, this unanimity masked a fundamental difference over the function of the truce in the organization's long-term strategy. For some members, the cease-fire was simply a temporary interruption of armed struggle, which would be resumed as soon as conditions—both internal and external—were ripe. For the followers of Pertur, however, the truce was the first in a long series of steps that would lead eventually to the negotiated self-dissolution of ETA (p-m). Given this difference of perspective, it was inevitable that the two factions would interpret differently the events of 1981. For the former group, the truce had been use-less since it had not led to the internal strengthening of (p-m) nor to a weakening of the position of the Spanish government. For the second, however, the cease-fire had been an essential ingredient in the strengthening of the democratic opposition, represented by Euzkadiko Ezkerra.

Through the summer of 1981, a nervous calm descended over the Basque Country. The truce of ETA (p-m) held; despite occa-sional so-called technical violations, the organization issued sev-eral communiqués declaring their continued commitment to a halt in hostilities. The military wing of ETA also reduced its violent attacks, perhaps because of the increased police presence in the Basque Country; perhaps, as those less optimistic argued, it was simply ETA's way of taking a "vacation" during the summer. There were continued rumors of talks between ETA and Madrid, but all we know for sure is that negotiations were proceeding for the re-lease of imprisoned poli-milis under the new "social reintegration" program being negotiated by Bandrés and Rosón. For whatever rea-son, ETA-inflicted deaths declined to thirty during the first six months of the year, compared with fifty-seven during the same period the year before.[19]

By late 1981, however, it had become clear that, aside from the limited progress made by Bandrés on the amnesty issue, nothing was being accomplished in the resolution of the other questions set forth by (p-m) when it declared the cease-fire. By mid-January 1982, it was fairly widely known that a debate was raging within (p-m) over the future of the cease-fire. In a newspaper interview that appeared in *Deia* on January 22, sources from within ETA (p-m) confirmed that the organization was reconsidering its posi-tion on the cease-fire since nothing had been accomplished on any of its key issues except the partial transfer of Basque prisoners to a prison closer to home. In any case, ETA (p-m) would never renounce armed struggle "as long as the objectives that drive the movement remain unfulfilled, that is, the freedom of Euskadi, socialism and the recovery of our national and cultural identity." The sources also stressed that "a truce should not be taken as something in-definite, since at any moment the circumstances can appear that finally break it."[20]

The debate went on within (p-m) for nearly two months, and

led eventually to a convocation of the eighth meeting of the Assembly, the maximum decision-making organ of the group, and referred to in ETA parlance as the VIII Asamblea. The principal point at issue—whether or not to continue to observe the truce—became transformed into a referendum on the future of ETA (p-m).[21] Those who favored terminating the truce believed (as they had always argued) that armed struggle by a small vanguard party was the only way Basque independence could be achieved. In the transition to democracy in Spain, they argued, violence would play a decisive role by sharpening mass consciousness. Their opponents, the ideological descendants of Pertur, argued that some gains were being registered by the Basque left parties such as Euzkadiko Ezkerra (EE); and if (p-m) resumed armed actions, they would make life very difficult for these parties.[22] They also believed that the general public in Euskadi was becoming alienated from their struggle by what they saw as excessive violence; and the organization was becoming increasingly isolated from the masses.

By early February, there were already rumors that ETA (p-m) was about to terminate the truce. France Press reported on February 4 that a (p-m) press conference was to be held at which the breaking of the truce would be announced; but sources within (p-m) hurried to notify the Basque media that this report was premature, and that no definitive vote had yet been taken on the matter.[23] However, on February 7 the Executive Committee of Euzkadiko Ezkerra issued a statement that the possibility of a break in the truce was genuine because "the objectives we hoped for have not been achieved."[24]

The vote was taken around February 18, after several weeks of meetings. Of the ninety-eight delegates to the Asamblea, seventy-four reportedly voted with the anti-truce faction.[25] The issue had been resolved, but at a high cost to the organization. The group split once again into an anti-truce faction—now called ETA (p-m) VIII—to reflect their origins in the VIII Asamblea, and a pro-truce faction—called ETA (p-m) VII—to lay claim to the ideological heritage of the preceding period, as well as to Pertur's legacy. In ETA jargon, the pro-truce wing became known as the séptimos while the anti-truce group called itself the octavos for the eighth assembly. The split was amicable (as some ETA splits have not been), but the damage was done. ETA (p-m) once again fell under the control of forces bitterly opposed to negotiations and to the idea of a cease-fire in general, and the violence resumed within days. On February 26, ETA (m) fired an explosive charge from a car at the headquarters of the Guardia Civil in San Sebastián; and on March 6, ETA (p-m) VIII detonated a bomb in Bilbao. Neither attack produced casualties, but it was clear that the calm of the preceding months had ended.

At the beginning of the summer of 1982, the anti-truce faction of (p-m) published a 150-page document that set forth the reasons justifying their return to armed attacks.[26] "The continuation of the truce," they wrote, "does not now make any sense unless we might think that revolutionary violence has no role to play. . . . In an eventual negotiation, an armed organization can only offer the elimination of armed action and of the organization itself. Therefore, if we begin from the conviction for the necessity of the exercise of revolutionary violence and of the existence of the armed organization that assures the accumulation of coercive power, we cannot presume the bilateral negotiation with the state. We begin from the fact that armed struggle is not negotiable; everything else, a temporary truce. Never armed struggle or the organization." This philosophy of the links between armed struggle and negotiation, born of the experiences of ETA (p-m) with the 1981 cease-fire, would eventually make its way into the thinking of ETA (m), and would in the years to come complicate attempts to negotiate with the organization's military wing.

The story of the remnants of the Pertur faction within ETA (p-m) was not completed, however. Shortly after the VIII Asamblea, the pro-truce wing held their own meeting, which they referred to as the second half of the VII Asamblea. In a press conference held on February 22, they issued their own analysis of the future of ETA's armed struggle. Their principal conclusions: "The acceptance of armed struggle by the Basque people . . . has declined substantially due to the participation of the masses in the political game and the social fatigue produced by the period of mobilization and agitation of the past decade; other reasons for the drop in acceptance of armed struggle would be its own errors and the mili dynamic that has even generated mass mobilizations against violence. . . . From the perspective of the negotiation of the pending matters, the truce has been a failure; but the truce has forced the milis to accept one of their own, and has allowed Euzkadiko Ezkerra to get out of the political fence on which it found itself by virtue of its 'conniving with terrorism'; the cease-fire has allowed EE to situate itself at an ideological and political level in the center of the left in Euskadi. . . . Armed struggle would provoke a confrontation with EE, with which ETA (p-m) would lose its political cover and would go on isolating itself more and more from the masses, evolving into an autonomous group with less and less influence on Basque society. . . . A break in the truce could lead to a possible renewal of the spiral of violence (such as that which took place at the end of 1980) which would benefit again the coup plotters, giving them reasons and excuses, although not causes. . . . Violence should be applied only when it is accepted by the masses as legitimate and effective, and felt by them to be inevitable and necessary. . . . This reconversion of ETA (p-m) is justified by the social and political transformations that are operating in Basque society. . . . Armed activism will pass to a very secondary level as long as we do not see new conditions of mobilization that correspond to a higher level of consciousness of the masses, an accumulation of [Basque] national power that can enter into open confrontation with the central power [i.e., Madrid], or a restriction or loss of the sociopolitical gains of the people."[27]

During the summer of 1982, contacts were made between the Spanish interior ministry and ETA (p-m) VII which led in late September to the dissolution of the Pertur wing of (p-m) and their return to civil society. Since this story is interwoven with the Bandrés negotiations for "social reintegration," we will discuss it at greater length in the following section. Most of the members were amnestied or given suspended jail sentences and allowed to take up their normal lives once again. The number of ETA members affected was not insignificant: some seventy living in exile in France and twenty-seven in prison. But, as these were the etarras least committed to a hard-line and to violence, their renunciation of armed struggle hardly affected their comrades who remained intransigent.[28] The octavos launched a wave of violent attacks that culminated with the October 1983 kidnapping of Spanish army captain Martín Barrios, after which most of their members either went over to ETA (m) or were deported to Cuba by the French government.

"Social Reintegration" and the Bandrés-Rosón Negotiations

In early 1981, before the two men began their historic negotiations, Juan María Bandrés held a very negative opinion of Spain's new interior minister, Juan José Rosón. As Bandrés later recounted, Rosón impressed him as a hard-line Francoist, a closed-minded *"cacique"* (a pejorative term for a traditional local political boss) from Galicia who harbored strong prejudices against Basques. Moreover, under his direction, torture was practiced extensively in Spain's jails and police stations.[29] Thus, when Mario Onaindia approached Bandrés about meeting with Rosón, Bandrés was skeptical that anything could come of it. Onaindia had already had several lengthy discussions with Rosón, however, and was convinced that the minister was more flexible than Bandrés believed. So Bandrés agreed to an initial meeting, which turned out to be the first in a series of negotiations that lasted more than a year, and which led to the dissolution of ETA (p-m) VII.

Informal talks went on between the two men throughout the first half of 1981. Gradually they discovered that they had a number of objectives in common, especially after the coup attempt of February 23 showed them that they had a common enemy in a resurgent neo-Francoism. As time went on, Bandrés found that Rosón was genuinely desirous of finding a solution to the problem of ETA violence. Rosón turned out to be an extremely effective spokesman for a negotiated settlement because he was a strong man in an otherwise weak government. The president, Calvo Sotelo, in effect gave him advance authority to discuss virtually any topic or question; and other ministers, such as Justice Minister Pio Cabanillas, were willing to let Rosón dictate the pace and the agenda of negotiations.

Despite this free hand, Rosón realized that he could not go farther and faster than the anti-negotiation elements within the government would permit, particularly the military, the police, and the Guardia Civil. He was quite careful to keep these groups fully informed of his progress in the talks with Bandrés and to consult with them on particularly controversial matters. He realized that any agreement he reached would be useless if it were not supported by a consensus on the government side of the table. Both Bandrés and Rosón were also careful to keep Felipe González, then leader of the opposition socialist party, fully informed of their negotiations. The first contact between Bandrés and González about this matter took place in late February 1981, shortly after they and a group of other deputies had finished watching a videotape of the abortive coup attempt.

If Rosón was careful to secure consensus from the government's side to support a negotiated settlement, he was also sensitive to the needs of ETA (p-m) to be able to claim some triumph, no matter how small. At one point in the discussions in 1982, the séptimos were close to making a public announcement of their self-dissolution. Rosón requested that the announcement be delayed so he could ensure some corresponding agreement from the government's side, even though he could have had the dissolution announcement more or less "for free."[30]

Talks between Rosón and Bandrés went on at two levels. At one level, the two men worked out the most important details between themselves. To ratify the agreements, however, plenary meetings were used to bring together the entire group of interested parties: from Euzkadiko Ezkerra, Bandrés, Onaindia, and Juan Infante; from the government, all the relevant ministers plus the police and the Guardia Civil. These meetings involved all the potential anti-negotiations elements in discussions, thereby co-opting them into the final agreement. Even the hard-line chief of the unified antiterrorist command, Manuel Ballesteros, eventually went along when he became convinced that ETA had to have an honorable way out of the insurgency.

Bandrés and Rosón realized that it would be difficult for both the government and ETA to admit openly that either had conceded something of real value in return for concessions from the other. The solution to this impasse lay in crafting a complex dynamic of action and response whose links would remain obscure except to those who were parties to the agreement.[31] Following the ETA (p-m) declaration of a truce, the government was to begin a series of symbolic "gestures" that would lead eventually to the release of a number of (p-m) prisoners. At the beginning of March 1981, there were 310 members of ETA in prison, of which 63 were from the (p-m) wing; but only 2 of these were in prisons located in the Basque provinces.[32] The plan was for the justice ministry to begin gradually to transfer to the new prison at Nanclares de la Oca (in the Basque province of Alava) as many of the (p-m) prisoners as possible, and eventually to secure their release on bond if necessary, but completely free of further punishment if possible. The full legal requirements of the Spanish penal code would be observed; but the objective would be to free the (p-m) prisoners as soon as it could feasibly be done. The pace of releasing the prisoners, or of moving them to Nanclares, depended on ETA (p-m)'s observing the terms of their own self-imposed cease-fire. The first group of twenty ETA prisoners were moved to Nanclares on December 15, 1981, and three of these had been released by the end of the year.[33]

According to Bandrés, the final agreement negotiated with Rosón consisted of two elements: in return for the dissolution of ETA (p-m) VII, all affected poli-mili prisoners and exiles would be freed of their charges, including even the worst cases (i.e., there would be no exception for so-called blood crimes). These were two hundred (plus or minus) cases divided into four categories. The easiest cases to deal with were the exiles who were "fichados," that is those who were known by the police to be ETA members, but who had no other pending charges against them. They were to be allowed to return home and the police would quietly drop their cases. For those in exile charged with crimes, the disposition of each case would be negotiated with the appropriate judge. The exile would return to Spain and appear before the judge to plead "not guilty." Since there was usually no proof except police testimony or confessions of other prisoners, these cases could easily be absolved or set aside for lack of evidence. Bandrés handled most of these cases himself as the defense attorney. The third category consisted of ETA members charged but not yet tried; they were either still in police custody awaiting trial or released on bond. The solution for these was to hold their trial immediately and either find them not guilty or commute their sentences if they were convicted. The last category was composed of those prisoners who had been tried, convicted, and were currently serving their sentences. They usually received a commutation, which Bandrés requested in their name.

At one point in early 1983, the Spanish government contemplated adopting the Italian model of selective amnesty, whereby the prisoner had to publicly repent for his wrongdoings and promise to collaborate with the government by giving them information about his fellow insurgents. (One extreme rightist politician even suggested that ETA members who were amnestied should be used to disarm ETA-laid bombs and booby traps to prove their change of heart.) Fortunately, cooler heads prevailed. The actual procedure adopted was such that no prisoner or exile was humiliated or required to do anything of a public nature in the way of repentance. In most cases, Bandrés prepared the legal request, which simply asked for the amnesty to be granted for reasons of *"utilidad pública,"* or "the public good." No further documents were required, there would be no further contact with police, and there was no public testimonial or humiliation. Despite these protective measures, the prisoners and exiles who accepted the amnesty were ridiculed by ETA and even threatened with death for having chosen to collaborate with the enemy.

In March 1982, following the split between the two wings of ETA (p-m), Bandrés and Rosón held the first of some thirty meetings to resolve the issues of amnesty and the dissolution of the séptimos. By midsummer, the negotiations had become public knowledge, and Mario Onaindia was openly predicting that there would be a general amnesty before the upcoming parliamentary elections. Despite opposition from the octavos who were in prison, by late July Bandrés had assembled a list of seventy exiles and twenty-seven prisoners who were willing to renounce armed struggle in return for amnesty.[34] On July 30, the Spanish attorney general, José María Gil Albert, suggested using a provision of the national penal code that allowed for absolution for convicted terrorists who would agree to cooperate "to avoid crimes or reduce their effects." This article, said Gil Albert, could be used to free many of the ETA prisoners.[35] But he also warned that the government could not accept the principle of general, unconditional pardons; amnesty, where it was given, had to be administered on an individual, selective basis. By early August, the list of the first twenty-five prisoners to solicit amnesty was published in the press. Rosón announced at that same time that the total number of prisoners and exiles being discussed was around one hundred.[36]

On August 3, Bandrés held a press conference with the first prisoner on his list to be released provisionally, Tomás Esnaola. Esnaola made a point of telling the reporters that "no one is going by way of the 'arrepentimiento' policy, since there is no reason to do so; but the present policy offers other avenues and other ways out." Nevertheless, five of the original list of twenty-seven had rejected the amnesty option, perhaps fearing ETA reprisals. And with good reason, for on August 10, ETA (p-m) VIII held a press conference at which they threatened to attack all prisoners or exiles who sought amnesty under the Bandrés program.[37]

The Dissolution of ETA (p-m) VII Assembly

By September 1, when twelve exiles and fourteen prisoners had been granted amnesty, news began to surface of the dissolution of ETA (p-m) VII Assembly.[38] The decision, which would affect perhaps twenty-five to thirty persons still at large and another twenty or so in prison, had been taken the preceding weekend, according to press reports. Bandrés was quick to warn that the news was premature, and that it was not yet certain that the definitive decision had been made. Nevertheless, on September 8 a séptimos spokesman told a Bilbao newspaper that the decision was definitive and would be announced on September 23. At about the same time, the Spanish magazine *Interviu* published an interview with séptimo leader José Mari Lara who confirmed that "last weekend we made the agreement, approved unanimously by the assembly, to dissolve the organization. The organizational measures for this dissolution will be undertaken throughout this month." The delay in announcing the decision was due, according to *Deia* columnist Eugenio Ibarzabal, to plans to free some twenty additional prisoners and permit the return to Spain of about thirty more exiles before September 20.[39]

Despite the failure of Bandrés and Rosón to reach this goal (by the end of September, only six more prisoners had been freed and ten exiles returned), the VII Assembly leaders proceeded with the public announcement of their dissolution. On September 30, at a packed press conference in France, ten of the best-known leaders of the séptimos confirmed the group's intention to disband and return to civil society. "We think," they said in a statement read to the journalists, "that we have fulfilled a fundamental role in the history of our people, in the degree to which we have helped

in the development and maintenance of the national consciousness of our people, in the achievement of important amounts of
self-government for which we will continue struggling with nonviolent methods, and in consolidating a patriotic left party from
a revolutionary perspective. Armed struggle and ETA have now
fulfilled their role."[40]

At the time of the séptimos press conference, the list being
negotiated by Bandrés contained thirty prisoners and seventy-five
exiles, including those already released. Bandrés was reported confident that another twenty-five exiles would be returned and twelve
more prisoners released, before the upcoming parliamentary elections scheduled for October 28. On October 4, the first six members
of the now-dissolved VII Assembly appeared in court to begin the
procedures to achieve their freedom.[41] By November 1, seventeen of
the original list of thirty prisoners had been amnestied, including
six who were pardoned after the dissolution of the VII Assembly.[42]
As time went on, however, additional names were placed on the
list, especially as séptimos who were living in France realized how
relatively easy it would be to return to Spain to take up a normal
life again.

One complication in the procedure were the threats made by
the octavos against the members of the VII Assembly who sought
amnesty. On several occasions in 1983, members of the séptimo
wing held news conferences to denounce this campaign of their
former comrades to dissuade them from abandoning the struggle.
At one such conference in January 1983, the séptimos read passages from a letter which they had all received that contained this
warning: "ETA, the armed organization for the Basque revolution,
addresses you, as one of the names on the lists negotiated between
Bandrés and Rosón, to have you understand that before any hypo-
thetical project to return to Euskadi Sur [i.e., the Spanish Basque
provinces] on your part, you must immediately contact the organization because of security problems that your position could
cause, and to solve these problems in the best way possible."[43] On
another occasion, ETA (p-m) VIII Assembly held a news conference
to threaten armed attacks against leaders of Euzkadiko Ezkerra for
having undermined ETA's solidarity through the negotiations.[44]

Partly because of these threats from the VIII Assembly, and
partly because of the agonizingly slow procedures required, the

actual freeing of prisoners and return of exiles went on for two more years. In January 1983, Bandrés and Juan Infante went to Madrid to negotiate with the new interior minister, José Barrionuevo, and found him supportive of the agreements made by his predecessor. There were still, at this time, nine prisoners awaiting disposition of their cases (three were to stand trial on February 3) and more than fifty exiles seeking to return.[45] In June, more than forty exiles returned to Spain, followed by a group of twenty-five in September, and a third group of six in January 1984. On December 17, 1983, the last prisoner on the Bandrés list, Santiago Cogolludo Vallejo, was released from prison. On January 14, 1985, the last exile on the list, Joseba Aulestia "Zotza," returned from France.[46] Four years after Bandrés first met with Juan José Rosón, this chapter in the story of negotiations with ETA was closed. In all, some two hundred exiles and prisoners, of whom 111 had been on one of the original lists of Bandrés, had been reintegrated into Basque society.[47]

The short-term consequence of the Bandrés-Rosón negotiations was to free several hundred exiles and prisoners from the Pertur wing of ETA (p-m). Prisoners and exiles from the VIII Assembly faction, the hard-line octavos, generally rejected "social reintegration" under the Bandrés plan. A few of them were incorporated into the negotiations between Joseba Azkarraga and the PSOE government in 1984. The remainder either passed over to ETA (m) or were deported to Cuba by the French government. By the mid-1980s, ETA (p-m) had ceased to exist in any significant sense.

The military wing of ETA, on the other hand, had a much more unbending view of amnesty. One of the "historic" leaders of ETA, José Manuel Pagoaga "Peixoto," expressed it this way in an interview with *Punto y Hora* in October 1982:[48] "Amnesty is the following: that the Spanish government recognize that the struggle we have maintained until now has been correct, and that the repression that has been deployed against us has been unjust. There should be an indemnization following the amnesty; but the only thing we ask is that they [the Spanish] go home, that they leave us in peace. . . . Five years ago [in 1977], the freeing of the prisoners and the return home of some refugees was like a drop of oil to grease the door of democracy as it opened. But then we got the division. Some affirmed: 'We have not left home only to gain the right to return; we left to achieve a reunified, socialist and

Basque-speaking Euskadi, and we will not return if not under those conditions.' The last five years [since the amnesty of 1977] have shown the impossibility of hiding the lies of yesterday with the lies of today."

Bandrés and the other EE leaders paid a heavy price personally for their involvement in these negotiations. ETA (m) and ETA (p-m) VIII Assembly, as well as hard-line leaders from the Basque Left parties, strongly criticized Bandrés for having arranged a betrayal of the insurgents' cause and for having played into the hands of the Spanish government.[49] EE was accused of having sold out to the interests of the status quo for the privilege of being accepted into the power structure of the Basque Autonomous Community. For years to come, relations between Bandrés, Onaindia, and EE on the one hand, and other elements of the Basque left more closely aligned with ETA (m) on the other, would be strained and tense.

In negotiations with ETA in later years, from 1986 on, much would be made of the difference between "political negotiations" and "tactical negotiations." The latter, which were allowed on the negotiating table by Madrid, included only law enforcement and security matters such as selective amnesty and the rejection by ETA of armed struggle. The former, which Madrid would not accept as legitimate issues for discussion, included the other ETA demands such as the integration of Navarra and the right of the Basques to self-determination. In fact, this distinction between legitimate and non-legitimate issues had its origins in the 1981–1982 negotiations over "social reintegration." Mario Onaindia is generally credited with having invented the distinction as a way of getting the various negotiating parties to focus their discussions on those issues where concessions were feasible and avoiding those questions where positions were hardened and intransigent.[50] In the 1981–1982 talks, the EE representatives never presented any political topics for negotiating for two reasons: first, because to do so would have subverted the democratic institutions, such as the Basque autonomous parliament and government, to which they had pledged their support; and second, because they assumed that the resolution of the more narrow security issues (amnesty, cease-fire) would bring as a more or less automatic consequence the resolution of the broader political questions as well. As late as 1988, Bandrés still opposed the negotiation of political questions,

believing that there would be immediate and positive political re-
percussions following the cessation of violence by ETA.[51] Thus,
while the Rosón-Bandrés negotiations had the immediate effect of
dissolving ETA (p-m) VII and freeing several hundred of its members, in the long run the negotiations served to introduce what
would prove to be one of the key conceptual distinctions between
what Madrid would discuss and what they would not, between
what could be gained through armed struggle and what could not.
This distinction complicated negotiations in the late 1980s; but it
is also true that separation of the questions into two classes contained then, and still contains today, the key to a successful end to
the insurgency.

CHAPTER FIVE

New Actors, New Initiatives, New Failures: 1982–1983

I N 1982 and 1983, new actors appeared in the negotiations arena and several new initiatives were attempted. After the self-dissolution of ETA (p-m) VII Assembly in September 1982, the poli-milis were never again to be a factor in negotiations; but the military wing of ETA launched a major offensive in the spring of 1982 that some said was designed to force Madrid to negotiate. In October 1982, Spanish parliamentary elections brought to power the Spanish Socialist Workers Party (PSOE). After a brief period of uncertainty in the socialists' approach to terrorism, the new government of Felipe González adopted a tough policy toward ETA which seemed to offer little hope of a negotiated settlement. In the Basque Country, on the other hand, new protagonists joined the effort to promote negotiations. The Basque socialist party, Herri Batasuna (HB), sought to define a new role for itself in Basque politics; but its attempts to become the intermediary between ETA and Madrid proved unsuccessful. The most dramatic attempt to launch negotiations was that of Basque president Carlos Garaikoetxea, whose *"mesa para la paz"* held everyone's attention during the early months of 1983. The outcome of all these efforts was the same as before—failure and continued violence.

The ETA Offensive and the Role of HB:
February–May 1982

The late winter and spring of 1982 was an especially tense period for Spain. Only a year after the Guardia Civil coup attempt, Spanish democracy still seemed weak and vulnerable; and the impending collapse of the governing party, the UCD, promised to aggravate even further the state's vulnerability. Elections scheduled for May in Andalucia were expected to go badly for the UCD, leading to an anticipated general election in the fall. And to make matters worse, the World Cup soccer matches were to be held in a number of Spanish cities (including Bilbao) during the summer, and for several weeks the eyes of the world would be focused on Spain.

Perhaps to take advantage of this unrest, ETA (m) announced in February a campaign of violent attacks that would last until May 15, although they gave assurances that they would not attack the soccer teams that would soon be gathering in Spain for the international matches.[1] On February 16, two members of the Civil Guard were killed in separate attacks; on March 15, another member of the Civil Guard was killed; on March 22, an attack on a bar left two police inspectors and the girlfriend of one of them killed and two more police wounded; on March 26, the head of the state telephone company in Guipúzcoa was killed, along with his bodyguard; and on March 30, a San Sebastián doctor was assassinated. During the first half of April, there were grenade launcher attacks against Guardia Civil or army facilities in four different cities, and those and other attacks left three more dead. The most provocative attack came early in the morning of April 18, when a powerful blast ripped through the central telephone exchange in Madrid, leaving virtually half of Spain without telephone service, and closing down more than 6,000 bank offices that depended on the company's computers to keep track of their accounts.[2]

The central question in all this violence was what it revealed about ETA's interest in negotiations. ETA's February announcement had laid down several conditions for avoiding the threatened attacks: withdrawal of all Spanish police and the Civil Guard from Euskadi; transfer of all law enforcement authority to the Basque government; and transfer of all Basque prisoners to prisons in the

Basque Country. These demands, which some called extreme, were put forward, according to press speculation, as an initial bargaining point in order to move Madrid to the bargaining table to discuss less controversial issues. If so, this strategy certainly failed. The crumbling UCD government, faced with almost certain electoral defeat in Andalucia within a month and a national election in six months, was certainly not disposed to negotiate with ETA.

Nevertheless, reports persisted that "ETA wants to negotiate."[3] In mid-April, just before the attack on the Madrid telephone office, ETA published a communiqué in the San Sebastián newspaper *Egin*, in which they called for the removal of all Spanish police stations and Guardia Civil barracks in the Basque Country within one month or they would attack the facilities. However, the communiqué contained passages seldom seen in an ETA message before, passages that seemed to suggest a certain weariness with the struggle and a hope that Madrid would soon find it possible to begin negotiations. "This political practice," begins the passage (referring to the recent armed attacks), "has become the only alternative offered to us from Madrid to resolve the so-called Basque problem. . . . Notwithstanding these indications [of Madrid's intransigence], in politics, in principle, there is nothing immovable. . . . If today the situation presents a clearly warlike picture on the part of the oppressive Spanish state, it cannot be discounted that in the near future a series of events—primarily the effort that we who hope fervently for a democratic and self-governing regime for Euskadi put forth—will bring about a qualitative change in the process and exchange those warrior songs for the sounds of political accords. . . . Those in political and military power in Spain should reflect deeply on the path taken by the struggle developed during the last five years by the Basque working class and calculate the balance of its results. . . . Where has their refusal to accede to the political claims demanded by the immense majority of the Basque population led them; and from here on, if they continue in their blindness, toward which dead end do they wish to drag us, with unsuspected consequences for the whole of the Spanish state?" These words, commented journalist Eugenio Ibarzabal, could not have been easy for ETA to write, and perhaps significantly, the message contained not a single reference to the KAS Alternative. "ETA want to negotiate," concluded Ibarzabal; "or perhaps it is already doing it."

It was at this point that the Basque socialist coalition, Herri Batasuna, entered the field of negotiations for the first time. The significance of this step can better be appreciated by understanding something of the relationship between HB and ETA.

In his book on ETA's strategic evolution, Pedro Ibarra argues that most of the groups on the left of the Basque political spectrum arose independent of the influence of ETA (m). Upon its creation in 1978, Herri Batasuna was a coalition of several groups, including the Basque Socialist Party (ESB) and Basque National Action (ANV), that had nothing whatever to do with ETA. In its earlier years, the HB coalition remained substantially autonomous from ETA's control. However, the reality of the situation was that HB and the other groups existed because ETA existed; and they were considered—and they considered themselves—members of a new Basque nationalist community that revolved around ETA. It was inevitable, therefore, that ETA's relationship with HB (as mediated through the KAS) would evolve toward greater mutual interdependence, and toward a greater dependence of the political organization on the military force. From 1982 onward, Ibarra concludes, HB "enters into a situation of strict dependence of its political activity on the tactical needs and plans of the military organization."[4] HB's attempts to wedge its way into the negotiations arena should be viewed, then, through this perspective. If Ibarra's analysis is correct, the offers by HB leaders to serve as intermediaries take on added significance, as they seem to suggest that ETA itself was looking for ways to facilitate negotiations.

On April 21, barely forty-eight hours after the Madrid telephone office bombing, five HB leaders, led by Jon Idígoras and Txomin Ziluaga, held a press conference to call for direct and public negotiations between ETA (m) and the Spanish government. HB offered its services as intermediaries to try to get the talks started. As always, the KAS Alternative was the basis for the proposal, but the leaders stated that there were only three non-negotiable points: the inclusion of Navarra in the Basque Autonomous Community; a constitutional amendment to give the Basque people the right of self-determination; and immediate and total amnesty for all ETA prisoners and exiles. Other features of the KAS Alternative could be negotiated.[5] They added, in their prepared statement, "We believe that ETA (m) has the desire to negotiate."

The response of the Spanish government was not long in coming. On April 22, in the midst of an intense debate in the Spanish Congress of Deputies over the recent wave of ETA attacks, Interior Minister Juan José Rosón said, "With ETA there is not nor will there be, neither now nor in the future, any possibility of negotiation. One does not negotiate with life or with freedom. The unity of the country is not for sale, and neither the government nor the people are ready to turn over or break up Spain, since the collective dignity cannot be the object of a trade, just as neither can we trade away our right to decide from freedom and according to the majority will." The words of the minister were supported by the chamber in its entirety, even including the Basque nationalist deputies.[6]

That same day, April 22, police moved to arrest the HB leaders who had participated in the press conference the preceding day. In Bilbao, police entered the headquarters of HB and arrested Jon Idígoras, but Txomin Ziluaga was not in the building and thus avoided detention. In a related step, the Spanish interior ministry asked the state prosecutor to examine the transcript of the HB press conference to give an opinion whether the HB leaders could be tried for apologia for terrorism.[7] Meanwhile, in Pamplona, an HB member of the provincial parliament of Navarra, Iñaki Aldecoa, and two other HB members were arrested and held incommunicado in the Pamplona police station on the grounds that they had helped the ETA squad that had carried out an attack in Pamplona the preceding week. By mid-May, a total of ten HB leaders, including Txomin Ziluaga and Santiago Brouard, had been imprisoned, allegedly for having taken part in demonstrations against King Juan Carlos during his visit to the Basque Country in February 1981, some fifteen months earlier.[8]

The May 15 deadline for the removal of all police and Guardia Civil installations came and went with little overall change in the positions of either ETA or the Spanish government. In June, ETA (m) declared a truce during the playing of the World Cup soccer matches. The soccer tournament ended on Sunday, July 11. The next Friday, an ETA team assassinated an executive of the state tobacco monopoly in the Bilbao suburb of Algorta. The killing raised to twenty-two the number of people killed by ETA thus far in 1982.[9]

The Socialists Come to Power:
September–December 1982

In 1982, as Spain neared a historic transfer of power into the hands of the Socialist Party, it would have been difficult to predict with certainty what the policy of that party would be regarding negotiations with ETA. One might have assumed, for example, that a left-wing party like the PSOE would take a more tolerant attitude toward an insurgent organization that derived at least part of its philosophy from Marxism. One might also have noted the intensive efforts by the secretary general of the party, Txiki Benegas, to get negotiations under way in 1978 when he was director of the Department of Interior of the Basque General Council, the interim pre-autonomy Basque government.

On the other hand, in his public writings in early 1982 (before the parliamentary election campaign began), Benegas sketched out a "global project" or "global accord" for meeting the challenge of terrorism in which negotiations were conspicuous by their absence. In April, for example, he revealed this five-point program for defeating ETA: the agreement of all the anti-ETA parties in Spain, including those in the Basque Country, to isolate ETA from its social support; full cooperation with the police and the Guardia Civil, providing them with the means necessary to eradicate terrorism; strengthening of measures to protect all those who feel threatened by ETA, especially those who refused to pay the "revolutionary tax"; a call to the workers' organizations to mobilize their members in the public fight against terrorism; and the guarantee that the government would not take any steps that might provoke or be seen as a pretext for terrorist actions.[10] The next month, writing in the Madrid magazine *Cambio 16*, Benegas added to his "global project" these measures: improvement of the law enforcement measures and techniques, including intelligence services (a phrase that many Basques interpreted to mean an increase in surveillance, spies, and police torture); and international discussions to eliminate support and cover for ETA from outside Spain (presumably primarily in France).[11] In all these proposals, there was no mention of negotiations or of any of the issues connected with ETA's demands, such as amnesty or law enforcement authority.

Admittedly, the atmosphere in Spain during the summer and fall of 1982 was not conducive to conciliatory statements or gestures from any politicians, much less from the party seemingly destined to win an overwhelming victory at the polls. A public opinion poll conducted in July but published in late October revealed that terrorism was seen as Spain's most important problem by more than 20 percent of the respondents, far behind the leading problem—unemployment—but far ahead of anything else.[12] In the weeks before the elections, both ETA (m) and ETA (p-m) VIII Assembly publicly rejected the idea of an interim cease-fire either before the elections or after, even assuming a new socialist government would be in power. Beginning on October 6 and continuing for several weeks, ETA (m) launched a series of bombing and shooting attacks against a variety of targets, including the Guardia Civil, that left three persons dead and six injured, one of them a young child.[13] And in early October details were uncovered of a military plot to overthrow the government on the day before the elections, which heightened the sense of crisis and urgency that surrounded the campaign.

It is not surprising, then, that the parliamentary election campaign leading up to the October 28 vote produced only tough anti-terrorist talk from all the candidates. None of the parties wanted to be seen as soft or weak on terrorism; and in their official campaign statements, they all pledged "intense" or "fundamental" or "frontal" attacks to wipe out terrorism in the country. All the parties vowed their support for the Guardia Civil and the military, and none of them even breathed a word of amnesty or any other negotiable issue.[14]

Throughout the campaign, PSOE leaders, including Felipe González, were adamant that they would not negotiate with ETA once in power. On September 15, in a press conference in Bilbao, Javier Solana, a member of the socialists' executive committee, said, "if the PSOE comes to power, there will be no negotiation with ETA. The problem of terrorism continues to be most serious, and the PSOE believes that there are two routes to its eradication: one based on police measures with the reinforcement of the state's security forces, and the second, of a political nature that involves the raising of citizen consciousness."[15] Several days later, also in a press conference, Felipe González echoed these sentiments and added a personal note: "We say 'No' to negotiation [with ETA]. I have already paid a certain price when at the beginning of the transition [to democracy] . . . we made it easy for a negotiated way out, when not so much blood had been spilled. That position was turned back against us in the electoral campaign of 1979 . . . I was accused of having proposed negotiations. And I did not respond in that campaign. . . . I was silent in the electoral campaign when there were accusations more stupid than unjust. That was something that we don't do any more: a gentlemen's agreement."[16] In an October press conference in Bilbao, González responded to a question about terrorism by saying that "words would have to be substituted for weapons" before there could be any solutions, and the amnesty measures taken by UCD Interior Minister Juan José Rosón, while not rejected by the PSOE, "must not condition the future."[17] Even a widely noted González speech in San Sebastián late in the campaign (the so-called spirit of Anoeta speech), while generally accepted as conciliatory toward Basque nationalism, still carefully avoided any specific comments about attitudes toward ending ETA violence.[18]

In the first days after the socialists' victory, however, there were signs that certain key party leaders might be interested in proposing cease-fire talks. On November 1, two days after the elections, Txiki Benegas was quoted in the press as suggesting that the PSOE could begin a dialogue with Herri Batasuna. "No one with a minimum sense of responsibility," he said, "and understanding that a new stage in history is opening, can be closed to a dialogue with anyone, because the objective we pursue, peace in Euskadi, is more important than certain hesitancies with regard to [dialogue]." Benegas went on to add, however, that "it is necessary that the weapons be silenced, because if not it will be enormously difficult [to conduct talks]."[19] On November 4, *Deia* reported from sources in the French Basque region that "perhaps negotiations between the PSOE and ETA (m) are already under way, although not at an official level."[20]

On November 5, ETA sought to force matters by assassinating in Madrid the commanding general of Spain's famous Brunete Division, Victor Lago Roman. According to one report, Benegas "panicked" at the thought of a potential military coup provoked by ETA, and made two calls to the office of an unnamed "well-known San Sebastián lawyer" to propose an agreement with ETA. In exchange for a cease-fire, Benegas offered to repeal the country's existing antiterrorist law, to put into effect immediately a law guaranteeing legal assistance for detainees and the transfer of ETA prisoners to local prisons. These offers were rejected by ETA and apparently repudiated by Benegas's fellow socialists, who believed that he had overreacted to the assassination.[21]

The day after the Lago Roman killing, HB leader Iñaki Esnaola said that "if the socialist government is ready to negotiate the issues important for Euskadi, expressed in the KAS Alternative, I believe that Herri Batasuna and ETA would be ready to negotiate, and HB could ask ETA for a truce."[22] Esnaola added that the Madrid assassination was not carried out to provoke the military into intervening, but rather to force the negotiations with the PSOE. Benegas's response the same day: "The PSOE does not talk, nor will it talk in the future, it does not negotiate, nor will it negotiate in the future, with anyone as long as attacks and assassinations are being carried out. Therefore, Iñaki Esnaola is radically mistaken when he affirms that the assassination of General Lago would have as an object the forcing of negotiations with the PSOE. If HB is capable of getting ETA to stop killing, then what it must do is get them to lay down their arms once and for all. If not, it will have to explain to the people why it does not do it."[23]

From prison, Iñaki Elorriaga, speaking in the name of the members of ETA (p-m) VIII Assembly then in jail, suggested that his group would give the new government "100 days of confidence" in which to test their true intentions regarding negotiations.[24] And on November 14, *Deia* printed excerpts from an interview with an ETA (m) spokesman in Mexico in which it was affirmed that ETA would condition its future actions on the behavior of the new PSOE government.[25]

In his investiture speech on December 1, President González claimed he was ready for a "dialogue" with Basque "political forces," but he later clarified that he would be willing to talk only with groups that rejected violence and that accepted as nonnegotiable the unity of Spain.[26] ETA (m) responded on December 6 with a communiqué in which it criticized the PSOE and announced that it would continue armed struggle.[27] González replied in a press conference the next day that "if what ETA pretends is to threaten and coerce the government of the nation, I must say that we are going to remain firm. In the face of this challenge, I call on the citizenry to react against this threat and contribute to peace in the Basque Country and all Spain."[28] And in an interview with *El País* published on December 13, González issued this clarification of his earlier offer of a dialogue: "I do not want to be misunderstood, and if people believe that I am offering a dialogue to those who act violently, I am being misunderstood. As far as I am concerned there can be only one kind of dialogue—the kind laid down by the limits of the constitution."[29]

On December 22, in a Madrid speech covered widely by the press, the new socialist interior minister, José Barrionuevo, insisted that "with ETA there are no possible terms for negotiation," but he said later in the same discussion that if ETA would suspend its violent actions for six months, the government might be willing to negotiate from that point.[30] In other words, while ETA insisted on negotiations that might lead to a cease-fire, Madrid wanted a cease-fire firmly in place before they would consider negotiations. ETA (m)'s answer to this proposal came on December 29, when they assassinated two members of the Guardia Civil in the Irun train station.[31]

Garaikoetxea's "Mesa para la Paz":
January–March 1983

At the beginning of 1983, it appeared that hopes for a negotiated settlement with ETA were dashed once again. In contrast to earlier periods, however, this time there was a new actor on the scene: a strong and popular Basque leader, Carlos Garaikoetxea, who was elected first president of the Basque autonomous government in March 1980. When it became clear that the González government was unable or unwilling to pursue negotiations, Garaikoetxea cautiously launched his own negotiation efforts, to be labeled the mesa para la paz.[32] (The phrase "mesa para la paz" would be translated literally as "peace table," although a better translation would be "peace commission.")

By the end of 1982, Garaikoetxea and other Basque leaders—especially those in Euzkadiko Ezkerra, such as Juan María Bandrés and Mario Onaindia—had concluded that the Spanish government and ETA were incapable of beginning cease-fire talks on their own initiative. The only way these two parties would ever be able to launch discussions would be through the intermediation of a third party. Although Herri Batasuna had offered its services as an intermediary, PNV and EE leaders were opposed to giving such an important role to HB because it would in their eyes legitimize HB's boycott of the Basques' own elected institutions. Their preferred solution was to work through the Basque government, and specifically through the person of President Garaikoetxea, who had acquired considerable mass popularity and legitimacy as spokesman for Basque nationalist aspirations.

The idea for such intermediation was dropped rather casually in a comment buried in a long interview Garaikoetxea granted to the press, which appeared in Basque and Spanish newspapers on January 7, 1983. In response to a question about how to avoid a violent confrontation between ETA and the newly formed Basque autonomous police force, Garaikoetxea remarked simply that the "confrontation could be avoided if a cessation of armed activities could be reached, and if a solution to the problem of violence is achieved, for which I believe that a meeting of the PNV, the PSOE, and HB could be very useful."[33] Press reports of the interview emphasized the remark in their treatment of the president's comments, and leaders of the various parties concerned began to respond cautiously. The PNV said it was "a proposition that ought to be tried"; and HB said they would have to study the proposal. PSOE leader Txiki Benegas said he needed to see a formal proposal, and anyway he doubted HB would accept. The socialist secretary general added that his party would have two preconditions before beginning any conversation: first, they would have to receive a formal proposal from Garaikoetxea, and not just an unofficial press report; and second, they would have to know that HB had accepted the offer. Over the next several days, HB issued statements reaffirming their desire to act as an intermediary with ETA (m) and calling the Garaikoetxea idea a step forward, although still not a clear proposal.[34]

Within a week, Garaikoetxea had made a major breakthrough in getting the PSOE and HB together. On January 13, he met for two and a half hours with Felipe González and laid out his own five points for negotiation: the termination of all violence; the legalization of political parties, including those (like HB) that advocated independence from Spain; the clarification and confirmation of a broad grant of home rule to the Basques through their autonomous government, especially in the field of police authority; the search for a solution to the integration of Navarra with the other three Basque provinces, while respecting the will of the Navarrese people; and the granting of amnesty to ETA members who would agree to abandon armed struggle.[35] It was clear that Garaikoetxea intended to use the opening created by the possible peace talks to press for greater autonomy for the Basque government as a way of encouraging ETA to discuss a cease-fire. González would not, of course, commit himself to any of these points, and indeed, some days later said that the unity of Spain was not negotiable and that all talks had to take place within the framework of the constitution. Nevertheless, the president assured Garaikoetxea of his support for the initiative.

By now, the three affected political parties had all expressed, with differing levels of reservations, their willingness to participate in the talks. HB, for example, emphasized that the KAS Alternative had to be the basis for the talks, and they had to be accepted as the valid intermediary to represent ETA in the talks. The PNV continued to stress the importance of simply getting the talks started; as far as they were concerned, strengthening the existing autonomy statute would have highest priority. The PSOE rejected the KAS Alternative as the basis for talks; and as for HB's role as intermediary, that would be proved if they could get ETA to stop the violence while the meetings were going on. The PSOE position was at this time, and remained throughout these discussions, that all violence had to cease before the negotiations could begin. Any armed attack by ETA before the talks began or while they were under way would be considered by the PSOE as cause to terminate negotiations.[36]

A second breakthrough came on January 16, when two leaders of HB, Iñaki Esnaola and Itziar Aizpurua, visited Garaikoetxea for more than two hours at Ajuria Enea, his official residence in Vitoria.[37] The mere fact that they met Garaikoetxea there was significant, since Herri Batasuna rejected the legitimacy of all the institutions of the Basque autonomous regime, including the Basque parliament (where they refused to take the seats they won in the

1980 elections) and the Basque government (over which Garaikoe-txea presided). The two HB leaders left the meeting without talking to reporters; and Garaikoetxea would say only that the meeting had been a "very important step" toward convening the commission. HB's assessment of the meeting was revealed the next day in a brief note presented to the press.[38] The note described the meeting as being "of positive value," and outlined the position maintained by HB in the meeting: the meetings would have to be "open, transparent and public"; and "for HB the achievement of the points of the KAS Alternative is an important and necessary step." Some observers professed to see in that last phrase an important shift by HB away from their rigid commitment to the KAS Alternative as non-negotiable. Subsequent interpretations were to prove these observers wrong.

On January 17, Garaikoetxea met in Ajuria Enea with Benegas and the PSOE leader in Vizcaya province, Ricardo Garcia Damborenea, to review their party's attitudes regarding the peace commission.[39] By the end of the day, the president had secured the socialists' acceptance of the invitation, followed the next day by the agreement of HB to meet. There were still a number of major obstacles to convening the talks. Both Garaikoetxea and the PSOE insisted that the talks could not proceed if there were any more violent attacks. The leading Navarrese parties complained that the fate of their province was being decided in a forum where they were not present; and Euzkadiko Ezkerra leader Bandrés said the negotiations would not be complete unless all the Basque parties were represented. Nevertheless, by January 20 Garaikoetxea felt sufficiently confident of the process that he ventured to convene the first meeting "within eight days." It began to appear as if Garaikoe-txea might actually succeed in arranging for representatives of HB, PNV, and PSOE to sit together in search of an end to ETA violence.

Such optimism proved to be unfounded. Almost immediately, both HB and PSOE began to pull back from their acceptance of the Garaikoetxea invitation. Alfonso Guerra, Spanish vice president and PSOE leader, said that Basque independence, amnesty for ETA members, and withdrawal of Spanish law enforcement agencies from the Basque provinces were all absolutely not negotiable.[40] Both Txiki Benegas and Ricardo Garcia Damborenea reiterated that there must be absolutely no ETA violence during the talks or the

PSOE would withdraw. HB replied that only ETA could grant that condition by declaring a truce; that they (HB) were not demanding an end to police brutality, mass arrests, or torture in prison as a precondition to starting negotiations; and that the cessation of violence should be the *end* of the negotiations, not the beginning. HB also offered new conditions related to agenda, participants, and location (they insisted on a meeting site in Navarra, which the other parties considered unnecessarily provocative of Navarrese public opinion).

Through all these exchanges, Garaikoetxea continued to labor to get the talks convened. At one point, a date had actually been set to begin the discussions: January 28. By January 26, the parties had reached the point of suggesting meeting sites and naming their representatives. Unfortunately, the meeting had to be postponed because of a disagreement over whether newspaper reporters would be allowed to cover the talks (HB insisted that they be admitted; Garaikoetxea resisted; PSOE sided with the president). Even though Garaikoetxea said that the peace commission was still going to move ahead, the delay turned out to be decisive.

On January 29, the HB governing council met and issued a new set of three conditions for the talks: that the KAS Alternative be placed on agenda for discussion; that the press be admitted; and that everyone agree that these talks would serve only as an intermediary device to prepare the way for direct negotiations between the only two forces that really mattered—ETA and the Spanish government.[41] Upon receipt of this communiqué, Garaikoetxea suspended the talks sine die on the grounds that HB was not serious about wanting to negotiate an end to the struggle. HB replied that the president had overreacted to their communiqué. Two of their conditions—the presence of the KAS Alternative on the agenda and the stipulation of their role as simply intermediation and not negotiation (which only ETA could do)—had been known from the beginning. Only the demand regarding press coverage was genuinely new.[42]

At this point, ETA (m) itself intervened in the process. On February 1, the press published an ETA communiqué that there could be no cease-fire until the KAS Alternative had been accepted. On February 2, ETA (m) attacked a Guardia Civil patrol in Guipúzcoa, killing one and wounding two others. Claiming that HB did not really want a dialogue and ETA did not genuinely want peace,

Garcia Damborenea responded to the attack by breaking off all PSOE participation in the Garaikoetxea proposal; and Garaikoetxea himself admitted that ETA had collapsed the negotiations. HB replied that if the PSOE wanted a cease-fire, they would have to talk directly with ETA. HB was not in a position to demand a cessation of violence.[43] Each side accused the other of not really wanting to meet and of looking for excuses to avoid negotiations.

On February 5, an ETA bomb exploded in the lobby of the central office of the Banco de Vizcaya in Bilbao, killing three and wounding nine bystanders. The bomb was exploded at about 9:45 A.M. when the bank was crowded with early Saturday morning customers. An estimated nine hundred persons were in the building at the time of the explosion. PSOE leader Benegas angrily commented that "In this atmosphere, Garaikoetxea can forget about counting on us for any effort to start a dialogue." Banks closed in protest throughout the Basque Country; and a rally against ETA violence in Bilbao on February 7 attracted several tens of thousands of people.[44]

The Basque president tried once more, on February 8, to set the date for talks to begin on March 1, on the condition that there be no more violence in the interim. HB replied that they would consider this new proposal, but Benegas said that Garaikoetxea's conditions were insufficient and that only a declaration by ETA of a cease-fire would get them to participate in the talks. On February 12, HB suggested that they might be willing to consider some other solution to the question of press coverage, but by now this was an unimportant side issue. On February 13, ETA struck again in the town of Tolosa, this time wounding an apparently innocent civilian (although ETA accused him of working undercover for a private detective) and killing his wife.

The peace talks were effectively ended. Benegas said that the PSOE would never sit down at the same table with "those who support assassins." HB said that the PSOE never did intend to negotiate seriously, and was only using the attacks as an excuse for not meeting with them. The PNV accused both sides of being unreasonable. And Garaikoetxea lamented the failure of his idea. "I am convinced," he said, "that sooner or later this is the way that will get us started, and those who today reject the 'mesa para la paz' will one day regret it."[45]

Was the mesa para la paz really possible, or was Garaikoetxea being unrealistic in even suggesting it? And if it was possible, what caused it to collapse even before it was started? Basque political scientist Gurutz Jáuregui Bereciartu, author of one of the leading books on ETA, wrote shortly after the failure of negotiations that "the 'mesa para la paz' was born fatally wounded. . . . This failure demonstrated clearly that at the present the fundamental problem is not one of reaching an agreement, . . . but of determining if there really exists a will to negotiate. The problem is not so much one of content as of political will."[46] On the other hand, Garaikoetxea suggested that before his January press conference he had sounded out the PSOE and the results of those soundings, plus HB's public declarations through 1982, had led him to a certain optimism regarding the willingness of these two groups to come to the bargaining table.[47]

Who, then, caused the talks to fail even before they were begun? As the neutral intermediary, Garaikoetxea's opinion must weigh especially heavy here. In the first days after the collapse of the talks, the president blamed hard-line elements within ETA and HB for causing the failure. But two months later, in the midst of the campaign preceding provincial and municipal elections, Garaikoetxea claimed that "before, during and after the 'mesa para la paz' the Spanish government tried to negotiate with ETA. And I have proof, and I am ready to confront publicly anyone who might ask me for it."[48] What the president apparently was referring to was an alleged effort by Txiki Benegas to establish his own negotiations with ETA and HB in early 1983. In order for this initiative to succeed, Benegas had to undermine the mesa para la paz, which he claimed he was going to do in a conversation with EE leader Mario Onaindia. This speculation remained essentially unconfirmed, and it was not known whether or not Benegas ever managed to establish contacts with ETA. What is known, however, is that these efforts, like so many both before and after, came to nought.[49]

The Socialists' First Year:
January–October 1983

On January 2, 1983, Basque journalist Eugenio Ibarzabal wrote in his weekly column in *Deia* that "there has been a lot of talk about contacts [with ETA], but the reality is that they have not existed. It seems surprising but so many declarations from one side and the other have not produced any conversation. . . . The distance to the opening of a negotiation is enormous. Nevertheless, I can see a variable that might be important in the future."[50] The "variable" to which Ibarzabal was referring was the attitude of the French government, which began to shift decisively against ETA in the year following the election of the socialists in Madrid. Still hoping that French pressure would be sufficient to move ETA to the bargaining table, the Spanish government worked for most of 1983 to start meeting with the insurgents. After the kidnapping and death of Alberto Martín Barrios in October, however, the socialists abandoned any hope of a negotiated settlement, at least for another year.

The first step taken in Madrid to encourage ETA (m) to give up armed struggle turned out to be a colossal blunder. In early March, the Spanish interior ministry revealed its plans to introduce in the parliament a bill that would provide for the pardoning of so-called repentant terrorists.[51] Modeled after the Italian law that had proved so successful in persuading members of the Red Brigades to give up their insurgency, the Spanish law would have allowed the courts to absolve ETA members of their crimes if they fulfilled these conditions: they must appear voluntarily before the court and confess their participation in all alleged illegal activities; they must prove that they did not participate directly in any violent attacks; they must pledge publicly not to participate in any violent acts in the future; and they must collaborate with police in gathering evidence that would lead to the identification and capture of other terrorists. The more the ETA member collaborated with police, the more he would see his sentence reduced. The bill also envisioned the possibility of granting the "repentant" etarras protection in case they feared reprisals from the organization. Provisional and conditional release was possible for those etarras in prison who had completed half of their sentence and who fulfilled all the other requirements.

The reaction against this proposed legislation was not long in coming. Euzkadiko Ezkerra leader Juan Infante, who, along with Juan María Bandrés, had been negotiating the gradual release of etarras from jail under the "social reintegration" policy of Juan José Rosón, immediately claimed that "there are no prisoners or exiles

in ETA who would be interested in such a possible 'law of repen-
tants'. . . . what the ETA members want is to take advantage of legal
measures that permit their release from prison or their return from
exile, even if they have to lay down their weapons beforehand, but
without the presumption of any type of repentance for informing
or collaboration." Bandrés himself added the next day that the proposed law would be a "serious error for our people," and "it would
be condemned to failure." He was especially concerned about the
fate of some twenty ex-etarras from (p-m) VII Assembly whose return from exile he was at that moment trying to negotiate. If they
thought that they would be classified with the "repentant terrorists" described under the proposed law, he feared they would refuse
to return to civil society. "We have to speed up the process," he
said, "before this new train runs over us."

Basque nationalist senator Joseba Azkarraga, later to play an
important role in the amnesty issue, also had a negative view of the
new bill. "To want to transplant the philosophy of the Italian model
to Euskadi," he said, "is to show complete ignorance of the struc-
tural reality of this country. Whether they like it or not, in Euskadi
the struggle of ETA has a series of components that the Red Brigades lack. A greater social support and the concept of the struggle
for national liberation are a good example of this." Accusing the
new socialist interior minister, José Barrionuevo, of having a "fascist approach," HB spokesman Jon Idígoras said that the law would
be a "most absolute failure" because it "ignores the true will of
Euskadi. In this country, no one is going to be an informer, and for
that reason, the law will not achieve anything."

Faced with such a general rejection of the "repentant terrorist"
approach, the Spanish government finally yielded to reality. In late
March, after a meeting of Minister Barrionuevo with parliamentary leaders of all the major parties, the proposed bill was quietly
withdrawn, and the subject was closed.

There were to be other initiatives, however, to open negotiations. One such attempt, by the former head of the unified antiterrorist command, Manuel Ballesteros, was revealed in late April by
newspaper columnist Eugenio Ibarzabal.[52] The subject was raised in
connection with an Ibarzabal column about the willingness of HB
to participate in provincial and municipal governments after the
upcoming May elections. "Reality has demonstrated," he wrote,

"that it is not necessary to participate in the institutions in order to get negotiations; the 'mesa para la paz' is a good example. But there also exist other attempts long after [the 'mesa'], only a *few short* weeks ago. Despite the fact that ETA is very far from the conditions that the PSOE affirmed that it was demanding to negotiate, their government has tried vainly to force a negotiation with ETA (m). Relatively recently, *Ballesteros, in the name of the socialist government, tried to negotiate with the armed organization.* Said attempt, one more following the line of forcing a negotiation with ETA (m) away from the Basque government, . . . ended in complete failure. The military organization again presented its well-known points. It is worth asking where the socialist government is going to go with its efforts now known by everyone and carried out after the initiative of the Basque government. *Could it be that negotiation with ETA, far from being insanity, is considered by the PSOE to be something they want to capitalize on?* In any case, this initiative has no relationship with what their spokesmen affirm and denounce."

Predictably, the Ibarzabal column created another controversy played out in the press over the next several days.[53] The spokesman for the Spanish government, Eduardo Sotillos, replied that Ibarzabal's charges were false and that they made no sense because Ballesteros was no longer a central figure in antiterrorist planning. This latter comment was not quite true since, even though he had been relieved as head of the unified command, Ballesteros had been kept on as special advisor to the director of state security, Rafael Vera. Ibarzabal stood steadfastly by his original comments. The delegate of the Spanish government in the Basque Autonomous Community, Ramon Jáuregui, said that "the government has made clear repeatedly its firm decision to not negotiate with terrorists. Therefore, the accusation is false." To which the spokesman for the Basque government, Pedro Miguel Etxenike, replied that "the attempts to negotiate with ETA have always been denied, and in fact there are more denials when the attempts to negotiate increase." Herri Batasuna, obviously enjoying the charges and countercharges flying back and forth between the Basque and Spanish governments, simply said that it "would not enter into the polemic," and instead they urged a public meeting of all the parties, with the press in attendance, so that the public would know what was going on.

As the year went on, it was clear that the socialist government was losing its patience with what they saw as a more conciliatory approach. It was during this period that the Plan ZEN was developed and put into practice; and it was also the time when the Spanish government increased its pressure on the French government to step up its actions against ETA. Negotiations seemed quite unlikely. In early June, at a press conference in Pamplona, the director of state security, Rafael Vera, said, "the only thing to negotiate with ETA is where they should deliver their weapons. All the rest is not negotiable." He added that the socialist government had discarded any initiative like that offered by Basque president Garaikoetxea earlier in the year.[54]

After some six months of gradually hardening its antiterrorist policy, the Spanish government reached a decisive turning point in October, almost exactly one year after coming to power. On October 5, Spanish army captain Alberto Martín Barrios was kidnapped from his home and held in exchange for the release of nine members of ETA (p-m) VIII Assembly, who were about to be tried for an attack on an army barracks three years earlier.[55] In the midst of negotiations for Martín Barrios's release, four Spanish police officers were arrested in France for allegedly trying to kidnap one of the leaders of the VIII Assembly, José María Larretxea. At about the same time, two other ETA members disappeared in France. These were the first attacks by what later became known as the GAL. ETA replied by killing Martín Barrios, whose body was discovered on October 19.

In reaction, the Spanish government launched a series of antiterrorist measures in Madrid and Paris to eliminate ETA by direct pressure. As Eugenio Ibarzabal pointed out in a column early in November, far from cleaning out all the old conservatives from the key leadership positions in the police, the socialists had kept them all in power and had even brought back such hard-line antiterrorist leaders as Manuel Ballesteros.[56] For the next year, the antiterrorist policy of the government would emphasize tough police measures and improved cooperation with the French. Negotiations were not only not emphasized; they were actually unthinkable. On November 9, for example, HB spokesmen held a press conference to charge that Txiki Benegas "has been for over a month asking us for official conversations about the KAS Alternative." Benegas charged back that the HB accusations were false, "at no time have I attempted to negotiate with HB on the KAS Alternative, either directly or indirectly through intermediaries."[57] In an interview with *El País*, Basque president Garaikoetxea put it succinctly in a classic understatement: "I believe sincerely that at this time the conditions do not exist to negotiate with ETA."[58]

New Negotiation Initiatives and a Second Attempt at "Social Reintegration": 1984–1986

B Y most measures, 1984 was a very bad year for ETA, perhaps the worst of any in its twenty-five-year history up to that point.[1] By mid-August, the French government had expelled twenty-four Basque refugees to Latin America, and another ten had been forced to move to other regions of France. Eight suspected ETA members had been arrested and were awaiting extradition to Spain, while five were in French prisons for crimes committed locally. Between December 1983 and August 1984, attacks by French or Spanish police, as well as by the GAL, killed eighteen members or suspected members of ETA, only two fewer victims than the organization itself killed in the same period. By late 1984, the first etarras had been extradited to Spain for trial; and the wave of French arrests had resulted in the detention of a number of key ETA leaders, including Juan Lorenzo Lasa Mitxelena "Txikierdi" and Isidro María Garalde "Mamarru."

Informed speculation held that the increased pressure on ETA on both sides of the Pyrenees had as its principal objective to force the organization to the bargaining table. To that end, the arrests and expulsions in France were orchestrated carefully to leave unmolested ETA leaders like Txomin Iturbe who were believed to be more inclined to support a negotiated settlement. Nevertheless, despite several major attempts to arrange negotiations, the period under consideration here—August 1984 to April 1986—ended with the insurgency situation no better than when it began. In some respects, in particular because of the assassination of Herri Batasuna leader Santiago Brouard, the atmosphere for negotiations had definitely worsened. One bright note was the second attempt at "social reintegration," engineered this time by Basque nationalist senator Joseba Azkarraga. Even that attempt ended in tragedy, however.

Brouard and Barrionuevo:
August–November 1984

In May 1984, GRUPO 16, a Madrid public policy discussion group, sponsored a series of roundtable meetings on the subject of "Political Violence and Terrorism."[2] The meetings brought together men who just a short time before had been sworn enemies. Recently amnestied poli-milis like Juan Miguel Goiburu Mendizabal sat across the table from leaders of the Spanish antiterrorist agencies, Manuel Ballesteros and Joaquin Domingo Martorell. In addition, virtually every political party in Euskadi was represented. The only significant forces not present were ETA (m) and Herri Batasuna. Spanish interior minister José Barrionuevo stressed that government policy toward terrorists was based on two principles: unremitting pursuit of still-active insurgents; and "flexibility, within the law, for those who abandon violence." All the Basque participants agreed that negotiations between ETA and Madrid should deal only with the cessation of violence and amnesty for prisoners and exiles; any other issues could be resolved only by the Basque democratic institutions. These basic principles would be the focus of the debate for years to come.

Notwithstanding this rather unpromising atmosphere, by early summer the subject of negotiations with ETA was an issue that refused to go away. Leaders of Herri Batasuna in particular continued to press for a negotiated settlement. On June 12, at a Pamplona press conference, HB leaders Jon Idígoras, Iñaki Esnaola, and Jokin Gorostidi stressed that "with the integration of Navarra with the other three provinces, the KAS Alternative would be 70 percent completed." They also promised that a negotiated settlement would permit HB to recognize the legitimacy of Basque institutions and they could occupy their elected seats in the autonomous parliament.[3] Idígoras returned to the theme in a newspaper interview in early July, with the remark that "if the constitution were amended to respect the personality of the peoples, violence would cease practically immediately." He also characterized the KAS Alternative as not the same as independence or socialism, and as being perfectly compatible with bourgeois democracy.[4]

In July, there were at least two attempts to contact ETA regarding negotiations. One involved a representative of the French government; the other, Euzkadiko Ezkerra leader Mario Onaindia. ETA refused to answer either inquiry.[5] On August 9, the French government arrested Eugenio Etxebeste "Antxon," the second in command of ETA (m) and reputed to be one of the hard-line opponents of negotiations. Even though Etxebeste was accused of no crime in France and there were no pending extradition requests against him, the French government expelled him to the Dominican Republic, where he resided under house arrest and practically incommunicado for nearly two years. It would not be unreasonable to speculate that Etxebeste was expelled in order to make it easier to deal with the ETA leaders believed to be more favorable toward negotiations, especially Txomin Iturbe.

On August 22, 1984, a spokesman for Interior Minister Barrionuevo informed the Madrid daily *El País* that the Spanish government was ready to negotiate with ETA, without intermediaries, wherever and whenever the insurgents might wish.[6] The statement affirmed Barrionuevo's willingness to meet directly or talk by telephone with Txomin Iturbe. The terms of the deal were clear: ETA was to cease all attacks and its members were to turn in their weapons; Madrid, for its part, would "facilitate the integration into society" of all etarras who would agree to observe the rules of Spanish political life. In a television interview shortly after the announcement, Barrionuevo emphasized that there would be no discussion of political issues, and in fact, he said, "the term 'negotiations' seems excessive." Nevertheless, the mere fact that the senior Spanish official in charge of the government's antiterrorist policy would offer publicly to meet face-to-face with the head of ETA was a dramatic change in Spanish policy.

While the terms of the August 22 communiqué differed little from earlier statements by Barrionuevo and other PSOE spokesmen, the announcement did contain the novel feature of direct Madrid-ETA talks, and so caught many political leaders by surprise.[7] (One report even suggested that President González himself was not informed of the proposal until Barrionuevo had already revealed it to *El País*, by which time it was too late to block the move without forcing the interior minister to resign.) Socialist secretary general Txiki Benegas denounced the offer, and threatened to resign from the party if the negotiations went beyond the purely technical cease-fire terms and began to touch on political questions. Other cabinet officers, particularly defense and justice, remained silent, perhaps, as was alleged, because they had not been consulted beforehand about the proposal. The director general of the Guardia Civil, José Antonio Saenz de Santa María, expressed his serious reservations about the plan and said that a government can never negotiate with a band of terrorists. PNV leaders were skeptical of the effectiveness of the offer; and Basque president Carlos Garaikoetxea criticized Madrid's intention to bypass Basque political institutions in their direct negotiations with Iturbe. An HB spokesman denounced the offer, calling it "politically unacceptable," adding that "ETA would only accept a true political negotiation." Both Barrionuevo and the director of state security, Rafael Vera, immediately publicly reaffirmed statements that there were no "political" issues open for negotiation, only the so-called functional matters having to do with surrender of weapons and so forth.[8] It is noteworthy, however, that Vera, in an interview that appeared just a few days after the original announcement, suggested that "one can imagine a political negotiation with minority political groups such as, for example, Herri Batasuna, but never with a terrorist band."[9]

The origins of Barrionuevo's offer are obscure. Some accounts suggest that the plan was merely a part of the government's original antiterrorist program; but other interpretations suggest that the interior minister was seeking to take advantage of a special confluence of events and circumstances in the summer of 1984. Foremost among these factors was a perception in Madrid that ETA's position in France was weakening, that public support for ETA was declining in the Basque Country, that police antiterrorist measures in Spain were improving, and that a rising number of etarras were seeking amnesty under the social reintegration policy. In addition, Felipe González had just returned from a trip to several Latin American countries, including Colombia, where he had been impressed with the success of Colombian president Betancur's negotiations of a cease-fire with rebel groups.

Not surprisingly, ETA's initial response to Barrionuevo's offer was negative. The organization claimed that "the present Spanish government is not for the democratic normalization [of the Basque Country], and we understand that the proposal that we add ourselves to the [group of repentants] is no change from previous governments." The statement added that the only basis for negotiations was the KAS Alternative.[10]

At this point, several attempts were made to establish links between Madrid and ETA through intermediaries. At the end of August, HB leaders Santiago "Santi" Brouard and Miguel Castells flew to the Dominican Republic to brief Etxebeste on the offer.[11] Also in late August, according to one of the participants, Barrionuevo sent a senior Spanish military official to San Sebastián to talk with an ETA representative about getting talks started. (Barrionuevo and others denied this report.)[12] Several weeks later, in mid-September, Santiago Brouard and Jokin Gorostidi were asked to come to Madrid to meet the French ambassador to Spain, allegedly with Felipe González's knowledge and approval. There they were asked to meet with ETA leaders and request a cease-fire for sixty days to allow time for the negotiations with Madrid to get under way. Paris, for its part, would agree to delay the impending extradition of four ETA members. An invitation was transmitted through Brouard to ETA to attend a meeting in France one week later, on September 22, to discuss this plan further. ETA's representatives failed to appear at the meeting; and the next day the French government approved the extradition orders of the four etarras.[13]

As a consequence of these meetings, Santi Brouard became an important factor in the discussions over the next two months. As Madrid sought to increase the pressure on ETA to negotiate, Brouard proved to be an invaluable intermediary. A medical doctor, Brouard became involved in Basque nationalist politics in 1973 when he was expelled from Spain for refusing to divulge information about a wounded etarra he had treated. He later entered pediatrics, and became widely known and respected in Bilbao for his humanitarian medical service. As a key leader of the Herri Bata-suna coalition, his credentials as a trustworthy Basque nationalist were impeccable. Brouard was, in sum, an ideal person to act as an intermediary in the cause of a cease-fire with ETA.

By mid-November, according to press reports, direct contacts had been established between the interior ministry and Txomin Iturbe.[14] *El País* revealed that there had been two contacts estab-lished in France, one through officers of the CESID, the Spanish military intelligence agency, and the other through two Catho-lic priests. These contacts were denied by Barrionuevo and gov-ernment spokesman Eduardo Sotillos. Despite sharp opposition within ETA, Txomin Iturbe was now thought to support an accord with Madrid that would stop the violence. (Several years later, after Txomin's death in Algeria, it was revealed that he had agreed to a negotiation with Madrid based on a six-stage plan that had been developed by persons in the CESID.[15] This six-stage calendar will be discussed in greater detail in the following section.)

The press reported on these contacts between Iturbe and Ma-drid between November 15 and 19. On November 20, two gunmen entered Santi Brouard's office in downtown Bilbao and, before his horrified patients, shot him to death. (As of late 1989, the trial of the men accused of Brouard's killing was still being processed through Spanish courts. However, it was generally thought that Brouard's killers were two professional assassins hired by the GAL.) Less than twenty-four hours later, an ETA team carried out a repri-sal attack in Madrid on Spanish army general Luís Rosón, brother of the former interior minister, Juan José Rosón.[16] General Rosón eventually recovered from his wounds, but the peace process had been interrupted once again by strategically timed acts of violence against symbolically significant targets.

Persons interviewed for this book in 1988 were in general agreement that Brouard had been killed by the GAL in an attempt to intimidate Herri Batasuna or as reprisal for an ETA killing in France. Most were reluctant to characterize the attack as an at-tempt to interrupt the negotiation process. Nevertheless, one is forced back to two key questions: why Brouard and why at that par-ticular moment? Regardless of the motivations behind the killing, which will probably always remain a mystery, the consequences

of the attack—and of the reprisal attack against General Rosón—
cannot be denied.

One week after the Brouard killing, ETA transmitted a long
letter to the Basque newsmagazine *Punto y Hora* in which the organization revealed a number of instances when Spanish government
officials had approached them to discuss a cessation of hostilities.[17] The report insisted that nothing short of the KAS Alternative
would ever be accepted by the organization; and future negotiations would have to be held directly between ETA and the "de facto
powers of the Spanish state," that is, the Spanish armed forces. ETA
thus served notice that they wanted nothing more to do with negotiations arranged through intermediaries. The tone of the report
left little doubt that the "duros," the anti-truce faction within ETA
(m), had managed to re-establish their control over the organization. Yet another opportunity for an end to violence in the Basque
Country had passed.

"Operation Wellington" and the Six-Stage Calendar:
August 1984–November 1985

On November 16, 1985, *El País* published a report alleging that
Spanish government representatives had held "dozens of contacts"
with members of ETA during the preceding fifteen months, that
is, following the Barrionuevo proposal of August 1984.[18] According
to this report, based on sources in the Spanish interior ministry,
these contacts had been carried out by several different government agencies, including the police and military intelligence, as
well as by political figures. Contacts on the other side had reached
as high as ETA chief Txomin Iturbe. Police sources were careful to
emphasize, however, that they were sent not to negotiate with ETA
but rather "to find out ETA's situation, what were their demands
of the government, and which aspects [of those demands] could be
answered."

The most controversial of these contacts were those allegedly
carried out between the CESID and Basque industrialist Juan Félix
Eriz.[19] This episode, which came to be known as "Operation Wellington," after the Madrid hotel where several of the meetings were

held, lasted more than a year. Eriz was involved in at least four significant meetings with CESID representatives, and a similar number with ETA leaders in France as well. Eriz had already become a controversial figure in Basque politics because of his role in the attempts to launch negotiations in 1978 that ended in José María Portell's assassination. He had also acted as an intermediary in five kidnapping cases; and on at least twenty occasions he had represented persons who sought relief from ETA's "revolutionary tax." In addition, he had negotiated the release from jail of about a dozen ETA prisoners.

Eriz's story began in late August 1984, with a telephone call from a person identified only as "Prat" (later identified as Barcelona industrialist José Prat). Prat had been approached by a friend of his in the CESID because of his intimate knowledge of the situation of Basque refugees in France. Prat and Eriz met in Barcelona on September 17 to discuss the possibility of negotiations. The next day, Prat introduced Eriz to a man known only as Gardeazabal, who claimed to be from the CESID. Their discussion lasted five hours, after which Gardeazabal told Eriz that he would inform his superiors about their conversation. Four days later, at the Hotel Wellington in Madrid, Eriz met another CESID official named Rafa, who agreed to draft a report to his superiors about the possibilities of negotiations. There was another meeting on September 30, also at the Hotel Wellington. On October 29 or 30 the talks were suspended indefinitely, for reasons Eriz did not disclose. On November 20, the Brouard assassination and the attempt against General Rosón caused all contacts with ETA to be broken.

Despite the suspension of talks with the CESID officials, Prat and Eriz continued to meet through the first half of 1985. In August, Eriz went to France to pick up a document that contained ETA's minimum demands to begin negotiations, and delivered it to Prat in Barcelona. On the basis of this document, Prat drafted a possible agenda for negotiations. Several days later, Eriz and Prat met again with Gardeazabal in Barcelona, who told them that CESID had given up on their contacts, but that he would try once more to interest them in pursuing the issue. Eriz called Prat shortly after that, insisting that they try again to meet with Gardeazabal. Prat could not attend that next meeting, which took place in Zaragoza;

but following that meeting, Eriz called Prat to ask him to prepare a complete proposal for further consideration. The chronology of events of the next month or so is confused and contradictory. What we do know is that in late October Gardeazabal approved the six-stage calendar for negotiations, and asked Eriz to show it to ETA for their approval. Eriz arranged a meeting with ETA for early November. On November 6, Gardeazabal called Eriz to tell him that the CESID had withdrawn its approval of the calendar and were definitively breaking off the contacts. Deeply disappointed, Eriz went to his meeting with ETA on November 7 to tell them that the six-stage calendar was no longer under consideration in Madrid. On November 21, two weeks later, ETA officially decided to end its own self-imposed "technical truce" and resume violent attacks.

The most significant product of these negotiations, the six-stage negotiation calendar, was surrounded by mystery. Eriz wrote that Prat had developed a rough draft of a negotiating agenda by early October 1984. We have also seen that Txomin Iturbe had agreed to a similar six-stage plan as early as November 1984. On the other hand, Eriz also claimed that he was given the calendar for negotiations in the autumn of 1985, perhaps in September. Exactly who created the calendar and who approved it for discussion with ETA were also not clear. Prat later claimed that he prepared the calendar and sent it to Eriz in the mail; but Eriz said that Gardeazabal delivered it to him at a meeting in late October. The calendar of negotiating steps was highly significant, however, because it was the first (and practically the only) public version of a detailed, step-by-step agenda that would resolve the principal KAS Alternative issues. In summary form, the calendar, which covered some ten years, contained the following steps:

STAGE ONE: Within two months, the cessation of all violence, including ETA armed attacks, collection of the revolutionary tax, attacks by the GAL, French extraditions and deportations; and the legalization of all parties.

STAGE TWO: By the end of 1988, agreement on a document providing for the integration of Navarra with the other three provinces, and a general amnesty for all ETA prisoners and exiles.

STAGE THREE: By the end of 1990, elections for Basque parliament, and amendment of autonomy statute to allow integration of Navarra.

STAGE FOUR: By the end of 1992, official bilingualism throughout the autonomous community.

STAGE FIVE: By the end of 1994, complete withdrawal of Spanish law enforcement authorities, replaced by Basque police.

STAGE SIX: By the end of 1996, an agreement among all political groups about proceeding to self-determination for the Basques.

ETA's "Technical Truce": July–November 1985

Operation Wellington was only one of several attempts undertaken during 1985 to get negotiations started with ETA. Almost from the beginning of the year, only a few months after Brouard's death, rumors were flying about impending negotiations, and messages were being planted in the press to indicate the willingness of one group or another to renew contacts. In February, for example, ETA's number two leader Antxon Etxebeste, from his exile in the Dominican Republic, gave an interview for a French magazine in which he admitted the real possibility that ETA would lay down its arms if only Madrid would "recognize Basque sovereignty and grant a real autonomy to Euskadi, that is, a state within a state."[20] This formula, plus the fact that Etxebeste avoided using terms like "independence" were deemed significant. Several days later, HB leader Iñaki Esnaola told a press conference that "Euskadi can be perfectly independent within the Spanish state," and that formal independence with boundaries and so forth was not necessary. He also made it clear that to accept the KAS Alternative on the agenda for negotiations was not the same thing as making a commitment to accept its five points. Others were welcome to bring other ideas to any bargaining table for discussion.[21]

In the late spring and early summer, the other Basque parties joined the dialogue over negotiations. In May, in the midst of an upsurge in ETA attacks, PNV president Jesús Insausti said that "due channels must be opened to negotiate with ETA," and he urged Madrid to make a gesture of good intentions, such as closing Spanish police installations in areas where the Basque autonomous police had begun to operate. Herri Batasuna responded by challenging the PNV head to a public debate on the negotiation issue.[22] Euzkadiko Ezkerra secretary general Kepa Aulestia told *El País* that the only real alternative to solving the problem of violence was negotiations based on social reintegration of prisoners and a political agreement, within the structure of the autonomy statute, among all the Basque parties.[23]

The *public* response of the Spanish government to all these calls for negotiations and to the wave of ETA attacks as well, was to reiterate its commitment not to negotiate. The official interior ministry position was that the Barrionuevo offer of August 1984 was still in effect if ETA wanted to talk. If not, there was nothing more to be discussed. Failing to force ETA to the bargaining table on these terms, the only option would be to toughen existing antiterrorist legislation.[24]

Behind this public posture of "no negotiations," however, Madrid was already moving to start talks once again.[25] Interior Minister Barrionuevo asked EE leader and parliamentary deputy Juan María Bandrés to contact Txomin Iturbe with an offer to begin discussions. The offer was based on the formula of "double negotiation" approved shortly before by the Basque government and parliament. According to this formula, Madrid and ETA would negotiate directly on issues such as amnesty and a cease-fire, while the Basque parliament (including Herri Batasuna) would discuss the other questions, among them the KAS Alternative.

At first it appeared as if Iturbe had rejected the government's offer. While Bandrés himself remained silent about the matter, some reports suggested that Iturbe had refused to receive him as a valid intermediary. Word of the offer filtered down from ETA back to Herri Batasuna, which immediately launched a public campaign to discredit Bandrés, a campaign that accused him of, among other things, instigating attacks by the GAL. (It was at this time that the polemic broke out between Bandrés and PNV leader Xabier Arzalluz over the latter's alleged role in persuading the poli-milis to abandon their cease-fire in 1982.)

It was revealed much later, however, that in July 1985, ETA leaders Juan Ramón Aramburu Garmendia "Juanra" and Francisco

Múgica Garmendia "Artapalo" began to meet in Paris with representatives of CESID.[26] Although he approved of and supported these talks, Txomin Iturbe did not participate personally in them. Some results began to be visible within weeks. On August 27, an ETA communiqué said that the organization "would not call a truce in our armed offensive against all the state apparatus while our objectives . . . are not a reality; a cease-fire, yes, but on the basis of a political negotiation with the de facto powers of the Spanish state."[27] In August and again in early September HB leader Esnaola reiterated his coalition's willingness to serve as intermediary between ETA and the Spanish government if there were a genuine disposition to negotiate political questions.[28]

On September 9, ETA decided to force the issue by exploding a large car bomb near a Guardia Civil bus on a crowded Madrid street, wounding seventeen of the bus passengers and killing an American business executive who was jogging nearby. In the communiqué that claimed responsibility for the attack, ETA repeated its willingness to "reach an agreement with the Spanish state and establish a cease-fire only on the basis of the minimum points of the KAS Alternative."[29] President Felipe González responded that "political negotiations with ETA would be a foolish blunder."[30] ETA, meanwhile, assassinated a member of the national police in Vitoria on September 14.

There then settled over the Basque Country an uneasy calm that was interpreted by some as a so-called technical truce imposed by ETA on itself as an unofficial sign of their desire to negotiate. Interior Minister Barrionuevo and others discounted the significance of the absence of attacks, saying in effect that ETA was not committing acts of violence because it lacked the capability to do so. Whatever the reason, ETA remained silent for seventy-two days until nearly the end of November, despite a bloody attack by the GAL on a bar in Bayonne that killed four Basque refugees.

Meanwhile, the talks went on more or less regularly through October. Another round of meetings was scheduled for the first half of November when the news reached the general public through an article in the Madrid daily *Diario 16*.[31] Subsequent reports even went so far as to claim that Spanish vice president Alfonso Guerra, up to that time a strong opponent of negotiations, had personally taken charge of the government's participation in the talks. These and other similar reports were all hotly denied in Madrid, where, as far as anyone would say, nothing out of the ordinary was going on with regard to ETA.[32]

At this point, the talks were halted, apparently on orders from Barrionuevo, who had managed to consolidate his position as the sole government spokesman in negotiations with ETA. The breaking of contacts with ETA coincided with the interruption of talks between ETA and CESID arranged by Juan Félix Eriz. The "technical truce" was officially broken on November 21 by a decision of ETA's executive committee meeting in France. Shortly after this decision, ETA resumed its armed attacks. On November 25, Juan Ramón Aramburu was arrested to be tried in Bayonne for violating French weapons laws, leaving Txomin Iturbe the sole veteran ETA leader still free and living in France.[33]

The Basque Government and Negotiations:
January 1985–March 1986

In late December 1984, a crisis in the Basque Nationalist Party and in the Basque government culminated in the resignation of president Carlos Garaikoetxea. One month later he was replaced by the deputy general (head of government) of Guipúzcoa province, José Antonio Ardanza, also of the PNV. By mid-1986 the crisis had worsened to the point that Garaikoetxea left the PNV to form his own party, Eusko Alkartasuna (EA), or Basque Solidarity.

The complex origins of the crisis, which cannot be explored here in any detail, involved personalities (President Garaikoetxea versus PNV leader Xabier Arzalluz), factional battles within the PNV (Vizcayans versus Guipuzcoans), and internal politics of the Basque Autonomous Community (the provinces versus the Basque government in Vitoria).[34] Also, however, the crisis reflected conflicting views within the party on the best way to deal with Madrid. Garaikoetxea advocated a more strongly independent policy that held the Spanish government at arm's length. His opponents within the party believed that a greater spirit of cooperation with Madrid would eventually bring a greater degree of autonomy to Euskadi. Partly because of this change in strategic philosophy, and partly because the crisis weakened the ability of Ardanza to govern without

support from the Basque socialists, the Basque government underwent a number of highly significant changes. The general character
of these changes was to make the Basque government less intransigent toward Madrid and more accommodating of the wishes of
the Spanish socialist government. In no policy area was this more
evident than the general question of dealing with ETA and, in particular, the issue of political negotiations.

During the period under consideration, on three separate occasions the Basque government had an opportunity to make a statement about political negotiations with ETA and its role in such
negotiations: the *pacto de legislatura* (legislative accord) of January
1985; the ten-point program on violence and pacification approved
by the Basque parliament in March 1985; and the final report of
the international commission of experts on violence, delivered in
March 1986. Taken both individually and as a set, these three statements made it clear that the Basque government would not be involved in direct negotiations with ETA, and negotiations involving
so-called political issues were absolutely prohibited. This was part
of the price the PNV paid for securing socialist collaboration in
governing the Basque Autonomous Community during the period
1985–1986.

Efforts to arrange an agreement between the Basque government, the PNV, and the Basque Socialist Party (PSE) actually began
in October 1984, when Garaikoetxea was still president.[35] The February 1984 elections had left the PNV with no margin at all with
which to govern the Basque Country; with HB's 11 deputies absent from the 75-seat chamber, the PNV's 32 seats were exactly
half of those who actually occupied their posts. Discussions had
begun with the socialists, the second largest body in the parliament, to secure their support without actually bringing them into
a coalition government. After Garaikoetxea resigned his position,
Ardanza made such an agreement an absolute requirement of his
accepting the position. Negotiations with the socialists went on
through January, and resulted in a seven-point accord between the
Basque government and the PSE by means of which the government
obtained socialist cooperation in the parliament.[36]

Point number two, by far the longest of the seven-point agreement, dealt with "violence, terrorism and democratic coexistence."
One of the most controversial parts of this section was in the pre-

amble, where the two parties expressed "their will to work jointly, within the requirements of a state of laws, in the struggle against violence and terrorism, *as well as the causes that give rise to it* . . ." [emphasis added]. For days the socialists resisted the inclusion of this last phrase in the statement on the grounds that in a democratic state, where speech and political activity are free and unrestricted, there are no causes that might legitimate terrorist violence. On this score, however, the Basque government insisted and won their point, a success that led to the commission of experts later in the year.[37]

The actual operative part of the section on terrorism consisted of six paragraphs. The first paragraph committed both parties to support the Basque autonomy statute, the full development of which must be the solution to historical conflicts between Euskadi and Spain. In the second paragraph, the parties agreed that there is no justification for terrorism in a democracy, where all points of view may be heard openly. Paragraph number three consisted simply of this statement: "The political problems of the Basque country must be negotiated only among the political forces with parliamentary representation, the Basque government, and, whenever it might act appropriately, the Spanish government." By means of this wording, the socialists made certain that there would be no political negotiations unless the government in Madrid authorized them; but the Basques also won a commitment that the Spanish government would not negotiate behind the back of the regional government. In addition, the special formula made it possible for Herri Batasuna to participate in the negotiations without actually entering the Basque parliament. Paragraph number four reiterated the parties' support for "social reintegration," or selective amnesty; while number five affirmed that international relations are the sole province of the central government and the Basque government has no role to play in relations with other governments, especially in the international struggle against terrorism. The final paragraph provided the mechanism by which the accord would go into effect, and by which other parliamentary parties could adhere to its sentiments and commitments.

In a matter of weeks the Basque government was presented with a dramatic challenge to its new policy. On March 7, in a café parking lot near Vitoria, an ETA bomb ripped through the car

of the chief of the Basque autonomous police, Carlos Diaz Arcocha, killing him instantly.[38] Officials of the Basque government
—from President Ardanza on down—condemned the killing as
"completely without justification" and a "frontal attack on Basque
institutions." Within days, the government had decided to convene
the regional parliament to issue a response to ETA's challenge.
In the interim, the parliament's committee of party leaders had
drafted a ten-point statement of principles on violence and pacification, which the parliament unanimously adopted in plenary
session on March 14.[39]

The statement began with a vigorous condemnation of the
attack on Diaz Arcocha, a reassurance to the people that "the worst
has passed," that terrorist violence "cannot threaten democracy or
autonomy," and an assertion that "the struggle against violence
in Euskadi is a responsibility of everyone" and "a problem of personal dignity." While admitting that the problem of violence would
not be resolved in the near future, the statement also emphasized
that "ambiguity and complacence" toward violence contributed to
making the problem worse.

Point number six stressed that both political and police measures would be necessary to eradicate violence; the former would
emerge from a full development of the autonomy statute, the latter
from the actions of the police strictly within the rule of law. "There
is no solution," the statement read, "to the problem of violence in
Euskadi outside the political and social normalization, which are
intimately linked to the fulfillment of the autonomy statute. . . . it
is necessary to affirm that the statute is a pact that we are ready to
defend to the ultimate consequences." The statement also pointed
out that in 1977 there was a general amnesty and no Basques in
prison, and that there was no justification for the resort to violence
after that time. Also, continued the statement, it was well known
that ETA had always rejected negotiation and dialogue, and therefore they would have to take the first steps to show their will to
come to an agreement.

Points seven and eight called upon political leaders and the
press to avoid using terrorist violence for partisan purposes and to
be aware of the impact of news about terrorism on public sentiments. In point nine, the government proposed to create an inter-

national commission of experts to "elaborate an analysis of the causes and mechanisms of the generation of violence in Euskadi." Finally, the government pledged to present to the parliament a plan to raise the awareness of the citizenry about the terrible damage ETA terrorism was doing to the Basque Country.

As so often happens with documents like this, the subsequent interpretations made by observers tended to weigh more heavily than the statement itself. President Ardanza said in a radio interview that the statement proved that "we [the Basque parliament and government] have the legitimacy of popular representation because we were the fruit of several elections, and those elections accredit us as the legitimate representatives of the will of this people." President González, on the other hand, claimed that the statement was of great importance because "the PNV condemned terrorist activity explicitly and unmistakenly, and it matches our idea that it does not make sense to negotiate with those who maintain [terrorism]." Jaime Mayor Oreja, leader of the Basque wing of the conservative Spanish party, Coalición Popular, said that the statement "reveals a unity of action against terrorism, and is a point of departure to struggle against it." Euzkadiko Ezkerra spokesman Mario Onaindia said that it showed that "the political measures that must be adopted to eradicate violence must be conceived and applied in Euskadi, because the only thing that Madrid can supply in this subject is the police aspect." Herri Batasuna, on the other hand, criticized the statement as nothing more than "rhetoric," a "grandstand gesture," and "supremely servile" to the wishes of Madrid. Several days later, the coalition presented its own ten-point program for the national reconstruction of Euskadi.[40]

All these steps led, then, to the creation of the international commission of experts on violence. Actually, the idea of asking a group of recognized international experts to study the ETA problem had been around for some time. In the early 1980s, the Basque government had hired two consulting firms, one British and one German, with a reputation for expertise in international security, to advise them on the organization of the new Basque autonomous police force. In April 1983, Xabier Arzalluz proposed the creation of an international commission to study terrorism. The list of men he suggested for the commission included several who had been consulted earlier on police policy.[41] Thus, when the idea of an international study commission was reborn in 1985, the people appointed to it were essentially those who had been consulted earlier.

The commission consisted of five persons who knew little about the Basque Country but who claimed expertise on terrorism generally. The head of the commission was Sir Clive Rose, former British ambassador to NATO. The other Briton on the commission was Peter Janke, a historian at the Royal College for Defense Studies. The other three members were a West German, Hans Horchem, a judge and law professor; a Frenchman, Jacques Leaute, a professor of law and head of the Institute of Criminology in Paris; and Franco Ferracuti, also a law professor as well as professor of psychology at the University of Rome. The commission was formally created on June 1, 1985, and asked to have its report completed within nine months.

Apart from the fact that there were no Basques on the commission, or even any persons with knowledge of or expertise in Basque affairs, there were other aspects of the commission's operations that could be easily criticized.[42] The commission was based in London, and made few visits to the Basque Country. Its contacts with Basques were limited to official circles, and included no one who could be considered sympathetic to ETA's cause or who would favor a negotiated settlement. Several members of the commission were criticized in the Basque press for being linked to an organization—the Institute for the Study of Conflict, in Great Britain—that had received money from the U.S. Central Intelligence Agency. One member—Peter Janke—was later accused of having a direct conflict of interest, since he was an employee of a subsidiary of Lloyd's of London called Control Risk, Inc., which sold very expensive insurance policies to wealthy Basque industrialists who feared being kidnapped and held for huge ransom payments.[43]

Even an ideologically neutral group of knowledgeable experts would have found themselves blocked on the question of negotiations, since it was obvious from the beginning that the commission was not going to disrupt the anti-negotiation agreements forged in January and March 1985 between the Basque government and the PSE. At the May 30 presentation of the commission to the press, Basque government spokesman Eugenio Ibarzabal assured reporters that "the autonomous government will respect the commitments signed in the legislative accord regarding negotiations with ETA and which discard a political dialogue with this armed organization."[44] And in early November 1985, only five months after the commission began its work and five months before it would present its final report, sources in the Basque government revealed to the press that the commission would advise against any kind of political negotiations with ETA.[45]

The commission presented its final report on March 5, 1986. Nearly two-thirds of the lengthy report, which filled 32 pages of the daily newspaper *Deia* were devoted to a discussion of terrorist violence *in other European countries*, including Britain, France, and Germany.[46] The report contains a brief introduction and a superficial summary of "violence in the Basque country." This latter section deals almost solely with violence allegedly done *by* ETA, and says almost nothing about the violence done *to* Basques by the GAL, police torture, and other agents of the state. The report concludes with a section called "Containment of Basque Terrorism," which deals with ethnic and sociological characteristics of the Basque population; legal and juridical aspects of antiterrorist policy; positive countermeasures, including police and intelligence activities; and a plan to raise the awareness of the Basque people about terrorism, including the media and education. At the very end of the report, the authors conclude with the following recommendation (the last of fifty-one separate recommendations): "Given that ETA is an unfortunate child of the dictatorship and that its activists are the offspring of the PNV [an observation that is factually incorrect], the commission emphatically recommends that negotiations not be excluded as a policy option."

Reactions to the report were almost uniformly negative except, of course, from the PNV, whose spokesman said that the commission's findings "reaffirm our position." HB spokesman Txomin Ziluaga said simply that the report lacked credibility; but the secretary general of Euzkadiko Ezkerra, Kepa Aulestia, called the report "ridiculous." About the commission's final recommendation regarding negotiations, he said simply that it was "solemn foolishness." No one else had much to say in the commission's defense; and the report passed into history leaving virtually nothing behind to help the Basque people or their government meet the problem of a violent society.

The Second Attempt at "Social Reintegration":
April 1984–September 1986

In the mid-1980s, there was a second attempt at social reintegration or selective amnesty, this time carried out by a PNV senator from Alava, Joseba Azkarraga.[47] Azkarraga had become involved with the problems of prisoners in 1980, and had, at the request of a number of them, served as an intermediary with the Spanish government to obtain improvement in their prison conditions. In late 1982, after the PSOE electoral victory, Azkarraga began to raise publicly the question of the fate of the prisoners who would remain after the first wave of selective amnesty cases—those who followed the Rosón-Bandrés route to freedom—had been concluded. He even went so far as to claim that at least 20 percent of the prisoners could be freed immediately without any special treatment or unusual interpretations of the law.[48]

In July 1983, a group of prisoners from the VIII Assembly of ETA (p-m) asked Azkarraga to look for a negotiated solution for their problem.[49] (It will be recalled that this was the wing of polimilis that had opposed the cease-fire in 1981–1982 and that had refused to accept the Rosón-Bandrés amnesty program.) Azkarraga agreed to take on their case, but he insisted that it be done not as his personal endeavor and not even as a political party matter, as Bandrés had done, but rather as a legitimate activity of a political institution. After some discussion it was decided that the Basque government would be the official agent through which amnesty would be sought. President Garaikoetxea agreed to support Azkarraga's efforts. Some time later, the Spanish government's Office of the Public Defender was brought into the project as the agency through which the requests were transmitted to the Ministry of Justice.

The prisoners also asked that Azkarraga discuss their case with the leaders of the VIII Assembly to secure their approval of the request. In early September 1983, Azkarraga met in France with three leaders of (p-m). During a tense meeting that lasted two hours, the (p-m) leaders denied the request. "The prisoners," they said, "will stay in prison until the organization says they can leave, and none of them should even think about making such a decision on their own initiative." They went on to add that while they wanted their comrades released, they wanted it done through political negotiations that included a general amnesty.

At this juncture, ETA (p-m) kidnapped and later killed Alberto Martín Barrios, a step that dramatically changed the dynamic of Spanish antiterrorist policy. Martín Barrios was kidnapped, ostensibly, to force the release of several prisoners of the VIII Assembly. Azkarraga and many of the poli-milis in prison believed that the attack was also intended to show the prisoners that the organization was still strong and that they should maintain their solidarity and reject social reintegration.

If anything, the attack had the opposite effect. Following the Martín Barrios killing, the Spanish government moved all the (p-m) prisoners out of the prison at Nanclares de Oca to the maximum security prison at Herrera de la Mancha. In early November, Azkarraga was called to the prison to continue his discussions with the prisoners, who wanted him to go ahead with the procedures for their amnesty. On December 30, Azkarraga met with Interior Minister Barrionuevo, who approved the process in principle. That same day, Azkarraga met with three representatives of the prisoners who were to communicate directly to the prisoners the outcome of these talks. On January 4, 1984, Azkarraga met with the head of the public defender's office, Joaquin Ruíz Jiménez, who agreed to transmit the petitions to the appropriate courts.

In the meantime, the Spanish government had decided that it wanted the prisoners to sign a public communiqué that would make clear their withdrawal from ETA and express their "rejection of armed struggle." Azkarraga negotiated the wording of such a document, which was signed by forty-three prisoners and made public on April 9, 1984. Of the forty-three, ten were in ETA (m), twenty-five in ETA (p-m) VIII Assembly, and eight in another wing of ETA known as Comandos Autonomos (CC. AA.). Over the course of the following year, about forty more prisoners sought to be included in the group, for a total of about eighty-five.

Even after the decision had been made in principle to facilitate the amnesty and release of a number of prisoners, there were still numerous problems that complicated the procedure in each individual case, and that threatened on more than one occasion to cause the entire effort to collapse. One such problem, for example, was the controversy that surrounded the amnesty plan whenever ETA committed an armed attack. The Spanish government found it very difficult to approve an individual amnesty request shortly after ETA had exploded a bomb or assassinated a Civil Guard; and these attacks usually caused the amnesty process to be suspended until public opinion had cooled down.

Another major problem stemmed from the slowness with which the Spanish government processed each amnesty petition. Even after the collective signature of the April 9 communiqué, each case still had to be presented and reviewed individually, and preliminary approvals at lower levels could be reversed upon review at the ministerial or cabinet level. Each petition had to be approved by the entire Spanish cabinet; and final decisions were often delayed for weeks. Azkarraga was frequently called to the prison to reassure a specific prisoner that his case was still going forward and that he should not give up hope.

Negotiations to persuade imprisoned etarras to accept social reintegration were extremely complex and had to be conducted with a maximum amount of discretion. ETA considered it absolutely essential that the prisoners remain in prison to serve out their sentences, and that solidarity among prisoners and their families and neighbors was crucial to the eventual success of the organization's strategy. Within prison, ETA maintained close surveillance over its members to ensure that none of them were negotiating with Azkarraga or other authorities. Outside the prisons, at the neighborhood level, the Gestoras Pro-Amnistía (Pro-Amnesty Committees) provided financial assistance to the families of the prisoners and helped them with emotional support to withstand the imprisonment of their loved ones. Once a prisoner had agreed to accept social reintegration, however, the Gestoras withdrew their financial support from the family.

Because ETA and the Gestoras Pro-Amnistía put so much pressure on the prisoners to remain in prison and in solidarity with the struggle, none of them wanted it known that they were negotiating for their release. There was always tension in prison when a member of ETA decided to seek social reintegration. He was usually shunned by the other prisoners and sometimes threatened physically. Many of them had to be moved to other prisons for their own safety. Negotiations had to be carried out through intermediaries, usually family members who carried messages back and forth between the prisoners and the persons dealing with that case. Even though each case was unique and each prisoner was dealt with individually, each negotiation was part of a larger and much more complex situation involving other prisoners. In some cases, for example, a prisoner was serving a sentence for a "blood crime" that was actually committed by another prisoner, who was eligible for release because of having been convicted of some lesser offense. The second prisoner did not want to be released unless the first was also, since the former prisoner was almost sure to reveal the truth to the authorities if the guilty etarra were released and he remained behind bars.[50]

One solution to these problems was to work on an individual basis to get sentences reduced gradually, thereby facilitating an early release. The etarra could return home to a hero's welcome and —officially at least—no one was the wiser. For those ETA members in exile in France who wanted to return home without fear of reprisals, another strategy was occasionally used. In July 1986, the French government launched a policy of expelling Basques without even holding an extradition hearing. In the first year of this program (until July 1987), a total of seventy were expelled this way, of whom twenty-eight were given quick judicial hearings and released almost immediately after their return to Spain. At least a few of these were in fact taking advantage of the social reintegration program; but this way they could make it look as if they had returned against their will and had not betrayed the organization.[51]

A final problem had to do with the difficulties these prisoners faced when they attempted to re-enter civil society. Spanish law provided a modest assistance for any released prisoner of 50,000 pesetas (about $400) per month for eighteen months to give him time to get adjusted and to find work. To Azkarraga's knowledge, none of the released etarras had difficulty finding work. Several of them had completed college degrees while in prison; and one, who had completed a law degree, eventually became the head of the Basque autonomous police in Guipúzcoa province. Most of them, however, returned to their hometowns where they usually sought work in farming, fishing, or some other outdoor occupation where they could try to forget their years in prison.

The first prisoners who signed the April 9 communiqué were

released on July 18, 1984, followed by other small groups on October 31 and December 26 of the same year. By March 1985, twenty of the original group of forty-three and about twelve of the second group had been released. Another group of about eighty exiles had been permitted to return and were immediately cleared of pending charges. Eventually, some eighty prisoners were released, although as late as 1988 five of the original forty-three were still in prison because they were serving sentences for "blood crimes," and their cases were much more difficult to resolve. In addition, about 150 exiles returned under the terms of this program. Of the hundreds of former etarras who sought social reintegration under either the Bandrés or the Azkarraga programs, not a single one ever returned to ETA or engaged in political violence.

As of 1988, the program of social reintegration was at a standstill, and indeed no one had sought amnesty through the Azkarraga program since 1986. One reason was that the ETA prisoners had lost faith in the Spanish government. They believed that simply by signing the April 9, 1984, communiqué pledging to reject armed struggle they would be allowed to go free. In some twenty cases, more than a year elapsed before they were freed and, as already noted, five of the forty-three signers were still in prison more than four years later. A second reason for the collapse of the program was its continued dependence on intermediaries. Bandrés in 1981–1982, and Azkarraga in 1984–1985, had done as much as they could, and they had secured the freedom of as many prisoners as possible without direct contact between Madrid and ETA. Any further amnesty would have to come as the result of direct ETA negotiations with the Spanish government.

But perhaps the principal reason for the failure of social reintegration after 1986 was the fear of reprisals from ETA (m). In this, the key event was the assassination of former mili leader María Dolores González Catarain "Yoyes." Ms. González was not the first amnestied etarra to be attacked; in February 1984 a former etarra named Mikel Solaun was shot to death in front of his wife and two daughters in his hometown of Algorta, allegedly for having collaborated with the police to secure his release under the Rosón-Bandrés program in 1982.[52]

But the case of "Yoyes" was of special importance both to ETA and to the government. González Catarain, from the Goierri town of Ordizia in Guipúzcoa province, had been head of ETA (m)'s political office from 1978 to 1980. In 1981 she broke connections with ETA and went into exile in Mexico. In 1984, she returned to France, where she initiated the procedures to be allowed to return to Spain under the Azkarraga program.[53] Her return attracted much attention in the press; not only was she one of the first members of ETA (m) to request amnesty, but she was the first leader of the organization ever to do so. Apparently, Yoyes had been assured by ETA head Txomin Iturbe that she would not be harmed by the organization; and for nearly a year, that promise was kept. However, in mid-1986 Iturbe was expelled from France and lost control over the organization. Those who sought reprisals against González were now free to carry out their threats. On September 10, 1986, while she was walking through Ordizia with her three-year-old son, Yoyes was approached from behind and shot several times in the back of the head at close range. Her death effectively closed the avenue opened by the Azkarraga amnesty program.[54] By 1989 it had still not been restored. While Azkarraga himself had arranged for the release or return from exile of nearly 230 former etarras, he did not consider it a success as long as so many still remained in jail. "If reintegration had succeeded," he told a reporter some time later, "this country would be different."[55]

CHAPTER SEVEN

The "Algerian Connection," Phase One: 1986–1987

A T about 8:00 on the evening of April 27, 1986, French police waiting at a roadblock on a country road about five kilometers from St.-Jean-de-Luz arrested the leader of ETA (m), Txomin Iturbe, and his brother, Angel.[1] Txomin's arrest and eventual deportation began the most serious and the most open attempt to negotiate an end to ETA's insurgency between 1978 and 1989. These negotiations (or "conversations," as Spanish officials preferred to call them) were conducted in Algeria between ETA and representatives of the Spanish government. The meetings took place in three phases: the first between November 1986 and February 1987; the second between July 1987 and February 1988; and the third between January and April 1989. (The third phase extends beyond the period covered by this book, and thus is not discussed in detail.) By late 1989, it appeared that these negotiations had failed; and, while there were still unofficial communications channels open between ETA and Madrid, officially at least all contacts were severed. Even the Algerian government had withdrawn as an intermediary and as the host for the talks; and the ETA members who had conducted the negotiations had all been expelled from the country. The "Algerian connection" proved to be vulnerable to many of the same obstacles to peace that have plagued Basques and Spaniards since the late 1970s.

Prelude to Iturbe's Arrest:
January–April 1986

Iturbe's arrest and confinement in France came at a moment when there was much public speculation about a possible breakthrough in talks with ETA. In March, the panel of international experts on violence hired by the Basque government to study the problem of ETA submitted its final report. Despite earlier press reports that the commission would recommend against negotiations,[2] the final version of the report had timidly concluded "that negotiations should never be excluded as a policy option."

Also in March, ETA (m) formulated several amendments to the KAS Alternative that were contained in an internal ETA document.[3] Some of the changes were minor; for example, point number one became "Amnesty, understood tactically as freedom for all Basque political prisoners." But there were two major changes in point number five. The new version added the demand that the autonomy statute must "enter into force in the four historic regions of Euskadi at the same time." This was to address the issue of the integration of Navarra with the other three provinces into a single autonomous community, an issue that did not exist in 1978. The new version also added the demand that the autonomy statute must recognize "the Basque right of self-determination, including the right to the creation of their own independent state." While some might have read these changes as making negotiations more difficult, another possible interpretation was that ETA's leadership was rethinking the whole question of their demands and a negotiated settlement, and that consequently 1986 might be a propitious time to renew discussions with the insurgents.

Basque president José Antonio Ardanza picked up this theme in a radio interview on April 7 when he asserted that the first step toward the solution of violence in the Basque Country was to propose a dialogue with ETA. The specific obstacles to peace, he claimed, were not insuperable; the demands of the KAS Alternative could be accommodated within existing laws and institutions.

The amnesty question could be resolved through a policy of social reintegration for both prisoners and refugees. The issue of the legalization of political parties was nearing solution through a court decision scheduled for May that was expected to give legal status to Herri Batasuna. A vigorous trade union movement would be sufficient to meet the demands for an improvement of the lot of the working class. The recently passed national police law respected the jurisdiction of the Basque autonomous police, so that issue was nearing resolution. The most complicated question, said Ardanza, continued to be the status of Navarra; but there were constitutional provisions that had to be respected, specifically those calling for a referendum. And finally, while he, like ETA, also desired the independence of the Basque people, Ardanza said for the time being they had to work within the constraints of the Basque autonomy statute.[4]

The answer from the other side came on April 10, when leaders of Herri Batasuna, Jon Idígoras, Txomin Ziluaga, and Iñaki Ruiz Pinedo, held a press conference in Bilbao to propose conversations with other Basque parties to discuss how to get negotiations started between ETA and "the powers of the state."[5] The HB spokesmen reaffirmed the party's conviction that the negotiations should be between "those that can guarantee the end of the violence, that is, ETA and the Spanish government." However, they offered their services to meet with other Basque parties to study other alternatives that they might suggest. While the HB proposal continued to be based on the KAS Alternative, they expressed a willingness to hear what other parties might propose to end the conflict. Perhaps most important, they proposed that the meetings be held without prior conditions, the first time that most observers could remember an offer with such flexibility. The last time the Basque president had sought to convene such a meeting—Carlos Garaikoetxea's ill-fated mesa para la paz three years earlier—the pre-conditions set by ETA and HB had been an insuperable stumbling block.

What had happened in the meantime (although this did not become generally known until much later) was that ETA, and Txomin Iturbe in particular, had become convinced of the need for (and the inevitability of) a negotiated settlement to the struggle. In 1984, one of the amnestied leaders of ETA (p-m) VII Assembly, Juan Miguel Goiburu "Goiherri," had talked with Iturbe shortly before he (Goiburu) was to return to Spain and to civil politics.[6] To Goiburu's comment that "things are not going well," Iturbe was said to reply: "I know that, too. The thing is to look for a way out. You [the poli-milis] don't have any 'blood crimes.' But we, how are we going to work it out?" Since then, things had gotten even worse, due primarily to the pressure from Paris. In another conversation, held before his arrest in 1986, Iturbe was quoted as saying "if we don't negotiate now, within a year the French will have dismantled everything, they will have decimated us, seized our weapons and money, and we will not have anything to negotiate." As time went on, even the political support of the other Basque parties had eroded, due partly to the need of the Basque Nationalist Party to cooperate with the socialists in the Basque autonomous government. Perhaps it was with this weakening of ETA's position in mind that *El País* columnist Patxo Unzueta wrote in September 1986: "It is highly revealing that [ETA], which some years ago seemed to aspire to nothing more than producing a military coup in Spain, has reduced its strategic objectives to obtaining a political negotiation. Not, as one might think, to the contents that are the object of the negotiations, but to the negotiation itself; that is to say, to the gesture by which [ETA's] status as the principal spokesman is recognized. More concretely, ETA does not aspire now to the independence of Euskadi or to socialism, but to someone's (it could be the Spanish army) admitting retrospectively the legitimacy of their actions, the heroic nature of their past, the nobility of their cause."[7]

President Ardanza did not delay in reacting to the HB proposal. "The doors to Ajuria Enea," he said, "are always open."[8] There were, in fact, not one but two responses to the offer. The first originated in ETA and remained secret; the second came from Herri Batasuna and was conducted in public.

In mid-April, the head of the Basque autonomous police, Genaro Garcia Andoain, held the first of six secret meetings with ETA leaders in France to explore the possible bases for talks.[9] A member of ETA who had known Garcia Andoain since the early 1960s when they had been members of the same mountain climbing club, approached the police chief about starting conversations with ETA leaders.[10] After receiving approval of the chief law enforcement officer of the Basque government—director of the department of interior, Luis María Retolaza—Garcia Andoain held several preliminary talks, followed by more or less official meetings with members of ETA's Executive Committee. Representing ETA, at least in the first meeting, was Francisco Múgica Garmendia "Artapalo," one of the alleged hard-line ETA leaders and the director of the organization's armed units since January 1985. Several days after the initial meeting, when Iturbe was arrested, Artapalo became the overall leader of ETA.

The talks between Garcia Andoain and ETA went on until October, when the police head was killed leading an attempt by Basque police to free an ETA hostage. Despite efforts to maintain absolute secrecy (the talks would not become known publicly until a year and a half later), Spanish police intelligence agencies knew about the contacts almost immediately. The purpose of the April meeting was to ask Garcia Andoain to sound out the leaders of the governing Spanish party, the PSOE, about the terms of a possible negotiation. At this first meeting, ETA offered the possibility of a cease-fire as a gesture of goodwill to support the meetings proposed by Herri Batasuna.

After Txomin Iturbe's arrest, however, the Garcia Andoain contacts were quickly converted into one of the channels by which ETA tried to have Iturbe released. Even after Iturbe's expulsion from France, the meetings continued, this time in hopes of generating direct talks with Madrid. All these efforts were failures, primarily, according to one close observer, because ETA overestimated the influence of the PNV and the Basque government in Madrid, and also because it was clear that the Spanish government did not want Basques serving as intermediaries in talks with ETA.[11]

The second channel was opened on April 25, when five leaders of Herri Batasuna (Txomin Ziluaga, Iñaki Esnaola, Jokin Gorostidi, Iñaki Aldekoa, and Jon Idígoras) met with an equal number of leaders of the Basque Nationalist Party (Xabier Arzalluz, Jesús Insausti, Markel Izaguirre, Xabier Aguirre, and Carlos Claveria) to (as the press reports put it) "find a way to make possible a negotiation between ETA and the Spanish state."[12] The site of the meeting, chosen by HB, was the headquarters of a gastronomical society in the town of Bergara.

Shortly before the meeting began, reports began to filter in to the group of another armed attack by ETA, this time a car bombing in Madrid that had killed five members of the Guardia Civil. The PNV representatives immediately questioned the HB leaders about the significance of this attack, and were told that there was no connection between the Madrid bombing and their meeting. While the PNV leaders could have broken off the talks, they stayed on because, as they put it later, they were in Bergara to talk with HB, not ETA. Moreover, "either the bombing was a coincidence, or a group in ETA did not want their talks to proceed. If the latter were the case, that was more than sufficient reason to maintain the conversations."

The Bergara meeting between the PNV and HB was, in the words of one participant, "brief and not profound." The HB representatives simply detailed their reasons for wanting the meeting, primarily to "make possible and support negotiation between ETA and the Spanish state." The PNV leaders replied that that seemed to them to be a "valid objective." The two groups then agreed to meet again, at which time each would clarify their respective positions regarding negotiations: HB would present the KAS Alternative; the PNV would show how these same objectives could be met through the Basque autonomy statute. In a communiqué several days later, ETA described the meeting as a "positive initiative . . . that creates a channel to make possible negotiation between our organization and those that really wield power in the Spanish state: the army."[13]

As the Bergara participants had planned, there was a second meeting in late May, but with a different agenda. Less than forty-eight hours after the Bergara meeting, Txomin Iturbe was arrested; and an entirely new dynamic imposed itself on the negotiation process.

Iturbe's Arrest and Deportation:
April–July 1986

The timing of Iturbe's arrest gave rise to considerable speculation in Basque political circles that his detention was not coincidental, but in fact had been deliberately engineered to ruin efforts to begin negotiations between ETA and the Basque government. On more than one occasion, Basque political leaders complained that Spanish officials wanted to prevent the Basques from opening any sort of independent dialogue with ETA, wishing to reserve that privilege for themselves.[14]

Madrid's desire to get Iturbe under their control on Spanish territory was long-standing. Their first request for his extradition dated back to March 6, 1979. Spanish interior minister José Barrionuevo had pressed French officials several times to detain Iturbe for questioning, especially after the kidnapping in January 1986 of Juan Pedro Guzman, a prominent Bilbao figure and member of the board of directors of Bilbao's athletic soccer team. Barrionuevo's pressure was intensified at a meeting at The Hague with his French counterpart, Charles Pascua, on April 23. It is impossible to say whether it was the PNV-HB meeting in Bergara on April 25, or, as Spanish officials claimed, the ETA car bombing in Madrid the same day that finally brought about Iturbe's arrest. But the fact remains that two days later, Iturbe was in French custody.[15]

The nature of Iturbe's arrest led also to speculation that this was not a random or coincidental police operation, but in fact had been carefully planned and directed from Paris. For one thing, his whereabouts had been common knowledge among French police for more than four years, and they had never before interfered with his freedom of movement within France. Witnesses reported that French police had Angel Iturbe's house under surveillance since early the morning of April 27, and the roadblock was carefully chosen to ensure that the Iturbe brothers would be seized in a remote area where escape would be impossible and innocent bystanders would not be involved. The arrest was conducted under the strictest and most scrupulous observance of French law to ensure that Iturbe could not be released on legal technicalities or because of flaws in the manner of his arrest.[16]

Immediately following his arrest, Txomin Iturbe was taken to the police station in the French Basque town of Hendaye, where he was confined for several days and interrogated. His brother, Angel, was released immediately; even though he was accused of several crimes in Spain, some dating back to 1975, in France he was not wanted by the police. Txomin Iturbe, however, had several French charges against him awaiting disposition. In June 1982, he had been arrested for carrying an illegal weapon, and the court at that time had granted him provisional release with the understanding that he remain in the city of Tours. Obviously he had violated the terms of that order, and the charge for carrying an illegal weapon still had to be answered.[17]

From the outset of his confinement, however, his advisors, family, and lawyer believed that France would eventually deport him to a third country as they had already done to three dozen ETA members since January 1984, including several key members of the group's executive committee: Pello Ansola Larrañaga "Peio el Viejo" and Carlos Ibarguren "Nervios," arrested in January 1984 and subsequently deported to Cuba; Eugenio Etxebeste "Antxon," deported in August 1984 to the Dominican Republic; Isidro María Garalde "Mamarru," deported in October 1984 to Cape Verde; and Juan Ramón Aramburu Garmendia "Juanra," arrested in November 1985 and deported to Cape Verde in February 1986.[18]

As it turned out, these concerns were well founded. The French government obviously had no desire to keep their controversial prisoner in jail in France, and in fact Iturbe remained in French custody for only seventy-six days. Upon learning of his arrest, the Spanish government immediately sent several police officers to Hendaye to interrogate Iturbe, and activated a long-standing request that he be extradited to Spain. The dilemma faced in Paris, however, was that Iturbe enjoyed the status of a political refugee in France, and was protected by French law from being extradited to Spain. As French minister of justice Albin Chalandon put it, Iturbe's case was "very delicate."[19]

In the short run, however, the machinery of French justice continued to process Iturbe's case. On April 29, he was taken from Hendaye to Bayonne where he was interrogated for nearly an hour by a French judge in the presence of several Spanish police officers, and then removed to the Grandignan prison near Bordeaux, where he would be held until his trial commenced.[20] On May 15, the court in Bayonne sentenced him to three months in prison for the 1982 offense of carrying an illegal weapon, and ordered him to appear again in a month or so to be tried for violating the terms of his provisional release four years earlier. In the meantime, he was to remain in French custody in Grandignan.[21] On June 24, an appeals court in Pau increased his earlier sentence for the illegal weapon violation from three months to one year; and on June 26, the Bayonne court added three months to the total sentence for having violated his earlier provisional release terms.[22]

Meanwhile, ETA made it known through several channels that if Iturbe were released promptly in France, they would be willing to discuss the terms of a cease-fire. On May 26, PNV and HB leaders held their second meeting, this time at PNV headquarters in Durango, at which time the HB representatives asked the PNV to ask Spanish president Felipe González to intervene in France to get Iturbe released. HB leader Iñaki Esnaola told the PNV representatives of ETA's willingness to negotiate once Iturbe was freed.[23] The PNV leaders conveyed the message to President Ardanza, who appealed directly to González in a secret meeting in Madrid shortly before the June 22 Spanish general elections.[24] HB was to criticize the PNV later for trying in these contacts to separate Txomin Iturbe's case as an individual from ETA as an organization. That is, the PNV saw this issue solely as one of an individual's rights, rather than an opportunity to raise in Madrid the question of a general amnesty.[25]

In addition to the HB contacts with the PNV, there were other attempts to get Madrid to intervene in France to free Iturbe. At about the same time as the contacts discussed above (mid-June), a senior PNV leader met directly with ETA representatives in France; and Garcia Andoain met on five separate occasions (early June, and July 14, 18, 23, and 28) in France with ETA spokesmen. The message that emerged from all of these meetings was the same: if Iturbe were released, ETA would be willing to negotiate and with "lowered expectations of the outcome."[26] Iturbe proposed that he be released for twenty days to try to get a cease-fire arranged; and ETA requested that Madrid send them a list of their "approved representatives" in these talks. These latter contacts were relayed through Luis María Retolaza of the Basque government to his counterpart in Madrid, Interior Minister Barrionuevo, with the request that he ask the French government to release Iturbe. This Barrionuevo refused to do.

At least one close observer of these contacts believes that Madrid responded with a counteroffer (that Iturbe be moved to another area of France, from where he could try to arrange a cease-fire), but that time ran out before anything could be negotiated.[27] Indeed, on July 10, hopes appeared high that Iturbe would be released in France. Prison officials completed some administrative procedures that led him to understand that he would soon be freed;

and that same day, an intermediary visited him to inform him of his imminent release. On the following day, however, Iturbe was removed from Grandignan and flown to a prison in the department of Ille-de-France, near Paris. Before leaving Grandignan, he was taken to the prison doctor and vaccinated against tropical diseases, a sure sign that the French intended to deport him, either to the Caribbean or to West Africa.[28]

Iturbe's lawyer, Christianne Fando, began efforts to prevent her client's deportation, but she was hampered by the refusal of French authorities to tell her where he was being confined. Whether by plan or by coincidence, the French had made their move over the Bastille Day holiday weekend; and most offices were closed and not answering their telephones. On July 11, Luis María Retolaza, acting for President Ardanza, telephoned Interior Minister Barrionuevo to ask for help in discovering where Iturbe was being held, since that was indispensable to lodging their appeal against the expulsion order. Barrionuevo refused to intercede, and replied to Retolaza that the French had already made the decision to expel Iturbe, and that nothing could be done to stop it.[29]

On Saturday, July 12, the French government expelled Iturbe and had him flown to the West African republic of Gabon. The next day, Txomin Ziluaga of Herri Batasuna warned "if the PSOE continues with this policy of repression and deportations, it will be responsible for the lack of a solution to all the problems we are living through, and for the maintenance of the current situation in Euskadi." On July 14, Bastille Day, an ETA comando blew up a Guardia Civil microbus in Madrid, killing eight immediately and wounding more than forty, of whom four died subsequently.[30] That same day, Garcia Andoain held his third meeting with ETA leaders in France. With Iturbe already in Gabon, it seems they had little to discuss.

From Gabon to Algeria:
July–September 1986

Upon his arrival in Libreville, the capital of Gabon, on July 13, Iturbe was told by local officials that Gabon had received him for humanitarian reasons, and that since he had committed no crime there, there were no charges pending against him and no request for his extradition to another country.[31] Therefore, at least in theory, he was free to come and go as he wished. In practice, however, while in Gabon, although he was relatively well treated, Iturbe lived under a modified form of house arrest.[32] He was given a small apartment in the center of Libreville, where he was virtually cut off from the outside world, without radio, television, or telephone. He was allowed to leave the apartment only to eat and to buy an occasional newspaper. In view of the several attempts on his life in France, Iturbe was accompanied constantly by two Gabonese police, and at times by French agents and his own security personnel. At first, he was extremely nervous and insecure about his fate. As he told a reporter soon after arriving in Libreville, "no one has told me if I am deported or if I can leave to go to any other country. I don't know anything about my situation; I don't even have a passport or identity papers." All the costs of his stay in Gabon were paid by the Spanish government, just as they paid the costs of the other three dozen ETA members who had been expelled to third countries from France.[33]

From the outset of his stay in Gabon, Iturbe knew he was there only temporarily.[34] In negotiations with the French government in Paris, the government of Gabon had agreed to receive him for only two to three months, after which he would have to be moved to another country. There seemed to be considerable confusion about who had the authority to decide where Iturbe would be moved. Officially, at least, the French government claimed the responsibility of finding a country that would permit him to stay more or less permanently, but the government of Gabon stressed repeatedly that it would allow Iturbe to go to any country he chose that would agree to receive him. However, in practice his eventual destination became the subject of considerable negotiation involving many different parties.

Iturbe himself would have preferred to go to a country where there were other ETA leaders, such as Cuba, where Ansola and Ibarguren had been deported. Even though Spain vetoed this choice, it looked for a while like Iturbe might actually reach Cuba, especially since Gabon made no pretense of controlling his departure from Libreville. The Spanish government would have preferred that he be confined in a relatively remote and inaccessible country, perhaps in the Caribbean or West Africa, so that it would be difficult for him to leave. Press reports in late July suggested that Madrid had tried unsuccessfully to move Iturbe to the island republic of São Tomé and Principe, off the west coast of Africa. In fact, it was even reported that they had sent a military aircraft to take him to São Tomé, but this was subsequently denied by his attorney, Christianne Fando.[35] The Basque government argued for Belgium, but Madrid refused to let him back on the European continent. It was later reported that Iñaki Esnaola had asked Basque government officials to seek Iturbe's transfer to Belgium, but Esnaola himself asserted that Iturbe did not trust the Belgians since they had just a short time before extradited several ETA members to Spain.[36]

Meanwhile back in the Basque Country the issue of negotiations with ETA had once again heated up. On August 3, the Bilbao daily *Deia* carried an article by Xabier Arzalluz in which he asserted that "ETA wants to negotiate, but Madrid does not." Arzalluz went on to accuse the Spanish government of blocking possible negotiations with ETA by having Iturbe arrested and then failing to prevent his expulsion from France.[37] Two days later, Felipe González responded to the charge with the demand that "those who favor negotiations with ETA should reveal exactly what they are willing to bargain away" to the terrorist group.[38] The Basque government answered the next day through its spokesman, Eugenio Ibarzabal, who characterized González's remarks as "frivolous." Parties attempting to enter into negotiations, he said, do not ordinarily detail in advance exactly what they are disposed to concede. Nevertheless, he quoted President Ardanza as being willing to discuss with ETA anything that did not violate the Spanish constitution or the Basque autonomy statute.[39] The Basques also revealed for the first time the efforts they had made during May and June to convince Madrid to accept ETA's offer to negotiate. The Basque government and the PNV were persuaded that ETA was sincere in its offer; and they accused Madrid of not being serious about ending ETA's violence.[40] Representatives of the Basque government had met with ETA more than a dozen times during the months of May, June, and July, according to these leaked reports, and Madrid had been informed of each of these meetings as they occurred. There were even reports much later that ETA during this time was observing a "technical truce" (i.e., an unacknowledged cessation of violence) until mid-October in hopes of getting talks started.[41]

On August 10, *El País* reported that the Spanish government had been in contact with Iturbe "at the highest level" for four months, from March until his expulsion from France in July. Thus, while HB and PNV leaders were meeting to explore the possibilities of negotiations, and while Garcia Andoain was meeting with ETA directly in France, this story suggested, there was yet another channel of communication opened up directly with Madrid.[42] Spanish President González at once rejected the story, denying that "there have been, are or will be" any negotiations with ETA.[43] Even people close to ETA doubted the validity of these stories, but they remained prominent news reports for several days.[44]

While Basque and Spanish political leaders hammered at each other over the negotiation issue, Iturbe remained in Gabon, unable to reach an agreement about his final destination. Madrid continued to block his transfer to Cuba to prevent the reuniting of several of ETA's key leaders; and on August 18, Christianne Fando was telling the press that no country had yet agreed to receive him permanently.[45] As late as the last weeks of August, the question was still unresolved. Gabon held fast to its position that Iturbe could not be made to go to a country not of his choosing; the ETA leader refused to go to one of the countries Spain had approved; no other country would agree to receive him (Cuba seemed uncertain as to what its position would be); and France seemed to want to distance itself from the controversy.

In this context, then, it is not entirely clear how the Algerian option unfolded. After Iturbe reached Algeria, there was much speculation in Spain that as early as June (while he was still in France) Algeria had begun to consider a plan to allow ETA to establish itself on Algerian soil.[46] While some observers speculated that Algeria was motivated by humanitarian concerns or by a historical association with ETA that went back to the 1960s when etarras were trained on Algerian territory, in fact, more immediate policy concerns probably enjoyed a higher priority in Algiers. For example, one purpose of bringing Iturbe to Algeria would be to pressure Madrid into siding with Algeria in its conflict with Morocco, and to halt the sale of arms to Rabat. But the more important objective apparently was to force the Spanish government to curtail the activities of the Algerian Democratic Movement, the illegal opposition party whose leader, deposed Algerian president Ahmed Ben Bella, was living at that time in Madrid. (Ben Bella left Spain in March 1987 to live in Switzerland after Madrid began to limit the activities of his organization.)[47]

Late in August, Iturbe left Gabon to fly to the capital of Angola, Luanda, where, he had been assured, he would be given a visa by Cuba.[48] Upon his arrival in Angola, however, Cuban embassy officials informed him that they had not received instructions from Havana, and he was not given permission to go to Cuba. After waiting forty-eight hours in the Luanda airport, Iturbe returned to Gabon. According to one report, when Cuba informed Iturbe that he would not be allowed to go to Havana, ETA then contacted the National Liberation Front, the official party in Algeria, to solicit their aid through the office they maintained to assist refugees.[49] This report also asserted that Algerian president Chadli Benyedid was presented with the proposal by unnamed persons at the meeting of the 101 countries of the Nonaligned Movement in Zimbabwe in September. On his return from that meeting, Benyedid stopped in Gabon early in September to discuss with Gabonese president Omar Bongo the transfer of Iturbe to his country.

On Friday, September 5, the government of Gabon confirmed that Iturbe had left Libreville "at the beginning of the week" to travel to Algeria, with a stop in the People's Republic of the Congo to arrange for an Algerian visa.[50] For a brief period, his whereabouts remained a mystery; but on September 10, Spanish diplomatic sources in Algeria informed Madrid of his presence in Algiers.[51] Sources in the Basque government suggested that Algeria was only a temporary residence for the ETA leader, and that eventually he would return to Europe, perhaps to Belgium. Whether true or not at the moment, these reports eventually proved to be wrong. Against his will, Txomin Iturbe had reached his final destination.

Initial Contacts in Algeria:
September–December 1986

There seems to be considerable confusion about whether or not the Spanish government approved of Iturbe's transfer to Algeria, or even whether they knew about it in advance. Sources I consulted on this question in 1988 offered a great variety of opinions. Some believed that Spain approved of the move in order to transfer Iturbe to a more accessible location; others thought the move was a French idea, as a prelude to moving him back to Europe; others believed that both France and Spain were genuinely caught off guard, and ignorant of the move until it had been completed.[52] Spanish officials complained later that Algerian authorities had not informed Madrid of Iturbe's arrival in their country; but since the Spanish press reported the trip within a matter of days after his arrival in Algiers, it stands to reason that Madrid knew of the move soon after it was completed, if not before.

Spain probably had mixed feelings about Iturbe's presence in Algeria. They certainly would have preferred to see him in a Spanish prison; and the Algerians used Iturbe's presence as leverage to influence Madrid to suppress (and eventually to expel) antigovernment Algerian exiles who were using Spain as a sanctuary. On the other hand, so long as Algeria did not become a haven from which ETA could launch armed attacks against Spain, Madrid was not completely displeased to have Iturbe in Algeria. He remained under Algerian control, relatively convenient to Spain when they wanted to contact him, but far enough from Europe to be unable to control events in the Basque Country. Indeed, the degree to which Iturbe's control over the organization might be slipping was vividly highlighted by the assassination on September 10 of María Dolores González Catarain "Yoyes," just a few days after his arrival in Algeria. Finally, with Iturbe in Algeria, the Spanish could undertake negotiations with him directly without having to go through Basque intermediaries, which would have been a problem so long as he remained in France.[53]

Meanwhile, several steps were being taken to move toward negotiations with ETA. In Madrid on September 17, Interior Minister Barrionuevo announced his willingness to establish "personal contacts" with a member of ETA to discuss a cessation of violence. As a gesture of goodwill, he also announced that ETA members living in France who had no charges pending against them should feel free to return to Spain, secure in the knowledge that they would not be "the object of any police or judicial action."[54] On September 11 and October 9, Genaro Garcia Andoain met with ETA representatives in France to discuss the possible resumption of talks. This channel was closed tragically on November 2 when Garcia Andoain was killed while leading Basque police forces freeing an ETA hostage, Basque businessman Lucio Aguinagalde.[55]

Although the Spanish had shown little interest in talking to Iturbe while he was in French custody, they did not wait long to contact him in Algeria. At first, Iturbe did not want to receive emissaries from the Spanish government; but Madrid appealed to the Algerians to intervene, and pressure from Algiers caused Iturbe to abandon his opposition to a meeting.[56] On November 12, a delegation of the Spanish interior ministry, headed by the director of state security, Rafael Vera, traveled secretly to Algeria.[57] The delegation also included two men with unsavory reputations among etarras: Jorge Argote, a lawyer for the Guardia Civil who had represented a number of civil guards accused of torture and abuse of prisoners; and Jesús Martínez Torres, the head of the intelligence service of the Spanish National Police, a man with a reputation as a torturer while with the National Police headquarters in Zaragoza.[58]

Vera did not talk personally with Iturbe; that responsibility was given to Jorge Argote. The choice of representative to make this initial contact was surprising. Argote had met with Iturbe in Gabon earlier in an attempt to have the ETA leader deported to São Tomé, a mission marked by failure and resentment. Moreover, Argote's reputation as a lawyer who defended civil guards accused of torturing Basques meant that he was not a person likely to be well received by the head of ETA.

The conversation between Argote and Iturbe took place in a villa located in a residential area about half an hour's drive from the center of Algiers. The talk lasted about an hour. Argote later characterized the meeting as "cordial"; ETA called it "poisonous." The Spanish representative insisted that ETA should cease its armed attacks at once, in return for which Madrid would be willing to discuss amnesty for ETA members in prison. Argote pressed Iturbe about the willingness of factions within ETA to stop the violence, but this line of discussion led nowhere. Iturbe reiterated ETA's offer to negotiate the KAS Alternative and rejected further talks with representatives of Spanish law enforcement agencies. According to one witness to the talks, Iturbe told Argote that he would not meet again with anyone who defended torturers; any

further discussions would have to be with people who had decision authority, including "a representative of the Spanish army who
could guarantee the agreements."[59] Despite the lack of any concrete
progress, the two agreed to schedule further discussions. A second
much briefer meeting between Argote and Iturbe on December 10
confirmed that serious talks would begin the following month,
although Iturbe showed Argote a note from ETA in which he (Argote) was rejected as an intermediary in future talks.

On November 26, the San Sebastián daily *Egin*, a newspaper
close to Herri Batasuna, published a lengthy interview with Txomin Iturbe.[60] Conducted by Basque sociologist and journalist Luis
Núñez in Iturbe's home in Algeria, this interview was the last time
Iturbe would be able to speak directly to the Basque people. The
interview ranged widely over such varied topics as Iturbe's child-
hood and his current physical and mental state, but the article
also touched on a number of important subjects in the negotiations
issue. With regard to the maintenance of law and order, for example, Iturbe made it clear that ETA would respect an all-Basque
police force. If the Spanish law enforcement agencies were withdrawn, leaving law and order in the hands of the Basque autonomous police, he said, "everyone in the Basque Country knows that
we will not go up against them [the Basque police]. Now of course
if at some point they come after us, then we will defend ourselves.
. . . But I want to leave it very clear that our enemy is not the Ert-
zantza [the Basque police] but rather the repressive Spanish forces
and their bosses."

On the subject of "social reintegration" Iturbe also had strong
opinions. When asked by Núñez if he thought that social reintegration might lead somewhere, Iturbe replied, "not in the least. With
reintegration we will go nowhere, despite the fact that the Spanish
communications media talk about this all the time. Reintegration
is a police measure . . . aimed at the most vulnerable sectors of the
liberation movement, that is, prisoners and refugees. . . . With that
policy of repression and reintegration they won't gain anything. If
they want to achieve something, they will have to negotiate political questions. We've seen many times that reintegration is nothing
more than a failure. A thousand times they have tried by that route
to break our unity, but they have not achieved it up until now and
they won't achieve it in the future. . . . the immense majority of

the prisoners and refugees see that [reintegration] is a false way out. What we need in the Basque country are not solutions or ways out for individuals, . . . but rather ways out for the community, solutions for the people in general."

Finally, in response to a question from Núñez, Iturbe had this to say about negotiations: "Well it's true that a lot has been said about this, and one day or another we'll get there, that's for sure. As they see their other policies fail, . . . and as they see that they cannot bring the Basque country to its knees, whether or not they want to, they will go to negotiations. . . . although they might not like it, sooner or later they will have to go to negotiations, and we have always said that we are ready to sit down at a table and look for a way out negotiated in the direction of the KAS alternative."

On December 7, the leaders of Herri Batasuna held what the press referred to as a "stormy meeting," at which the subject of negotiations was the central issue. Iñaki Esnaola found himself virtually alone in defending the idea that negotiations were a means to an end, not an end in themselves. Perhaps the most significant development surrounding this meeting went relatively unnoticed, however. The day before the meeting, Esnaola was reported as declaring that "we have never said that negotiations with ETA are the only channel. We have defended them because no one offered others; but if now new channels are opened, in HB we would study them."[61] This was not the first time that a "two-track" strategy had been suggested for negotiations; but it was the first time that anyone from ETA or HB had publicly supported such an option.

In mid-December, several days after the second contact between Iturbe and Argote, there apparently was an informal meeting in Algeria between Iturbe and several of the Spanish officials who would meet officially with him later in January.[62] This contact lasted only two hours and dealt only with relatively superficial generalities. The meeting was later described as a preliminary attempt by both sides to feel out the intentions of the other. Real negotiations would await the important meeting coming up in January.

Negotiations and Iturbe's Death:
January–February 1987

Before 1989, the closest ETA and the Spanish government came
to real negotiations were the talks in Algeria that began on January 11, 1987, and extended into a second session the following
day.[63] In all, the conversations lasted more than seven hours. Iturbe
represented ETA, while the Spanish government's three-man delegation showed that it still regarded the question as a police matter.
The head of the delegation was Julian Sancristobal, predecessor
to Rafael Vera as director of state security in 1984 and 1985. The
second man on the delegation was well known to ETA—Manuel
Ballesteros. Ballesteros was head of the Intelligence Service of the
National Police in early 1981 when Joseba Arregi was arrested
and tortured to death, and shortly thereafter was placed in charge
of the Unified Antiterrorist Command.[64] In 1985, Ballesteros had
been found guilty of assisting three Spanish police to cross back
into Spain illegally shortly after they attacked a Basque bar in Hendaye, killing two people. He was sentenced to leave his government
post for three years and to pay a fine of 100,000 pesetas.[65] A second
police official, Pedro Martínez Suárez, acted as interpreter between
the group and the Algerians. Several other people have been identified as participants or observers, but they have denied stories of
their involvement.[66] In addition to the working sessions on January 11 and 12, the Algerians hosted a dinner for the negotiators,
a symbolic event that suggested to the Spaniards that Algeria regarded ETA as a legitimate organization with status approaching
that of a "quasi-state." In fact, one participant noted that Algeria's
treatment of Iturbe as an official government representative both
surprised and rankled the Spanish delegation.[67]

The negotiating parties made little real progress on any of the
substantial issues. From ETA's perspective, the meetings were very
tense and punctuated with repeated "habitual poisonous charges
and warlike and genocidal language." At the first meeting, on January 11, Iturbe repeated the demands of the KAS Alternative, and
questioned the Spanish delegation about a possible evolution of
the government's position. The Spanish representatives replied by
reiterating the offer extended by Interior Minister Barrionuevo in

August 1984: if ETA ceased its armed attacks, there would be amnesty for those who had not been charged or convicted of "blood crimes." Persons in prison would be pardoned on an individual basis, and those in exile would be permitted to return, so long as they had agreed to lay down their weapons and abandon armed struggle. The Spaniards emphasized, however, that the constitution prohibits general amnesties or pardons for groups of people unless authorized by the king. The Spaniards also made clear that a cessation of violence had to occur before there could be any other negotiations, and they reaffirmed the Spanish position opposed to political negotiations. Iturbe replied that ETA was ready to sit down at the bargaining table without any pre-conditions, so long as the Spanish delegation had the authority to commit Madrid. But, he added, the cease-fire would have to come after the negotiations, not before.

Iturbe also succeeded in getting on the agenda the two major political questions: self-determination and Navarra. On the subject of the status of Navarra, he proposed that the two autonomous communities—Basque and Navarrese—establish joint commissions or working groups in specific fields to facilitate an eventual union of the two governments. The affirmation of the Basques' right of self-determination, perhaps by the creation of a federal state, would be much more difficult. Iturbe reminded the Spaniards that the Basque voters had not accepted the 1978 constitution as legitimate, but the Spaniards replied that "there would be great difficulty in changing the constitution" to meet ETA's demands.

The second working meeting, held the next day, unfolded around more or less the same issues "in an atmosphere," according to ETA, "of evident nervousness and contradictions among the members of the Spanish delegation." The group did agree to meet again, however, and Iturbe made an additional request: the transfer to Algeria of another of ETA's senior leaders, Eugenio Etxebeste "Antxon," at that time confined in exile in Ecuador. Iturbe felt uncomfortable negotiating issues of substance, and wanted Etxebeste involved if the discussions moved to another level. The Spanish representatives agreed to consider the request, although subsequent reports have suggested that they never really took seriously the possibility that Iturbe and Etxebeste might be allowed to be reunited again. In any case, this request, as well as whatever substantive progress the negotiators achieved, were all rendered irrelevant by events of the coming month.

While ETA and Madrid had been maneuvering toward the January 1987 meeting in Algeria, there were important developments in the Basque Country as well. On November 30, 1986, elections for a new Basque parliament had produced a bitterly fragmented legislature in which no party held enough seats to form a one-party government. Throughout December and January, the various parties had sparred and negotiated with each other over the terms of a coalition, but without success. Finally, in February, the parties with the two largest blocs of seats—the Basque Nationalist Party and the Basque Socialist Party—reached an agreement on a coalition government. The PSE, acting to advance the interests of their parent party, the Spanish PSOE, used these negotiations to move the PNV toward a less intransigent and more cooperative position vis-à-vis Madrid. One of the most important areas in which the PNV shifted ground had to do with negotiations with ETA. Thus, the final PNV-PSE accord, published on February 28,[68] contained this significant passage: ". . . a global strategy to face the problem of violence must include (1) An analysis and a declaration of principles coincident with the Institutional Declaration of the Basque Parliament, March 15, 1985. In fulfillment of what was expressed in that declaration approved unanimously by the Parliamentary Groups, we denounce the lack of legitimacy of organizations that use violence to express the will of the Basque people, and consequently, we reject their pretention to negotiate the political problems of the Basque people, which must be done only among the political parties with parliamentary representation, the Basque government, and, as appropriate ["*en su caso*"], the Spanish government." This declaration closed the door on any separate negotiations between ETA and the Basque government over political issues, but left open the very real possibility of conducting such negotiations with Herri Batasuna acting as an ETA surrogate.

On the morning of Friday, February 27, the car in which Txomin Iturbe was riding spun out of control on an Algerian country road and struck a tree. Iturbe and his Algerian driver were killed instantly. Two other passengers in the car, Iñaki Arakama and Belen González Peñalba, both ETA members living in exile, escaped with light to moderate injuries.[69] (It subsequently came to light that there were some thirty ETA members in Algeria whose residence there had not been communicated by the Algerian government to Madrid, a fact that caused considerable consternation in Spain.)[70] After several days of bureaucratic delays, Iturbe's body was finally returned to be buried in his hometown of Mondragon on March 8. The funeral was marked by an emotional demonstration of a crowd estimated at tens of thousands shouting their support for ETA and for Txomin.[71] People close to ETA and to Iturbe were inclined to believe the official Algerian reports on the cause of death, largely because they had a chance to talk with the car's other occupants. However, there were still lingering doubts when I talked with some of them in 1988. One person told me that, remembering everything that had happened to those who had favored a negotiated settlement (Pertur, Portell, Argala, Brouard, and others), he had warned Iturbe to take precautions to protect his own life. Another, one of the last people to see Iturbe alive, told me that he really did not doubt the official reports, but that Algeria was such a closed society it would probably be impossible to ascertain the truth with any certainty.

With Txomin Iturbe's death, the first phase of the Algerian connection came to an end. Whether or not his death would bring about the collapse of talks with ETA would depend on Madrid's desire to continue. As Iñaki Esnaola told reporters aboard the airplane that brought Iturbe's remains back for burial, "the important thing about all this is whether or not there is really a will to negotiate."[72]

CHAPTER EIGHT

The "Algerian Connection,"
Phase Two: 1987–1988

TXOMIN Iturbe's death forced a number of adjustments on the parties interested in negotiations. In France, the ETA leadership passed to a new generation, the third since the early 1970s. The new leader was Francisco Múgica Garmendia "Artapalo," born in 1954 near Ordizia in Guipúzcoa province. Originally a hard-line activist within ETA (p-m), Artapalo became disillusioned with the overly cautious approach of this wing and joined the military wing in the mid-1970s. Before taking over from Iturbe, Múgica had been in charge of ETA's armed cells. Unlike Iturbe and some of the other older leaders, Múgica had avoided detection by never registering as a refugee and never requesting a French residence card. Since he had lived in almost complete isolation and secrecy, little was known about him at the time he assumed control of the organization.[1]

ETA's attitude toward negotiations at this time was revealed by an internal document drafted sometime in the first half of 1987 and discovered when French police arrested ETA leader Santiago Arrospide "Santi Potros" on September 30.[2] The document argued that Spain's political transition had either eliminated or suppressed conditions that might lead to a mass uprising of workers or a mili-

tary insurrection, and thereby presented Euskadi with an adversary
—the Spanish state—that was virtually invulnerable to armed assault. As a consequence, ETA would be forced to negotiate at least
a temporary cessation of violence while the organization worked
for its revolutionary aims in other ways. "Negotiations," the document claimed, "are situated clearly in the context of the strategy
of a prolonged war of attrition that the Basque revolutionary process has always defended. In the face of insurrectionist theses, and
taking into account the characteristics of Euskadi as a geographic
enclave, . . . we understand that a military victory over the states
that oppress and divide us is not viable in the present conditions,
and we are adopting a tactic of irreversible conquests by means of
the creation of favorable correlations of forces that emerge through
negotiations."

The second half of the document was titled "Negotiate, what
and how?" It opened with a warning of the difference between
"negotiations" and "conversations." "Negotiations" seemed highly
unlikely because "the option of negotiations is not yet 'swallowed'
by the powers of the state, nor is it legitimized in the Spanish
government and public opinion. . . . Conversations are more possible. For the state, conversations are instruments for sizing up
our positions, the level of security and confidence of our forces,
etc. Conversations are a useful element within a strategy of con-
founding, dividing, poisoning, as well as a card to use with public
opinion as proof of our intransigence and their generosity." However, the document asserted, conversations could also be useful to
ETA, and for the same reasons; i.e., to show public opinion that
Madrid accepted ETA as a legitimate bargaining party. To engage
the Spanish government at the level of conversations, however,
ETA would have to be flexible and expert in its use of the mass
communications media, to make sure that it would win the battle
for public opinion. To take full advantage of the "conversations"
strategy, the document sketched out a six-step negotiating process: (1) preliminary contacts to know who is talking with whom,
and how representative they are; (2) an agreement on the principal negotiator; (3) formation of a commission and agreement on a
minimal set of procedural rules; (4) presentation of proposals and
discussion; (5) partial agreements with possible consequences to
be analyzed; and (6) final agreement, including an accord on follow-

up and control of the agreement. It was a sign of how far ETA had come in its negotiation strategy that these "conversations" were not to become public until step four, when formal proposals were due to be presented and debated.

Attitudes were changing in Madrid as well; and for evidence of that we have this intriguing anecdote.[3] In June 1987, Basque nationalist senator Joseba Azkarraga was in Madrid for a meeting with Rafael Vera, director of state security. Vera commented that police methods would be insufficient to eliminate ETA, and that negotiations would be necessary. Basque political parties would be included in the negotiations, but they would be asked to give concessions to Herri Batasuna. Madrid could not be seen to negotiate political issues such as the status of Navarra with ETA, but would be willing to let the Basque parliament negotiate a solution to these issues. Azkarraga replied that his party, Eusko Alkartasuna, would find it difficult to accept this because it would be an affront to those parties that had accepted the legitimacy of the Basque institutions from the beginning. Vera's only reaction was that all parties concerned would have to find a way to make concessions to find a middle ground.

With attitudes on both sides seemingly resigned to seeking a negotiated settlement, the stage was set for the most extensive negotiations ever undertaken with ETA, the second phase of the Algerian connection.

Etxebeste in Algeria:
July–August 1987

In Algiers, the governments of Spain and Algeria launched a series of discussions to lessen tension between the two countries caused by what Madrid perceived as unwarranted Algerian intervention in Spanish affairs. Until Iturbe's death, Spain had not been officially informed by the Algerians that they were receiving more ETA members from France, and Spain responded sharply to the news. On March 23, Spanish representatives met with their Algerian counterparts to draft a new understanding that would enable Algeria to receive a mutually acceptable number of ETA members (press reports suggested thirty), so long as they were not permitted to engage in any activities directed against Spanish security. On March 30, Spanish foreign minister Francisco Fernández Ordóñez began a two-day visit to Algeria to firm up this accord, and this trip was followed in early May with a visit by Rafael Vera.[4]

Negotiations with ETA remained a low priority for the Spanish government until June 19. On that date, an ETA cell placed a car bomb in the crowded parking garage of Hipercor, a supermarket in Barcelona. The explosion killed twenty-one persons (not all of whom died instantly) and wounded thirty-nine. The revulsion and condemnation of this atrocity were almost universal. Even some leaders of Herri Batasuna were compelled to condemn the attack, even though they were careful to point out that they did so not in the name of the party but as a reflection of their personal opinion. One can only speculate on ETA's motivations in launching this attack, but if their aim was to get Madrid back to the negotiating table in Algeria, they certainly achieved that objective.

The instrument by which Spain sought to resume negotiations was the transfer of Eugenio Etxebeste "Antxon" from his confinement in Ecuador to Algeria. Etxebeste was born in 1951 and joined ETA (p-m) in 1976. He went over to ETA (m) the following year, and assumed the leadership of ETA's political office after the death of Argala in 1978. From that time until his arrest by French police in 1984, he was a member of the executive committee of ETA. Following his arrest, the French government deported him to the Dominican Republic where he lived in confinement until May 1986. Shortly after Iturbe's detention in France, Etxebeste was moved to Ecuador.[5] At the January 1987 meetings, Iturbe had requested that Etxebeste be transferred to Algeria to join him in the negotiations, a request that Madrid probably did not seriously consider. Etxebeste was believed by Spanish police to be one of the hard-liners in the ETA leadership, not a man apt to facilitate negotiations. Moreover, since he had been out of direct contact with the organization for nearly four years, his influence with the current leadership was likely to be low. After the Hipercor bombing, however, the Spanish moved quickly to resume negotiations; and on July 9 or 10, Etxebeste left Ecuador for Algeria.[6] His arrival one day later began phase two of the Algerian connection.

Once Etxebeste was in Algeria, Spanish officials wasted little time in contacting him. On August 11, a three-man delegation consisting of Rafael Vera, Manuel Ballesteros, and Jesús Martínez Torres visited Algeria.[7] In Madrid, officials denied that the trip was to meet with Etxebeste; Vera and the others had gone to Algiers, they said, to discuss the Spanish-Algerian agreement regarding the transfer of additional ETA members from France. Etxebeste met just with Ballesteros on this occasion. The meeting lasted only about an hour and dealt only with superficial issues. Etxebeste emphasized that he was meeting with them simply as an individual, and that he could accept the role of intermediary only if ETA agreed to the arrangement. He stressed that he was not empowered to negotiate in the name of ETA, and could only transmit to the ETA leadership in France a report of what was discussed in Algeria. ETA's view of the meeting was that it was extremely tense and disrespectful. The Spanish representative simply repeated the offer of amnesty for individual ETA members in prison, a proposal that ETA had already rejected many times. From ETA's perspective, the meeting had only one purpose—to sound out Etxebeste on the terms of a possible negotiation.[8] The only new element in the discussion was a slight shift of Spanish policy regarding amnesty for ETA prisoners convicted of blood crimes. Whereas before Madrid had steadfastly maintained that amnesty would be impossible for these people, it now appeared possible that some of them could be released with the understanding that they live outside Spain—perhaps in Algeria—for a lengthy period, perhaps as long as ten years.[9]

Meanwhile, in the Basque Country press reports on August 23 and 25 confirmed that secret ETA-Madrid talks were under way in Algeria. These accounts suggested that ETA would be satisfied simply to get Madrid officials to meet with them at a negotiating table, and that the only three issues remaining for negotiation were amnesty, the status of Navarra, and self-determination. On the Spanish side, unnamed persons in the interior ministry were reported discussing seriously the possibility of negotiating a settlement with Herri Batasuna so that they could not be accused of giving in to an illegal insurgent group.[10]

In response to these reports, Spanish vice president Alfonso Guerra replied, "there is only one possible negotiation: that they lay down their weapons and stop the killing."[11] Nevertheless, when President Felipe González emerged from a meeting with French president François Mitterrand on August 25 and was asked about these reports, to everyone's surprise he announced that dialogue with ETA was indeed a possibility. Even though he continued to reject political negotiations, he did leave open the possibility of discussions or contacts with the insurgents on other subjects. Even this modest admission was a major change from the official Spanish position, which was that they would never negotiate with ETA over anything other than the terms of their surrender.

On August 28, the official spokesman of the Spanish government, Javier Solana, told a press conference that "there have been, there are and there will be" contacts with ETA, thus admitting publicly for the first time that negotiations were a possibility and that meetings with ETA were not only common in the past but that they would continue into the future.[12] Solana was careful to add, however, the standard Spanish line: that the meetings were simply to get ETA to stop killing and turn over their weapons. "ETA and their followers," he said, "should give up any hope that there might be a political negotiation." If Madrid thought that the issue would be resolved that easily, however, they were mistaken. On August 26, Basque president José Antonio Ardanza insisted that his government, the Basque parliament, and all Basque political parties would have to be involved in negotiations if they were to succeed.[13] And on August 30, the Barcelona daily *La Vanguardia* reported that ETA's executive committee had held an emergency meeting in Paris and had categorically rejected any dialogue with Madrid that avoided political negotiations.[14] As a consequence, Antxon Etxebeste was reported to have withdrawn from further contacts with Spanish representatives.

ETA's Communiqué:
September 1987

On September 5, the San Sebastián daily *Egin* published a communiqué from ETA that summarized the organization's response to the August meeting with Ballesteros and the several press reports cited above.[15] Because of the communiqué's significance in the development of the Algerian negotiations, it deserves to be cited in detail.

The communiqué was necessary, according to ETA, in order to clarify relations between ETA and the Spanish government after what the communiqué called "poisonous leaks and speculations about the contacts carried out in Algeria between a delegation of the Spanish government and our organization." The communiqué confirmed in detail three of the contacts held with Spanish officials: November 12, 1986, between Txomin Iturbe and Jorge Argote; January 11–12, 1987, between Iturbe and the delegation headed by Julian Sancristobal; and August 11, 1987, between Antxon Etxebeste, Manuel Ballesteros, and Jesús Martínez Torres.

The assessment by ETA of these three meetings was decidedly negative. The statement accused Madrid of intransigence, of not really wanting to negotiate a settlement, and of continuing to regard the insurgency as nothing more than a police problem, as evidenced by their sending only police officials to Algeria. The communiqué asserted that only ETA had maintained a clear and unambiguous intent to carry on the dialogue and an openly negotiating attitude. The Algerian contacts, the communiqué claimed, were viewed by Madrid as an opportunity to sound out ETA's willingness to bargain and to gain information about the organization. The communiqué also charged that the Spanish government had unleashed a campaign of distorted press leaks intended to drop a "smoke screen over the process of Basque national liberation and over our organization." A key part of this process was for Madrid to project an image of wanting to negotiate, which was nothing more than a cover for an increase in their "repressive strategy" and their "policy of genocide." Finally, charged the communiqué, the escalation in repression was masked behind an image of wanting to negotiate so as to "create false expectations within the Basque working class organized around the Basque National Liberation Movement (MLNV), seeking to generate frustrations and divisions within it."

The communiqué then continued on to analyze current Spanish and French policy towards ETA. Far from wanting to negotiate an end to the violence, Madrid was attempting to eradicate ETA through increased activity of the GAL as well as much tougher anti-ETA actions by the French government, including more arrests and expulsions. These policies were linked to efforts in Spain to outlaw organizations linked to the MLNV, and to prevent these

organizations from expressing their opposition to Madrid's bla-
tant anti-Basque and anti-worker policies. However, the "inherent
contradictions" in the post-Franco reforms were becoming sharper,
and signs were appearing of weakening among the "forces of occupation." One such sign was the proposal for a *"pacto de Estado,"*
or an antiterrorist pact that would bind all the Spanish and Basque
political parties to this "repressive strategy" of the PSOE. To their
discredit, the other Basque nationalist parties—the PNV, EA, and
EE—had allowed themselves to be drawn into collaboration with
this strategy. These Basque parties must bear much of the blame,
said the communiqué, for permitting themselves to be used in this
way simply to gain a short-term political advantage. But, the communiqué went on, the fact that Madrid had chosen to make public
the contacts with ETA showed clearly the failure of its policy to
liquidate the MLNV and to assimilate the Basque people. ETA concluded this section of the message by calling on the Basque people
to stay alert, and to not let themselves be diverted from claiming
"our national sovereignty." The people were urged to continue to
support the KAS and Herri Batasuna as the only organizations still
faithful to the objectives of the Basque struggle. The communiqué
also warned of even greater repressive measures to come, but said
they would be the consequence "of the unstoppable advance of the
process of national liberation, in which only our frontal struggle
against the oppressor Spanish state can guarantee the attainment
of irreversible achievements."

The last three paragraphs of the communiqué are quoted here
in full as an indication of ETA's views on negotiation at the moment: "We repeat once more the offer of a cease-fire in return for
the conclusion of a process of political negotiations between ETA
and the real powers of the [Spanish] state, from which is clear [*"del
que se desprenda"*] the acceptance of the KAS tactical alternative
in its entirety. ETA rejects any attempt to force it to a negotiation
from weakness, to which it will never bend, and likewise it points
out that only the formal aspects of the [KAS] alternative have a
place on the negotiating table and not its content, which must be
adopted in its entirety. Euskadi ta Askatasuna reaffirms its commitment to struggle contracted with the Basque working people, in
whose service it will continue putting all its military and political
power, leading the process of national and social liberation to the

achievement of our strategic objectives, an independent, socialist, reunified and Basque-speaking Euskadi."

Reaction to the ETA communiqué was not long in appearing. From Madrid, Julian Sancristobal charged that ETA's message contained "clear falsehoods."[16] The chief flaw in the communiqué, according to Sancristobal, was its misrepresentation of the position of Txomin Iturbe on several key points. According to notes taken by the Spanish delegate at the time of the Algeria meetings, Iturbe assured him that "the contents of the KAS alternative were not a sine qua non for opening negotiations," and that "there would be a cease-fire as soon as the negotiating panels were established." Sancristobal also charged that Iturbe himself felt it was unwise for ETA to insist on meeting with a high representative of the Spanish armed forces. Other sources from the interior ministry claimed that the communiqué offered a distorted view of the meeting of August 11, which, these sources claimed, was conducted in a completely normal atmosphere. Ministry sources went on to characterize the communiqué as simply "playing to the gallery" and intended for internal consumption by ETA rank-and-file members. The Spanish government would not be deterred, however, by the harsh tone of the communiqué from continuing to seek a settlement negotiated on the basis of a cessation of violence and amnesty for individual prisoners.

Several days later, on a trip to Barcelona, interior minister José Barrionuevo asserted that the government "will continue to maintain contacts and dialogue with ETA whenever possible," even though the organization might launch violent attacks such as that on September 8, when a Guardia Civil officer was killed in Bilbao. The minister added, however, that "the dialogue is open, but it doesn't have to be permanently or indefinitely."[17]

On September 16, leaders of Herri Batasuna in a press conference announced that they were calling for a mass demonstration on October 3 to press for negotiations between the Spanish government and ETA. The leaders said they were convoking the rally in Bilbao to demonstrate their conviction that the process of negotiations was now irreversible.[18]

A few days later, on September 18, Etxebeste and Ballesteros met in Algeria for the second time. At this meeting, the ETA leader stressed again that Madrid must send "a political spokesman at the highest level with the objective of initiating a phase of conversations of a political character leading to the preparation of a possible future framework of accords."[19] ETA's objective here was to move beyond the stage of discussions or contacts that Madrid could characterize as "police matters," and into the discussion of "political issues" as well. Within a month after the Etxebeste-Ballesteros meeting, such contacts were indeed made.

Renewed Contacts:
September–October 1987

On September 30, French police captured an important ETA leader, Santiago Arrospide Sarasola "Santi Potros," in the French Basque town of Anglet.[20] The arrest of Arrospide, the person in charge of ETA's comandos liberados, or armed cells, also yielded a great quantity of documents and other information that enabled police to launch a series of raids against suspected ETA cells through early October. More than one hundred Basque refugees alleged to be ETA members were arrested in France and fifty-five were deported to Spain. About a dozen were sent to Algeria, where the number of ETA members living in exile rose to more than thirty.[21] In Spain as well, police measures seemed to be having an effect on ETA. In November, the Guardia Civil claimed it had dismantled ETA's infrastructure in Guipúzcoa by capturing the cell that had assassinated María Dolores González Catarain "Yoyes" in September 1986.[22]

As a result of these and other police actions dating back to 1984, as well as the death of Txomin Iturbe and the arrest and deportation of other "historic leaders" like Antxon Etxebeste, ETA was now in the hands of four relatively young and unknown leaders.[23] Francisco Múgica "Artapalo" remained in charge of the comandos liberados, but he now shared overall control of the organization with three others. José Antonio Urruticoechea Bengoechea "Josu Ternera," born in 1950, had been a member of ETA since the age of 17. He came from a poor farm near the small Vizcayan town of Miravalles, completed high school in Bilbao and worked in a bank before going over to ETA full time. He had lived in France since 1971 and had served on the executive committee of ETA since 1975. He was reportedly in charge of the organization's international connections. The second man, José Javier Zabaleta Elosegui "Waldo," was born in 1957 in the Guipuzcoan town of Hernani, near San Sebastián. He joined ETA in 1975 and had lived in France since the following year. He was in charge of the comandos legales, the support infrastructure of the organization. Finally, José Luis Alvarez Santacristina "Txelis" was the only non-Basque in the leadership group. With a master's degree in philosophy from the Sorbonne, Alvarez was the ideological and intellectual leader of the organization. Although Alvarez had never taken part in any act of violence, he was regarded by police as the leader most deeply committed to a hard-line nationalist position.

In spite of the French police raids and arrests and the rising number of ETA members being deported from France, Spanish government spokesman Javier Solana continued to hold open the possibility for a dialogue with ETA. In a press conference in Bilbao on October 6, where he was accompanied by the civil governor of Vizcaya, Iñaki Lopez, and the Spanish government representative to the Basque Autonomous Community, Julen Elgorriaga, Solana asserted that such contacts were not under way at that time, but that in principle the way was open for them to resume.[24] However, he reiterated that Spain's approach to dealing with ETA rested on four pillars: police and other law enforcement measures; international cooperation, especially with the French; social reintegration, or selective amnesty; and a broadly based political accord in Spain against terrorism. There was little in his remarks that would lead ETA to believe that Spain would look with favor on political negotiations.

Nevertheless, during the first half of October the two parties were discreetly seeking ways to initiate contacts once again. The French newspaper *Le Monde* reported on October 10 that the Spanish government was in contact with ETA in Algeria, a report immediately denied at the Spanish interior ministry.[25] On October 12, there was allegedly another meeting in Algeria between Etxebeste and Ballesteros, also subsequently denied by Madrid when press accounts of the meeting appeared nearly three weeks later.[26] President González, on a trip to Argentina when the reports were made public, refused comment about contacts in Algeria.[27] He added, however, that "the Spanish government said publicly that it was ready to carry out contacts that might facilitate a way out of the violence, as long as that is not interpreted as political negotiation; that was our position when we said it, it is still our position today, and it will continue being our position, because my obligation is to try to eliminate terrorism."[28] He might also have added that the Algerian connection had reached a turning point.

The Elgorriaga-Etxebeste Meetings: October–November 1987

Barely two weeks after the arrest of Arrospide and the intensified police pressure in France, a highly significant series of meetings began in Algeria between Antxon Etxebeste and the Spanish government delegate to the Basque Autonomous Community, Julen Elgorriaga. These meetings were held in two phases: the first on October 15 and 16, the second on November 21. The significance of these talks lay not only in the topics included in their agenda but also in the symbolic importance attached to the representatives. For the first time, Spain sent to the talks someone who was not a police official, and who could speak for the country's political leadership. In the Spanish system of autonomous communities, the post of delegate is an important one, since it is this person's responsibility to ensure that laws and policies of the central government in Madrid are properly implemented and enforced at the level of the autonomous community. In naming Elgorriaga to this position in the Basque Autonomous Community, one of the most sensitive of such posts in the country, the Spanish government had already expressed their complete confidence in him, and had vested in him considerable stature. Persons close to ETA were later to criticize the choice of Elgorriaga, partly because he was not from the inner circle of the PSOE leadership and partly because he was thought to be a man of limited intelligence and ability.[29]

There was also a major change on ETA's side of the table. In earlier contacts with Ballesteros, Etxebeste had maintained that he was consenting to meet only out of deference to the expressed wishes of the Algerians, and that he was acting simply as an intermediary to convey information from one party to the other. The arrest of Arrospide, the disruption of ETA's leadership in France, and the deportation of more ETA members to Algeria increased Etxebeste's importance to the organization. Accordingly, the ETA leadership now gave him the authority necessary to engage in negotiations.[30]

Despite this symbolic significance, the meetings were not especially productive at first.[31] According to ETA's version, the talks showed that Madrid's position had not evolved, and that it continued to be based on the legitimacy of the post-Franco reforms. When Etxebeste raised the issues in the KAS Alternative, especially the status of Navarra, Elgorriaga responded that the Spanish government would not enter into political negotiations with ETA because there already existed a suitable framework for dealing with these issues, which was the Spanish constitution and the Basque autonomy statute. The most he could promise was to fulfill the autonomy statute to the fullest extent possible, to reduce Spanish police and other law enforcement agencies in the Basque Country, and to treat the question of Navarra within the channels already existing in the two autonomous communities. While the question of Navarra offered one serious obstacle to an accord, a much more difficult barrier was ETA's insistence that an end to violence must incorporate a recognition by Madrid of the Basques' right of self-determination. Elgorriaga replied that such a recognition would be impossible in Spain's existing constitutional structure, and it would be politically suicidal for Felipe González as well.

In response, Etxebeste charged that the so-called reforms were imposed by Madrid, that they were little more than Francoism with some vestiges of democracy, and that they had been rejected by the Basques in earlier referenda. Other signs that the Basques regarded the current system as nonlegitimate were the heavy "no" vote on the NATO referendum in March 1986 and the steady increase in the popular vote for Herri Batasuna, which demonstrated that the Basque electorate was rejecting the moderate "reformist" parties such as the PNV. In the 1987 municipal and provincial elections, for example, HB emerged as the leading Basque party in the four provinces, including Navarra, with about one-fifth of the total vote.

Etxebeste also raised the question of the treatment of ETA members in the event of a cessation of hostilities. The ETA communiqué quotes Elgorriaga's offer of "a dignified way out, incorporation of prisoners into the country's political and social life with their heads high, as well as the gradual freedom of the prisoners." Later press accounts suggested that Elgorriaga and Etxebeste discussed the possibility of a "covered amnesty" (amnistía encubierta) for ETA prisoners convicted of blood crimes. According to this formula, if ETA would renounce the use of violence, Spain would begin to release these prisoners gradually with the understanding that they would leave Spain and not return for a long time.

Despite the fact that there had been no narrowing of the gap between the two positions, Etxebeste requested another meeting while keeping the contacts secret. The two men agreed to meet again in about three weeks. In the meantime, the Spanish government sought to strengthen its bargaining position both at home and in France. On November 5, the non-partisan antiterrorist pact was signed in Madrid by all political parties except the Basque party, Eusko Alkartasuna. This pact was subsequently ratified by the Spanish parliament on November 10. On November 9, Felipe González met with French president Mitterand and Prime Minister Chirac to request that they step up the pressure against the ETA leadership still in France. Apparently, it was González's hope that Paris could detain the members of the ETA executive committee and deport them to Algeria, where Madrid could then negotiate directly with the organization's leaders.

The second meeting between Etxebeste and Elgorriaga took place on November 21, at which time a highly significant exchange occurred. According to ETA's version of this meeting, as contained in its January 1988 communiqué, Elgorriaga affirmed "that the Spanish government was ready to take up political questions with ETA, and that the continuation of conversations is conditioned on there not being any more 'executions,' in response to which the ETA representative stressed that to place conditions on the will to establish a channel to reach a fundamental agreement casts a dark shadow over the talks, which totally blocks the supposed will of the PSOE to resolve the conflict. With the repeated leaks of information, as well as in this question of principle, there is underlying a kind of formula to provoke the breakdown of conversations, an indication that, upon reaching this point, the real powers and their agents are dragging along serious contradictions, and they are trying to undermine the [negotiating] table with sophistries that are difficult to explain, but which will serve them as justification before international public opinion to accuse ETA of having broken off the conversations."[32]

Elgorriaga's version differs from the ETA communiqué slightly, but significantly. In an interview published in February 1988, Elgorriaga said, "when Antxon understood that the government would never negotiate with ETA on political questions, which in a democracy is the responsibility of the political parties, he asked what I thought about the PSOE talking directly to HB. I answered that that might be acceptable, that that was what we were trying to do, to talk and to stop the killing, and that where you discussed political questions was in the parliament."[33] With that brief exchange, the ground had been prepared for what would prove to be the most significant achievement of these talks, the fashioning of the two-track formula.

Actually, there had been hints of a two-track approach earlier than this November 1987 meeting, which we will review in our concluding chapter. So long as ETA insisted, however, that they had to be directly involved in all political negotiations, and so long as Madrid refused adamantly to be involved in such talks, the issue of political negotiations continued to block real progress on these deeply rooted questions.

Through the latter half of November, however, there was considerable speculation in the Spanish and Basque press that ETA and Madrid were close to establishing the two-track formula as a way of resolving the impasse over political negotiations. On November 15, *El País* reported that the Spanish government was holding "sporadic contacts" with HB leaders parallel to the conversations going on in Algeria, and that ETA was willing to go along with this approach because of the serious reverses the organization had suffered during the preceding several months.[34] On November 22, one day after the second meeting between Etxebeste and Elgorriaga, *Deia* reported that Madrid was eager to achieve a settlement of the conflict before the PSOE had to convene new elections. While elections were mandated by 1990, PSOE leaders envisioned moving them up to 1989 to make them coincide with voting for members of the European parliament. Having negotiated a settlement with ETA would be the best possible campaign propaganda, and would ensure the election of the socialists to another four-year term. This article also cited the two-track approach as an attempt to avoid the problem of political negotiations, and listed as the principal issues to be resolved amnesty, the status of Navarra, the removal of Spanish police from the Basque Country, and the recognition of the right of self-determination. Unquestionably, the chief obstacles remained Navarra and self-determination.

Once again, however, a tragic event interrupted progress in negotiations. The gains registered in the two meetings between Elgorriaga and Etxebeste were all but cancelled out by yet another strategically timed act of violence. On December 11, ETA placed a car bomb, estimated at forty to fifty kilograms of plastic explosive or amonal, near the family living quarters of the Guardia Civil barracks in Zaragoza. The bomb, which was detonated at 6:30 in the morning on a Friday, killed eleven, including five young children. The repulsion and condemnation of this act of violence were virtually universal throughout Spain and the Basque Country. One week later, on December 18, the Spanish government formally broke off further talks with ETA as long as killings of this sort continued.

The Madrid Antiterrorist Pact:
September–November 1987

The idea of an anti-ETA pact or accord among all the political parties in Spain, including those in the Basque Country, was not a new initiative. In April 1982, PSOE secretary general Txiki Benegas had proposed a five-point antiterrorist program that included "a political agreement of the democratic institutions, parties, and labor and cultural organizations."[35] Socialist senator Ana Miranda had proposed a similar antiterrorist pact in an article that appeared in a 1984 publication.[36] These early proposals had as their principal objective the isolation of both ETA and Herri Batasuna from the rest of the Basque political spectrum.

Shortly after the Hipercor bombing on June 19, Benegas began a series of secret meetings with key leaders of Spain's principal political parties.[37] These meetings, held in discreet restaurants or private homes in Madrid, were to explore the possibility of fashioning an antiterrorist statement of principles that all the country's parties would subscribe to in order to demonstrate their solidarity in the face of similar attacks in the future. Basque parties, particularly the PNV, were invited to these sessions even though they felt generally irrelevant to the process, and they so informed Benegas. By the end of the summer, the socialist leader had sufficient support for his idea to reveal his initiative to the public.

There then followed another round of meetings that were openly acknowledged but closed to the press. By the middle of September, Benegas had met with leaders of the following: the principal conservative opposition party, Alianza Popular (AP); the key center-right party of Adolfo Suárez, the Centro Democrático Social (CDS); the smaller center-right Partido Demócrata Popular (PDP); the Catalan party, Convergència i Unió (CiU); the Partido Liberal (PL); and the left-wing Izquierda Unida (IU).[38] By the end of the month, he had added the three Basque parties likely to be willing to sign such a document—PNV, Eusko Alkartasuna (EA), and Euskadiko Ezkerra (EE). Herri Batasuna was not included in this (or any other) round of meetings.

Out of these discussions, Benegas concluded that there was enough sentiment for an antiterrorist agreement to warrant pursuing the idea further. The next step would be for President González to talk with other political party leaders to secure their commitment and support. However, these initial talks also led to the conclusion that an antiterrorist pact signed in Madrid would be of little value unless it were matched by an equivalent accord among the Basque parties and the Basque government in Vitoria. The involvement of the Basque parties was especially stressed by Adolfo Suárez in his meeting with González in early October. Thus, a second track of discussions was launched by Basque President Ardanza on September 25 in a speech to the Basque parliament in which he issued a call to all parties with parliamentary representation (including Herri Batasuna, even though their seats in the parliament remained unoccupied) to meet with him in preliminary talks leading to a Basque antiterrorist accord. This second agreement eventually became much more controversial and more significant than the Madrid pact.

By early October, Benegas had circulated among the leaders of all the political parties a draft statement that consisted of six points.[39] Even though this draft bore little resemblance to the statement eventually approved, it is worth noting its principal provisions. Points one and two were general statements that rejected the use of violence in a democratic system and asserted the obligation of the state to combat terrorism while maintaining a regime of laws and individual rights. Point three underscored the need to improve police methods and intelligence gathering, and called for improved coordination between Spanish and Basque law enforcement authorities. Point four dealt with the need for improved international cooperation to meet the terrorist challenge; while point five called upon all citizens to work for the elimination of fanaticism and intolerance in Spanish society.

For our purposes, point six held the key statements. After stressing the need to avoid public discussions of terrorism, the last paragraph rejected "the imposition of the political pretensions of a minority over the majority will of the citizens. This would be the equivalent of replacing the popular will and the legitimation of the efficacy of violence to achieve political objectives. [Therefore], there is no room for negotiations with terrorists over institutional and political questions, these aspects being reserved for the democratic decisions of the citizens through their organs of representation and government." The last paragraph closed with a reiteration of the application of "social reintegration" measures for terrorists who give up their violent activity.

In October, Ardanza held his first round of talks with Basque party leaders. On October 8, Julen Guimon and José Manuel Barquero of AP and Alfredo Marco Tobar of CDS visited the president's residence, Ajuria Enea, in separate meetings; and on October 14, the president met with representatives of EA (Iñaki Oliberi and Juan Porres) and of EE (Kepa Aulestia and Martin Auzmendi). On October 13, Ardanza, through his chief of staff, Jon Azua, invited Herri Batasuna to send its representatives to Ajuria Enea; and on October 20, HB leaders Tasio Erkizia and Josu Iraeta met with Ardanza—only the second time the coalition had gone to the president's residence, the first time since Ardanza became president.[40] The next day, October 21, Ardanza met with PNV president Xabier Arzalluz and another PNV leader, Josu Bergara. This round of meetings was concluded on November 2, when Ardanza met with Txiki Benegas to resolve a number of pressing issues facing the governing coalition, including the Basque antiterrorist pact.

Meanwhile in Madrid González continued his meetings with

key Spanish leaders: on October 5 with CDS leader Adolfo Suárez; on the sixth with AP chief Antonio Hernandez Mancha; and on the ninth with Arzalluz. By this time a new ingredient had been injected into the picture: pressure from France.[41] The police raids that stemmed from the arrest of ETA leader Santiago Arrospide on September 30 had provoked much criticism of the Chirac government from French human rights activists; and Paris now insisted that there be a statement from Spain that unequivocally condemned ETA terrorism and invited international collaboration in the antiterrorist struggle. Such a document would justify further police pressure against Basques in France should it be necessary.

On October 22, presidents González and Ardanza met in Madrid to coordinate the preparation of the two antiterrorist statements. Ardanza emphasized to the Spanish president that the question of Basque self-determination would not be raised in the Vitoria statement since he had made it clear that these discussions were being conducted within the existing statutory framework, that is, the Basque autonomy statute. However, the Basque president also stressed his belief that a suitable solution to the violence of ETA would include amnesty for blood crimes and some formula that would draw Navarra and the Basque Autonomous Community closer together.[42] The two leaders also discussed the relative priority of the two statements and the proper sequence that they would follow in signing and ratifying them. They agreed that the Basque statement would come first, and the Spanish pact would follow with commitments to the principles incorporated in the Basque agreement. As we shall see, this sequence proved to be impossible to achieve, and the Basque accord was signed more than two months after the Spanish agreement.[43]

As a result of the discussions González and Benegas held with other party leaders during October, the initial draft statement underwent major modifications. The final statement consisted of five points, the first of which was most significant for our analysis.[44] The opening paragraph began by reiterating that the basis for the country's antiterrorist policy continued to be the March 1985 resolution of the Basque parliament, especially in that document's rejection of "political negotiations." In language that recalled the PNV-PSE agreement of the preceding February, the paragraph continued: "We denounce the lack of legitimacy of ETA to express the

will of the Basque people, and, consequently, we reject their pre-
tension to negotiate the political problems of the Basque people,
which must only be done between the political parties with parliamentary representation, the Basque government and the Spanish
government." The remainder of the pact contained these principles:
that the Spanish antiterrorist law should be abolished and its principal provisions absorbed into the country's regular penal code,
thereby eliminating terrorism as a crime meriting special treatment; that judges and courts throughout the European Community
should have the authority to punish terrorist acts committed in any
other EC member country; that information mechanisms should
be established between the government and the signatory parties
to facilitate the fight against terrorism; and finally, that the signa-
tories of the Spanish pact support the Basque initiative and would,
at the appropriate time, "share" the principles of the Basque accord.
Without knowing the exact shape of the Basque agreement, many
Spanish leaders were unwilling to commit themselves to anything
more decisive than this.[45]

As the proposed date for signing the Madrid pact drew near, two
major problems threatened to block what Benegas and González
most wanted: a consensus among all the parties of Spain and of
the Basque Country, which they defined as near unanimity, with
only Herri Batasuna refusing to sign. After meeting with Benegas
in Madrid on November 4, EA representative Joseba Azkarraga announced that his party would not sign the pact for two reasons:
first, because EA opposed references to European Community involvement, fearing that this formula would be used to cover and
justify increased anti-Basque pressure in France; and second, the
refusal of Madrid to guarantee that the Spanish government would
uphold the commitments undertaken in the Basque antiterrorist
accord, still to be written and signed. In this objection, EA was
simply reiterating their oft-stated position, that a final solution to
the problem of ETA insurgency had to lie with the democratically
elected representatives of the Basque people.[46]

Much more serious was the refusal of the PNV to sign the
accord until several other long-standing conflicts between Madrid
and Vitoria were cleared away. Of these, the most pressing had to do
with the negotiation of a new *cupo*, the sum of money the Basque
government had to pay to Madrid in return for services rendered by

the Spanish government in the Basque Autonomous Community. The PNV believed that the existing cupo was disadvantageous and unfair to the Basque government, and they chose this opportunity to hold the antiterrorist pact hostage in order to gain some ground on the unrelated issue.[47] The PNV and the Basque government were also angered by the refusal of Benegas to affirm Spanish guarantees of the elements of the Basque agreement still in the discussion stage.

In the end, EA refused to sign the accord, as did, of course, Herri Batasuna. The PNV did finally sign, but only after Benegas personally threatened to dissolve the PNV-PSE governing coalition in Vitoria if the PNV did not sign. Thus, the Madrid antiterrorist pact was signed on November 5 and ratified by the Spanish parliament on November 10. The scene now shifted to Vitoria, where, for the next two months, Basque political leaders would try to fashion their own antiterrorism statement.

The Vitoria Antiterrorist Pact:
November 1987–January 1988

President Ardanza began the second round of talks with Basque party leaders on November 18, buoyed by the news that HB had decided to continue to participate, at least for the time being.[48] It was apparent from the beginning, however, that finding a meaningful formula that would satisfy everyone would be extremely difficult. All parties were agreed that the current accord should go beyond the 1985 Basque parliament resolution, but there was little consensus beyond that about what should go into the pact.[49] Herri Batasuna wanted to use the statement as an opportunity to sketch out a radical restructuring of the Basque status in Spain that emphasized their inherent right of self-determination. Eusko Alkartasuna supported a strong statement on self-determination, but also wanted more pragmatic issues addressed, including the scope of authority of the Basque police and the problem of Navarra. The party of Carlos Garaikoetxea also wanted to form a commission of the Basque parliament charged with defining what was meant by "the full development of the autonomy statute."[50] The Spanish parties, especially the more conservative Alianza Popular, were opposed to including such "political" issues in the antiterrorist statement, since to do so seemed to suggest that ETA's insurgency had some legitimate justification rooted in questions that could be resolved through political measures. The issue of amnesty for persons convicted of blood crimes also promised to be a major obstacle. HB supported a total amnesty, but said it did not go far enough; the other Basque parties wanted general amnesty after ETA ceased its attacks; the PSOE said that individual amnesty or social reintegration was as far as they would go at that time; the other Spanish parties were totally opposed to amnesty under any circumstances.

The opening stages of this second round of meetings did not go well for Ardanza. After a second meeting of HB representatives with the president, the radical coalition announced on November 26 that it was withdrawing from the consultation process, and would shortly present its own plan for "national reconstruction." On November 30, HB unveiled its plan to secure 500,000 signatures on a petition calling for Madrid to recognize the right of the Basques to self-determination. An attempt to bring together leaders of the PNV, the PSOE, and HB to negotiate some of these difficult questions away from public scrutiny was vetoed by the socialists. The one hopeful sign was an agreement achieved with Euskadiko Ezkerra on December 2 that they would sign the pact as it was presently being drafted.[51]

On December 4, Ardanza sent to all the parties an initial draft statement (what came to be referred to as the "zero draft") for reactions and comments. The agreement, whose official title was "Accord for the Democratic Normalization and Pacification of Euskadi," consisted of a preamble and thirteen points. Among other things, the text reaffirmed the validity of the Basque autonomy statute but claimed that it was being developed too slowly. Without naming them, the draft appealed to ETA to lay down its weapons, and to HB to participate in the representative institutions of the Basque Country. Amnesty was supported for all ETA members who agreed to abandon armed struggle, including implicitly those convicted of blood crimes. As for Navarra, the draft called for the creation of joint commissions that could develop linkages between the two autonomous communities. Finally, the text reaffirmed the 1985 resolution in rejecting any political negotiations with ETA, asserting that such issues had to be decided by the democratically elected representatives of the people.

Ardanza hoped to have the draft signed and ready for parliamentary ratification by December 23, before the Christmas holiday season interrupted the business of politics. He was unduly optimistic. Criticisms of the zero draft were voiced as soon as it appeared. Eusko Alkartasuna complained that the document did not go far enough in defending the right of self-determination; the socialists opposed any statement dealing with self-government or questioning the status of the autonomy statute. Both the PSOE and Alianza Popular opposed the wording of the amnesty provision, which seemed to favor pardons for all ETA members, including those convicted of blood crimes. From several Navarrese parties came thunderous criticism that the status of Navarra should even be considered in a document about which they were not consulted. Benegas delivered to Ardanza a completely new proposed draft and Garaikoetxea submitted a number of amendments, primarily having to do with the question of self-determination and the scope of the autonomy statute. On December 11, while Ardanza was completing the second round of discussions on the pact, ETA bombed the Guardia Civil barracks in Zaragoza. The popular reaction against this act changed the dynamics of the Basque discussions, stiffening conservative opposition to a general amnesty and making it more difficult to discover a formula satisfactory to all parties concerned.[52]

The week of December 21 was filled with numerous meetings, some open and others private, at which these many details were discussed. Ardanza and Benegas met on December 21, at which time the president assured the PSOE leader that the pact would not mention the subject of self-determination (the same assurance he had given President González in October).[53] On December 22, Ardanza met again with Xabier Arzalluz, who stressed the importance of having general consensus on the agreement (excluding HB) in order to show ETA that they now stood alone.[54]

On Christmas Eve, Ardanza sent to all the parties his second draft, slightly shortened to twelve points.[55] There were some nuanced changes in the references to Navarra, and the wording of the amnesty section was changed to make it clear that persons convicted of blood crimes would not be given pardons. The second draft, now referred to as "draft one," included a commitment that the Basque government would seek to mobilize "social reaction against terrorism," and would undertake an agreement with Madrid that would guarantee coordinated action against ETA. Again, ETA and HB were not mentioned by name but only by allusion.[56] Immediate reactions were negative. The Spanish parties still objected to the wording—indeed, even to its very inclusion—on the Navarra problem; and EA still complained that the document was too weak on the self-determination question. What did not change was the wording on negotiations; it was clear that no one wanted to alter their stance on political negotiations with ETA.

Ardanza now took a calculated risk to achieve a breakthrough on the pact. Despite the major obstacles that remained to an accord, he convoked a "summit" meeting of all the parties on January 5, 1988, and announced that he intended to keep the representatives in session more or less continuously until they either signed the pact or walked out and declared the process ended in failure. The first session lasted from 11:00 A.M. on Tuesday, January 5, until 1:30 A.M. on Wednesday. Each of the six parties was represented by its president or general secretary (Benegas for PSOE; Arzalluz for PNV; Aulestia for EE; Guimon for AP; and Marco Tobar for CDS) except for EA, which sent Oliberi as a substitute for Garaikoetxea who was recovering from a knee operation.[57] Because of a news blackout agreed to by the participants, the degree of progress registered by the meeting was not immediately apparent; but Ardanza professed to be "optimistic" about the prospects for an agreement.

The second session of the summit was convened at 11:30 A.M. on Sunday, January 10, and lasted until nearly midnight. Guimon from AP proposed that the pact be separated into two documents; one a condemnation of terrorism, the other aimed at clarifying the issues of self-government and the autonomy statute. This proposal was rejected by all the other participants. The session concluded without agreement, but with positive signs that one was within reach.[58]

The third and final session began at 10:00 A.M. on Monday, January 11, and would not come to a close until nearly 3:00 A.M. on Tuesday. Emotions were high throughout the day. News reporters peering through the windows of the meeting room saw Benegas at one point gather his papers and prepare to leave, only to be persuaded to resume his seat. Marco Tobar of CDS at one point threatened to leave as well. Shortly before 3:00 A.M. Oliberi of EA walked out of the meeting, announcing that his party would not sign the pact because of its inadequate statements on Navarra and the Basque police.[59]

Ardanza now made plans to have the pact signed by the remaining five parties at noon that same day, January 12. After a number of hurried telephone calls, including several by Txiki Benegas, it was agreed that EA should be allowed to sign the pact with reservations. This option was transmitted to Garaikoetxea, who accepted it. The signing was postponed until later in the day. At 4:00 P.M. Oliberi returned to the meeting; and at 5:00 the document was signed. Its content was little changed from the second Ardanza draft. There was one reservation, that by EA to the wording on the Basque police.[60] On January 19, the Basque parliament formally ratified the pact unanimously.

Reactions to the Basque antiterrorist pact were predictable. Herri Batasuna called it "a declaration of war against the patriotic left," and rejected the accord as the result of manipulations by the socialists.[61] ETA labeled as "shameful" the participation of the PNV and EA in the agreement, and claimed that the accord had been based on the false premise that ETA was weakened after the French police raids the preceding autumn.[62] All other parties generally approved of the document, some with greater fervor than others. Press reaction throughout Spain was overwhelmingly favorable. At last, it seemed, ETA and HB were isolated from the rest of the Basque political parties.[63] In a public opinion survey conducted for Basque television between January 12 and 15, 46 percent of the respondents in the Basque Country thought that the accord would be "decisive" for the pacification of Euskadi; 23 percent thought it would be worthless; and 28 percent had doubts about its effectiveness.[64]

Despite the intensity with which the Vitoria antiterrorist pact was debated, it seems in retrospect to have had little if any real impact on the ETA insurgency. On several occasions in early 1988, President Ardanza attempted to reconvene the group of six leaders who had hammered out the final document to try to restore some of the momentum and solidarity that emerged in those marathon bargaining sessions. These efforts failed when the PSOE and EA refused to attend.[65] It was not until mid-May that the Spanish parliament fulfilled its part of the bargain by ratifying their support for the Vitoria pact, again without the signature of Eusko Alkartasuna.[66]

On one thing, however, the parties to the Vitoria pact remained in complete accord: the question of political negotiations with ETA. In July 1988, the newly appointed head of the Basque government's department of the interior, Juan Lasa, declared his support for a negotiated settlement with ETA. When asked by reporters if such negotiations could have a "political character," Lasa replied: "If such a case were to appear, why not? Political negotiations are a difficult subject, but to put an end to the conflict that way would be well worth the effort, and the majority of the people are anxious for us to make that attempt. We will not lack the will or the energy to make the effort, and neither will Madrid."[67] The public outcry from across the political spectrum against Lasa's statement forced not only a correction by Lasa himself but a reaffirmation by Basque government spokesman Joseba Arregui that the government had no intention of withdrawing from the Vitoria pact.

The Truce Communiqué:
December 1987–February 1988

Julen Elgorriaga had planned to fly to Algeria in mid-December to hear from Etxebeste what ETA's response would be to the proposal delivered to the insurgents at the November meeting of the two men.[68] The Zaragoza bombing caused these plans to be suspended, at least temporarily. While it was official Spanish policy that talks could not be resumed as long as violent attacks like that of Zaragoza were being carried out, informally it was generally accepted that the meetings between Elgorriaga and Etxebeste were only postponed, and that they would probably resume, perhaps within a month.

Such an interpretation seems warranted judging from the next communication ETA received from Madrid. On December 18, the same day that the Spanish government formally broke off contacts, Rafael Vera flew to Algeria to deliver an important message to Etxebeste. He did not meet directly with the ETA representative, but instead sent him a message through Algerian authorities. In the message, Madrid requested a truce of sixty days to give them time to renew contacts, and asked that ETA refrain from any provocative armed attacks like the Zaragoza barracks bombing during this time. If ETA would accept this proposal and avoid violent actions, Madrid would commit itself to renewing the meetings to prepare a "negotiating commission" (mesa de negociaciones). At the same time, contacts would be established between the PSOE and HB, subsequently to be expanded to other Basque parties, presumably to begin discussing political questions. Apparently ETA perceived the Vera message as an offer to begin political negotiations if the insurgents would refrain from armed attacks for sixty days.[69]

Press accounts of the period suggest that the Spanish government was not going to let the Zaragoza bombing deter them from further meetings with ETA; but the insurgents had to understand the terms of continuing the meetings.[70] El País, quoting government sources, reported that "the government will probably not demand a formal ETA truce declaration, but what is clear is that the terrorists will have to be convinced that no one is going to negotiate anything under the blackmail of terror."

Thus, as the new year began, ETA sought to follow up on what appeared to them to be a grand opportunity to get Madrid to the negotiating table. Despite serious opposition within the ETA leadership to a renewal of further talks, the organization had gone so far as to seek the assistance of a group of legal experts who were asked to elaborate a constitutional formula that would permit a declaration of the Basque right of self-determination. There were even being circulated within ETA statements that looked beyond the Algerian negotiations to define the new role of the organization when armed struggle was no longer being employed.[71]

In retrospect, it is difficult to see how the various parties to the conflict could imagine that they were actually close to a negotiated settlement. The Spanish government's absolute opposition to any sort of political negotiations was made clear in the course of the discussions that led to the two antiterrorist pacts. Moreover, with the exception of Herri Batasuna, Basque political parties also rejected any negotiations that went beyond relatively simple matters of security, public order, and amnesty. On the other side, HB leader Iñaki Esnaola said in a televised debate on January 20 that "ETA is not going to sit down at the [negotiating] table just so their prisoners can return to the street."[72] There remained, then, several serious obstacles to a settlement that seem not to have been accurately perceived—or at least not taken seriously—by either side.

Despite these missed perceptions, the dynamic of proposal and counterproposal went forward. According to El País, citing a report in the Madrid weekly El Globo, the truce proposal had its origins in a document drafted by the ETA leadership in France and debated by the leading elements of the KAS on January 11 and 12.[73] ETA members in prison as well as those still in hiding in Spain were delivered copies and given a chance to comment on its terms. Spanish police later claimed that their intelligence service had obtained a copy of this early version, and they were well informed about the proposal before it was received in Madrid. On about January 20, Iñaki Esnaola delivered a copy of the original draft to Antxon Etxebeste, who was given the chance to comment on it as well. Sometime between January 20 and January 27, Algerian intermediaries delivered the final version of the communiqué to Spanish authorities; and on January 29, the San Sebastián daily Egin published the full communiqué.[74]

According to one close observer, Spanish officials were infuriated at what they deemed to be the premature disclosure of the truce proposal, thus making it appear as if ETA had taken the initiative in the negotiations.[75] Actually, however, ETA had earlier transmitted an unofficial version of the proposal to Madrid, and were waiting on an informal response before proceeding with its publication. In fact, according to one observer, ETA had even prepared several different versions of the actual truce proposal, depending on which response they got from Madrid. As time passed, however, and no response from Madrid was received, the organization decided to go ahead with the publication of the communiqué.[76]

The communiqué is actually addressed to several audiences, first of which is the Basque people. ETA issued the communiqué, according to the opening paragraph, to give the Basque people the full story on the meetings that had been going on in Algeria, to counteract the "poisonous psychological offensive unfolded by the oppressor Spanish state." The communiqué makes clear from the outset that "the only accord that can lead to an armistice is the signing of the KAS Alternative." Any other hope is based on "false expectations" and "ignores the Basque national reality." The Spanish government was waging a vigorous anti-ETA policy both within Spain and abroad, covered over by what appeared to be a willingness to negotiate. Despite this offensive, ETA wanted to reiterate once again its willingness to negotiate a settlement. The communiqué then went on to describe the several contacts between ETA and Spanish representatives, including Ballesteros on September 18, 1987, Elgorriaga on October 15 and 16 and November 21, and Vera on December 18. Several paragraphs of the communiqué were devoted to the antiterrorist pacts, which were seen by ETA as not only illegitimate, but based on an incorrect perception of the organization's weakness.

The final paragraphs of the communiqué contained the specific ETA proposal. First, there had to be a preliminary meeting between representatives of the Spanish government and the Basque National Liberation Movement (MLNV), which would give each party an opportunity to verify the other's "authentic disposition to dialogue." An extremely important point in the communiqué, but one frequently overlooked by subsequent interpretations, was that the rest of the truce offer was conditioned on the outcome of this preliminary meeting.[77] Assuming that the preliminary meeting concluded successfully, then ETA was prepared to make this four-point offer:

1. "As a sample of their disposition to dialogue, during a mutually agreed upon period no longer than 60 days, ETA would observe an official partial truce that would involve the provisional cessation of executions, except in the case of chance confrontations."

2. "During this same period, as a counterpart [to the above], police hostilities should cease throughout Euskal Herria." [Note: This formula would also include the Basque region of France.]

3. "The conversations should be renewed in the period immediately following the official confirmation of the truce, under the premise of a future [negotiating] commission made up of both delegations at the highest level, whose composition should be studied by each of the parties, along with the agenda,

with a political content, to be established by both delegations, and with the expressed willingness to constitute a negotiating framework leading to a negotiated political solution to the conflict."

4. "[The offer also urges] the acceptance of the mediating role of the Algerian government in the conversations, in effect as their political guarantor, with the commitment to enforce the respect of the accords."

With this communiqué, ETA sought a solution to the two long-standing obstacles to a settlement. To solve the problem of the timing of a cease-fire, ETA proposed a two-stage meeting. First, before hostilities ceased, a preliminary meeting would confirm the willingness of both sides to continue negotiations. Then, a cease-fire would take effect, followed by further negotiations. To solve the problem of political negotiations, ETA accepted the two-track approach by agreeing to vest their negotiating authority in the hands of another organization, the MLNV, led by Herri Batasuna. Nevertheless, the initial reaction of the Spanish government, through its spokesman, Javier Solana, was disappointing. Virtually all of the points in the communiqué were rejected: there would be no political negotiations; the cease-fire had to be in place before any further talks began; Madrid would not reduce its level of police activity in pursuit of ETA; and the role of Algeria as a mediator was unacceptable.[78]

Shortly after the publication of the communiqué in *Egin*, the matter was confused considerably when Julen Elgorriaga revealed that two truce proposals had been drafted by ETA. The first, an internal document meant solely for circulation among ETA rank-and-file members, differed substantially from the public version. Where the *Egin* version made the KAS Alternative the sine qua non of negotiations, the internal document makes no such reference. And while the public proposal quotes Elgorriaga at the November 21 meeting as saying "the government is ready to take up political questions with ETA" (a quote denied by Elgorriaga himself), the internal version has the Spanish representative saying simply that "the government makes the continuation of talks conditional on a cessation of executions."[79] Spanish experts in terrorism believed that the "softer" version had been favored by those in Algeria, but the organization's leadership in France wanted a "harder" version in order not to appear too conciliatory, especially to their own rank-and-file members.[80] Persons interviewed in the preparation of this book believed that the different versions were prepared so that ETA could present a public proposal that would match what they anticipated would be the Spanish public response. Since ETA had sounded out Madrid informally on the "soft" version and received no response, they went ahead with the publication of the "hard" version. Once again, observers were led to interpret these differences as significant or not depending on their view of negotiations generally.

For the next several weeks, the press buzzed with analyses of the ETA proposal, rumors, and leaked reports of meetings, either under way or in the offing.[81] One well-informed observer, Basque journalist Luis Aizpeolea, writing in the San Sebastián daily *El Diario Vasco*, speculated that the ETA truce proposal was an attempt by the insurgents to gain the initiative after suffering several major reversals in the preceding months, especially the Basque antiterrorist pact, public revulsion at the Hipercor and Zaragoza bombings, and the massive arrests in France.[82] Madrid, momentarily caught off guard by the proposal, reacted cautiously and continued to insist on a verifiable cease-fire before joining ETA at the negotiating table. On both sides, concluded Aizpeolea, there were elements that genuinely wanted to re-open negotiations, but there were others who merely wanted to use the current proposals and counterproposals to manipulate the images held of their organization by the public. It was premature, he wrote, to say which elements would gain the upper hand, but "soon we will know."[83]

On Wednesday, February 3, *Deia* reported that Julen Elgorriaga would be in Algeria the following Sunday, February 7, to "sound out" ETA representatives about their willingness to comply with Madrid's demand for a cease-fire prior to renewing negotiations.[84] Elgorriaga immediately denied the reports, saying "I like Algeria, but not *that* much."[85] The next day, February 5, *El País* repeated the report, accompanied by a picture of Elgorriaga, that "the government will send a delegate to Algeria to talk with ETA about the cease-fire."[86] According to this report, Elgorriaga was going to suggest that Herri Batasuna take over negotiations about "political affairs," and the Spanish government would facilitate "a dignified way out" for the organization to abandon armed struggle.[87] This time, the response was a bit more ambiguous. Government spokesman Solana said simply that "at this time there are no contacts with ETA," but he refused to confirm or deny the possibility of such contacts in the near future.[88]

On February 7, the day Elgorriaga was supposed to be in Algeria, *El Diario Vasco* published a long interview with him in which he asserted that contacts were not about to be renewed with ETA, that they would be re-established when the government was certain that ETA had stopped the killing, and that there was no truce yet.[89] "We will know," he said, "in several months."

Nevertheless, the desire to cease the violence and to get talks started was so strong that persons on both sides began to see tacit agreements where there were none. On February 12, *El País* reported that "a government emissary will talk with ETA leaders in Algiers at the end of the month or the beginning of March."[90] According to this report, the Spanish government was inclined to date the beginning of the cease-fire from January 29, the date of the publication of the truce proposal, so they could renew talks in Algeria on their own terms. Again, they overlooked the ETA demand that there be a preliminary meeting in Algeria before the cease-fire would take effect. On February 13, *Deia* quoted Herri Batasuna leader Jon Idígoras as saying that "members of HB and a [Spanish government] minister will go to Algiers in March" to form two negotiating commissions.[91] Again, the Spanish government misunderstood ETA's position on the cease-fire; ETA misunderstood the government's position on political negotiations.

If there was continued misunderstanding of both positions, it was not without clear warnings. On February 15, *Deia* published a report from the French news agency, France Press, that carried ETA's latest communiqué.[92] In the message, ETA warned that there was no truce in effect since "there has not been a full response to the requirements previously pointed out in our earlier communiqué." ETA said that to talk about a truce already in effect was an attempt by Madrid to manipulate the process, waiting for some ETA action to declare the truce violated and using this as the pretext for breaking off the talks. Once again the organization warned that a preliminary meeting had to take place before a truce could go into effect. Such a meeting had been planned for February 7 (as press reports had claimed), but had been postponed by Madrid. The Spanish government position was equally clearly spelled out. On February 16, *El País* reported that "the government demands guarantee that there will be no armed attacks during the negotiating process."[93]

As late as February 19, there were press reports that "ETA and the Spanish government could sign the Algiers accord before the end of the year."[94] These reports confirmed the acceptability of the two-track negotiating process, with Madrid and ETA resolving the issues of amnesty and a cease-fire, and with PSOE and HB representatives discussing political questions. Elgorriaga would continue his trips to Algeria to meet with Etxebeste, and a cease-fire was expected momentarily. What still remained unresolved, however, was the crucial question of timing. Even after the ETA communiqué of February 14, persons in Madrid were claiming that this was only a "war of words" more for the purpose of swaying public opinion than for conveying real content.

On February 20, Elgorriaga went to Algeria for what would prove to be his final meeting with Etxebeste. The ETA leader was expecting Elgorriaga to have for him the definitive answer to the January 29 proposal, including details on the negotiating commissions (names of those who would be sent from Madrid, the agenda, and so forth). Instead, Elgorriaga responded that he had not been given any of that information and that he was not empowered to discuss any political negotiations with ETA. His only mission was to discuss the much more limited question of a cease-fire. Press reports later emphasized that Elgorriaga said that the government would negotiate only amnesty and cease-fire questions, leaving the political issues to be negotiated elsewhere.[95] Etxebeste was furious at what he perceived to be betrayal. Elgorriaga was, in the words of one close observer, "left hanging in the air by Madrid."[96] The mutual misunderstandings, so clear in retrospect, had led finally to their inevitable conclusion: deadlock and a breakdown in negotiations.

Whatever the source of this confusion, the damage was done. On February 24, even while press reports continued to claim that a settlement was near,[97] ETA kidnapped a wealthy Spanish businessman named Emiliano Revilla from his Madrid home. In its follow-up communiqué, the organization denied that there had ever been a cease-fire in effect just because the Spanish government had claimed there was; and they declared that they had taken this action because of Madrid's slow response to their truce offer.[98] Others saw the kidnapping as a sign that ETA was desperate for money, or as an attempt by the organization to show the Spanish government that they were still capable of audacious attacks in the heart of Madrid, in "the mouth of the wolf" as one observer put it.[99] Whether impressed or not, the Spanish government declared that as long as Revilla was in ETA's control, there could be no negotiations.

During the summer of 1988, while I was in Euskadi conducting interviews for this book, there was a general feeling that beneath the surface efforts were being made to get talks started again with ETA. Even though officially nothing could be done until Revilla was released, unofficially the Spanish government was in contact with ETA so that upon the hostage's release, talks could begin almost immediately. Some people believed, as the Madrid daily *Diario 16* reported on August 16, that Algeria would not be the site for the next round of discussions, and Etxebeste would not be the intermediary.[100] In July, changes in the Spanish cabinet brought two Basques—José Luis Corcuera and Enrique Múgica—to head the ministries of interior and justice, respectively, a move seen by some as designed to place in these key positions people who would be more favorable toward a negotiated settlement. The government was also reported looking for someone who could serve as an intermediary to get negotiations started again.

Even ETA seemed disposed to talk in conciliatory terms. In an interview published by the magazine *Avui* on May 25, an ETA spokesman described the KAS Alternative as "a minimum program that could not be reduced." However, he continued, "what can be talked about and discussed and played around with are the forms of application of the points, of the formal aspects of the KAS Alternative. We can talk about the terms and modes of application, and in that we are totally open to dialogue. The Alternative cannot be discarded, but we can talk about how to install that new statute, what to do with the current one, . . . and what commissions need to be established so that the process can be developed."[101]

Early Sunday morning, October 30, 1988, ETA finally released

Emiliano Revilla, only a few meters from his home in the center of Madrid. His captivity, at 249 days the longest ever carried out by ETA, was brought to an end when his family finally succeeded in delivering ransom payments estimated in the press at some $10 million.[102] The following Wednesday, November 2, *Egin* published an ETA communiqué that repeated the offer of a cease-fire under the same terms that were offered in its January truce communiqué, and invited Madrid to return to the negotiating table in Algeria with Antxon Etxebeste. The Spanish government's response was to insist that there must be a cease-fire in effect before talks could begin. In the period between the two ETA communiqués, from January 29 to November 2, 1988, 13 people were killed by ETA attacks and 7 more were wounded.[103] These attacks brought to 562 the number of deaths attributed to ETA since 1968.

CHAPTER NINE

Obstacles to Peace

O N April 4, 1989, Euzkadi ta Askatasuna issued a communiqué in which they declared ended a cease-fire they had established eighty-five days earlier, on January 8. Despite a number of bombs placed alongside railroad tracks and in other public places, the absence of any bloodshed for the next few days gave hope that the organization would not immediately resume its violent attacks; but this hope was shattered on April 12 when a member of the Guardia Civil was shot to death in his car in the Bilbao suburb of Las Arenas.[1] By December, 19 more killings had been attributed to ETA to be added to the estimated 568 victims of ETA violence inflicted through the end of 1988.

What made this act of violence even more tragic was that it signaled the failure of a three-month-long attempt to negotiate an end to the war between ETA and the Spanish state. While it appears that the negotiators, meeting in Algeria, came closer to an agreement than at any time in the past, the collapse of the 1989 talks should not have surprised anyone, for the unfortunate fact is that, as we have seen, attempts to negotiate an end to this conflict have been going on literally since the day General Francisco Franco was buried. By my own count, based largely on materials in the public record and reviewed in the preceding pages, since November 1975 there have been at least twenty, and probably closer to thirty, separate and identifiable attempts to negotiate a cease-fire with ETA —an average of about one every six to eight months during the period up to July 1989 (see table 9.1). Some of these attempts were abortive and failed to lead even to preliminary contacts; some were little more than a single contact lasting several hours; others have extended over periods of three months or more, and have involved many meetings of perhaps a half dozen negotiators. All these efforts have one thing in common: with a few limited exceptions, they have all ended in failure.

It is comparatively easy to discard some of the more frequently heard reasons why these attempts have failed. For one thing, it is obvious that a lack of communication channels is not a problem. All the parties involved (and they are numerous) know each other very well, and they are in frequent contact with one another whenever it suits their purposes. There is also clear evidence that both ETA and the Spanish government want the violence to end. With many of its key leaders either in French jails or in distant exile, and with five hundred of its rank-and-file members in Spanish prisons, ETA itself may be reaching the point of exhaustion, both materially and psychologically. For its own reasons, the Spanish government would also like to bring the conflict to a close before 1992, the year when Spain will be very much in the international eye because of the Barcelona Olympics and the celebration of the 500th anniversary of the discovery of America. Nearly all other Basque parties and government agencies stand to gain significantly from a cessation of violence, depending of course on the terms of such a cease-fire.[2] Outside support for the insurgents is also not a factor; more than other such conflicts, ETA's struggle is almost completely self-contained and independent of outside assistance. Finally, public opinion supports a negotiated settlement. In Spain generally, a clear majority favor a negotiated end to the struggle, while in the Basque Country itself, where the great majority of ETA's attacks occur, three-fourths of the population advocate a negotiated settlement.[3]

How, then, are we to explain the many frustrated attempts to negotiate an end to this insurgency, now the worst on the European continent? Finding an answer to this question has been the principal objective of this book.

Table 9.1 Summary of Attempts to Negotiate with ETA, and Related
Events, 1975–1989.

Approximate Date(s)	Summary of Event
November 1975	Marcelino Oreja meetings in France
July 1976	Pertur's assassination
December 1976– January 1977	Meetings with ETA (p-m) in Geneva
May–June 1977	Amnesty negotiations prior to elections
February 1978	KAS Alternative published
May 1978	Abortive Martín Villa trip to Geneva
June 1978	Portell assassination
Summer 1978	Attempts by Benegas to start negotiations
December 1978	Argala assassination
Summer 1979	ETA (p-m) bombing campaign
November 1979	Ruperéz kidnapping
Summer 1980	ETA (p-m) bombing campaign
February 1981– February 1982	ETA (p-m) cease-fire
Summer 1982	Arzalluz contacts with ETA (p-m)
February 1982– September 1982	ETA (p-m) VII Assembly dissolved
1981–1982	Social reintegration "via Bandrés"
February–May 1982	ETA (m) offensive; HB offers to mediate
December 1982	PSOE offers to negotiate
January–March 1983	Garaikoetxea's mesa para la paz
April 1983	Ballesteros attempts negotiations
August–November 1984	Barrionuevo offer; Brouard assassination
August 1984– November 1985	CESID negotiations with Eriz; Operation Wellington and six-stage calendar
September– November 1985	ETA's technical truce and direct talks
June 1985– March 1986	International Commission of Experts on Violence gives weak pro-negotiation recommendation
April 1984– September 1986	Social reintegration "via Azkarraga"
April–May 1986	HB-PNV contacts
Spring–Summer 1986	Garcia Andoain contacts
November 1986– February 1987	Algerian Connection, Phase One. Iturbe's death
July 1987– February 1988	Algerian Connection, Phase Two. Revilla kidnapping
January–April 1989	Algerian Connection, Phase Three. Etxebeste expulsion from Algeria

The obstacles to negotiations that I have uncovered can be clustered into three sets. One set involves the political, cultural, and social context within which negotiations take place, and in the ways in which that setting intrudes into and shapes the negotiations. A second set has to do with the linkages between the cessation of violence and the conduct of negotiations. While superficially these obstacles may appear to be nothing more than a problem of timing, in fact the difficulties are much more deeply rooted in the very nature of armed struggle. A third cluster of obstacles involves the nature of the negotiation itself, particularly the topics to be allowed on the agenda. What is involved here is the distinction between "political" and "technical" negotiations, and who has the legitimate right to bargain in which policy area. This section concludes with some discussion of a possible two-track negotiation strategy that could be useful in removing this obstacle. (There may also be cultural factors that affect Basque-Spanish relations, or that impede the ability of one or the other culture to engage in the bargaining and compromise necessary to conduct negotiations to end conflict. I will have to leave to the anthropologists the discovery and explanation of these obstacles, if indeed there are any.)[4]

Contextual Obstacles to Negotiations

Since the parties in conflict—ETA and the Basque and Spanish governments—have been engaged in numerous negotiation attempts over the past fourteen years, one would expect that by now they would have learned whatever they need to know about the political, cultural, and social context within which these negotiations take place. Nevertheless, an outside observer can still identify a number of obstacles to negotiation at this level whose importance the negotiating parties do not seem to appreciate.[5]

First, all parties must recognize the extremely complex institutional milieu within which they operate. As we have seen, the conflict is not a simple one of ETA versus Madrid; many contending political forces and groups are involved, with constantly shifting agendas and priorities. As many as two dozen identifiable groups have something at stake in negotiations with ETA, and the number could easily rise higher if we were to sub-divide the groups more precisely.

The complexity of this universe of interested parties provides a challenging environment within which to negotiate with ETA. Most of these groups have multiple priorities; a settlement with ETA is an important goal for them, but not overwhelmingly so, and certainly not the sole objective of any of them. Of all the interested parties, in fact, I would speculate that the only group that places a higher priority on a cease-fire than on any other goal would be the prisoners and their families.

Most of the other groups want an end to the violence, to be sure, but they want it on their terms. The parties and media, for example, want a settlement, but many of them want it achieved in ways that benefit them politically. There is tension between the Basque and Spanish governments over which of them should take the lead in conducting negotiations; and on more than one occasion each has kept its negotiating attempts secret from the other. Within each government as well there is tension between and among the various ministries (e.g., interior versus justice) as each tries to advance its own bureaucratic goals. The history of ETA itself is littered with internal divisions and splits, many of which turned on the questions of a negotiated settlement. Finally, there is tension between the goals and priorities of the leaders and of the rank-and-file members of most of these groups; and leaders on both sides appear reluctant to move too fast toward negotiations lest they appear too conciliatory toward their group's enemies. Under these circumstances, coalitions in support of negotiations are extraordinarily difficult to assemble and easy to break apart. Yet, leaders must continue to try to assemble such coalitions because no single political force controls all the resources (economic, political, legal, and so forth) necessary to secure a settlement.

One of the reasons why coalitions must be formed to support negotiations is that on all sides of the dispute there are key actors strongly opposed to a negotiated settlement. Up to now, the anti-truce elements have been able to frustrate negotiations, usually by withdrawing their support or by an act of disruptive violence at strategic moments. For example, the assassination of José María Portell, in June 1978, took place just as he was about to arrange negotiations between a faction of ETA and the Spanish government. His death not only ended this attempt, but set in motion a major increase in antiterrorist activity that made it impossible for several years even to suggest publicly the option of negotiations. Something similar has happened at least a half dozen times in the intervening years. It would be tempting to lay all the blame for these acts of sabotage at the feet of ETA or one of its anti-negotiation factions; but the truth is that in most instances it is simply not possible to discover who actually committed the act, much less the motivations for doing so.

One way to blunt the ability of anti-negotiation elements to torpedo negotiations is by controlling the agenda. People trying to arrange a cease-fire should identify those who favor negotiations and engage their support by keeping the initial agenda general and limited to administrative and technical questions such as site, participants, etc., until talks have firmly begun. Once talks have begun, they should not reject out of hand any agenda item. Placing an item on the agenda is never a commitment of action on that item, one way or the other; and it likewise does not necessarily confer legitimacy on that demand if contending parties do not wish to do so. At the same time, pro-truce elements should identify those who oppose negotiations, and defuse their opposition by refusing to state beforehand that a given act will be taken as reason to suspend the talks. By stating that an armed attack will cause a suspension of the talks, one gives the anti-truce forces the power to block negotiations simply by committing that act. In addition, those on the government side should recognize that within ETA the question of a negotiated settlement is not a simple matter of disagreement among friends; it can be a life-and-death issue. At least two ETA leaders, and one other leader of the Basque Left, who favored negotiations have been killed, a third survived an attack that killed his wife, and a fourth died in an automobile accident under mysterious circumstances; and it is at least a reasonable possibility that their deaths had something to do with their position on negotiations.

A third point: skilled intermediaries are absolutely crucial to the successful conduct of negotiations. As I have already observed, a scarcity of lines of communication is not the problem here; ETA leaders know how to reach their opposite numbers in Madrid, and vice versa. Trust and confidence are the principal elements in short supply; and intermediaries trusted by all the parties to the struggle are few in number. Moreover, it is obvious that tremendous physical and political courage is needed to undertake the role of intermediary in these situations. At least two men who undertook to act

as intermediaries—Portell in 1978 and Santiago Brouard in 1984—
were killed in the midst of their negotiations, again by persons still
unknown. (As of late 1989, the Brouard case was still being pro-
cessed through Spanish courts. Those accused of his murder were
apparently mercenaries contracted for by the GAL.) It should also
be remembered that acting as an intermediary with terrorists has
technically been a violation of Spain's antiterrorism laws, and at
least one person who acted as an intermediary in a hostage case was
arrested and charged with complicity in the kidnapping. Thus, it
is essential that intermediaries be protected—both physically and
legally—throughout any negotiation effort.

How the parties use their intermediaries is another source of
concern. Several persons with whom I spoke in my research observed that both ETA and the Spanish government were deeply
suspicious of anyone who might offer his services as an intermediary, believing (perhaps with justification) that the intermediary was
trying to capitalize on his strategic position between the two sides.
One person who has performed this service a number of times told
me he would never offer to do so again unless requested in writing by both parties, so that if things did not work out as expected,
they could not repudiate him or deny that he was acting at their
request.[6]

I would also suggest that the Spanish government think carefully about the kinds of persons they dispatch as envoys to talk
with ETA. ETA has said repeatedly that they want to talk with the
representatives of the country's *political* sectors, not those who
represent the *police* agencies in the government. Yet, with the exception of the Elgorriaga missions in late 1987 and early 1988,
Madrid has insisted on sending only interior ministry officials
and senior police administrators. This affront might be overlooked
were it not for the fact that several of their most frequently used
envoys have reputations as being torturers of arrested Basques; and
in some cases, meetings have been held in which the torturer and
his victim confronted one another across the bargaining table. It
is inconceivable how Madrid could expect that productive talks
could take place under these circumstances.

Finally, the press in Spain generally, and in the Basque Country
in particular, must exercise self-control and behave responsibly in
their coverage of negotiations. There are few news media in Spain

that could be considered neutral and disinterested. Many news-papers and newsmagazines are connected to a specific party (or even a faction within a party) or ideology, and will try to advance their group's perceptions of an event. Television is even less well suited for a role in these matters as it is still a state monopoly (although steps are now under way to diversify the television indus-try by adding one or more private companies). There is a regional television station in the Basque Country; but it too is govern-ment owned and operated. The press cannot be kept completely out of negotiations, however, since newspapers are used frequently as conduits of information among parties who are not in direct contact with one another. Moreover, the role of the press in such delicate matters in a more or less open society is always supremely sensitive. Nevertheless, all parties—especially ETA, which in the past has been the most intransigent group on this question—should recognize the positive benefits to be derived from keeping negotia-tions out of the public eye, at least at the beginning. There is some evidence that this admonition was observed in the third round of negotiations in Algeria, even though eventually the collapse of the talks stemmed from press reports of what were essentially two dif-ferent versions—ETA's and Madrid's—of what had been agreed to in Algiers.

Violence as an Obstacle to Negotiations

On more than one occasion, talks with ETA have broken down because of a disagreement about the linkage between a cease-fire and the negotiation process. What is at stake here is the timing of a cease-fire; i.e., whether it should come before, during, or after the resolution of the issues. From the beginning, Madrid has in-sisted that violence must be halted before negotiations could begin, and there would have to be ironclad guarantees that the violence would not be resumed as long as the talks were under way, a posi-tion we could describe as "first truce, then talks." Regardless of the kind of regime in Madrid, or the personalities involved, the Span-ish government's position has been clear: they will not sit across the table from ETA while the killing is going on. ETA's position on this issue, on the other hand, has undergone substantial change over the years, and cannot be easily or simply characterized.[7]

From the mid-1960s until 1974, ETA operated from the strategic premise of "revolutionary war," wherein violence had a key role to play until the final objectives of the struggle—an independent, reunified, socialist, and Basque-speaking Euskadi—were obtained. The organization's leaders knew that ETA was too weak to confront the Spanish military directly; but, by means of the "action-repression spiral theory," they believed that violence could be used to provoke Madrid into destabilizing repression, leading to increased turmoil and finally civil war. This position could be described as "first final victory, then a cease-fire."

ETA's first real experience with the revolutionary war strategy, in 1968, was so damaging, however, that they began to reassess the wisdom of this approach. The result was the adoption, by 1974, of a two-stage strategy. The first stage would culminate in autonomy, which, while substantial, would fall well short of independence, which would be achieved in stage two. While it was implicit in this strategy that the potential for armed struggle would be maintained during both stages, it gradually became ETA policy to reduce violence during the second stage; in other words, to reduce violence after the first-stage goals had been achieved. This approach might be called "first autonomy, then we'll consider a truce."

By February 1978, the two-stage theory had evolved into the negotiating posture that ETA maintained for a decade. The end of stage one would be signaled by the achievement of a set of five demands, known as the KAS Alternative. Violence would continue until these five demands were achieved, at which time there would be a cease-fire; in other words, "first the KAS Alternative, then truce." However, the organization would continue to exist even after these demands were met, and would retain its right to resume violence in the pursuit of its second-stage goals.

Until their truce proposal communiqué of January 28, 1988, then, ETA's position was that the cessation of violence was the *objective* of negotiations, not a *precondition* as Madrid insisted. The January 28 communiqué was widely interpreted as an offer of a sixty-day cease-fire to take effect the moment talks began. Instead of waiting until the KAS Alternative had been achieved,

ETA was willing to cease violence as soon as the Spanish government agreed to begin "political negotiations" (an issue to be discussed in the next section). This position we might characterize as "truce begins when talks do." Madrid, however, still wanted a cessation of violence as well as guarantees for the future *before* coming to the negotiating table; and, since ETA was unwilling to yield on that point, talks were broken off. Most recently, in 1989, ETA has adjusted its position on the cease-fire question once more. The January 1989 statement declared the cease-fire to be in effect before political negotiations began, so long as the Spanish government would meet with ETA and accepted openly that eventually political negotiations would be undertaken. This position would be characterized as "truce when talks are promised." The 1989 talks collapsed at least partly because Madrid was unwilling to accept this condition. However, it is clear that over the years ETA has changed its position on the linkage between a truce and a settlement, each time coming closer to the position held by the Spanish government.

This obstacle will continue to complicate negotiations until all the parties recognize that negotiations serve to try to *resolve* conflicts, *not* simply to confirm some prior resolution. Negotiations must *precede*, not follow, the termination of the conflict. Thus, ETA's insistence on acceptance of the KAS Alternative or of political negotiations before a cease-fire, like the Spanish government's insistence on a cessation of violence before talks can begin, is both unrealistic and unreasonable. The principal problem here is the continuation of violence while negotiations are going on. ETA leaders must know that it is impossible for their adversaries to enter into negotiations while provocative violent attacks are still being launched; on the other hand, by making a cessation of violence an absolute pre-condition to beginning negotiations, the Spanish government has—wittingly or not—played into the hands of elements, both those within ETA and others, who do not want talks to proceed.

One major problem here is that both sides want to negotiate from a position of strength, and neither wants to be seen as seeking peace from a position of weakness. Many Basques believe that Madrid uses an incorrect psychological approach in its frequent claims that ETA is growing weaker and will soon be forced to sue for a cease-fire. With these kinds of public comments, what Spanish officials do is provoke ETA into acts of violence simply to prove that the organization is entering into negotiations not out of weakness but from a position of strength.[8] The fact that these attacks are especially dramatic and timed for maximum disruption (e.g., the car bombing of the Guardia Civil barracks in Zaragoza) magnifies their harmful impact on the dynamic of negotiations.

It would also be helpful to remember that the very nature of armed struggle makes it impossible to renounce the use of force before securing one's aims. As numerous ETA strategists have pointed out, the only thing they have to offer at the bargaining table is their ability to turn off the violence. If they have already played that card before the game even begins, Madrid has no incentive to negotiate in good faith. Therefore, so long as ETA exists, the threat of violence will always loom over the bargaining table, no matter what kinds of verbal commitments there may be between the two sides.

"Political" versus "Technical" Issues as an Obstacle to Negotiations

The distinction between "political" and "technical" negotiations was first suggested by Euzkadiko Ezkerra leader Mario Onaindia in 1981.[9] At the time, Onaindia and Juan María Bandrés had just begun the negotiations that led to the dissolution of ETA (p-m) and the freeing or return of some two hundred prisoners and exiles, one of the few instances of successful negotiations on record. The reason for the success of this negotiation effort lay not only in the skill and persistence of the two Basques and in the flexibility of the Spanish interior minister, Juan José Rosón, but also in the separation of the agenda into two sets of issues: those that are "technical," and open for discussion, and those that are "political" and cannot be placed on the agenda.

A schematic comparison of the negotiating positions of the two parties suggests some of the differences between the two sets of issues (see table 9.2). The differences will become clearer as we examine a way to overcome this obstacle: the two-track approach to negotiations.

Table 9.2 The Negotiating Positions of ETA, Spanish Government, 1989.

ETA's 1978 Position	Status in 1989	Spanish Position	ETA's Position
1. Truce after agreement on KAS Alternative	Temporary truce ended 4-89	Truce before talks	Truce and talks together
2. KAS Alternative			
1. Immediate, unconditional amnesty	Selective amnesty	Selective amnesty	Immediate unconditional amnesty
2. Legalization of all parties	Done	Not an issue	Not an issue
3. Withdrawal of all Spanish police, Civil Guards	Basque police, but no withdrawal of Spanish forces	Phased reduction after cease-fire	Phased total withdrawal
4. Improvement of conditions for workers	Possible under Basque autonomy statute	Not an issue	Not an issue
5. Autonomy statute	Done, but not complete	Existing institutions acceptable	Statute not legitimate
1. Self-determination	No	Not possible	Essential
2. Navarra integrated	No	Navarrese decide	Process negotiable
3. Euskera official	Co-official	Basque issue	Acceptable
4. Control over police, army	No	Irrelevant	See #3 above

The two-track strategy for dealing with ETA's demands has been recognized and discussed in Spain since at least 1984, although not by the name I have given it. The earliest public reference I have found to such an approach was a comment made in August 1984 by the Spanish government's director of state security, Rafael Vera, that political negotiations, while unthinkable with ETA directly, could be conducted with the political party that has close ties to ETA, Herri Batasuna.[10] In August 1985, the president of the Basque government, José Antonio Ardanza, was quoted by *Le Monde* as rejecting political negotiations with ETA, but admitting the possibility of such negotiations with "forces that have shown that they represent a portion of the electorate."[11] In December 1986, Herri Batasuna leader Iñaki Esnaola was reported as declaring that "we have never said that negotiations with ETA are the only channel. We have defended them because no one offered others, but if now new channels are opened, in HB we would study them."[12] There is ample evidence that by summer of 1987 a two-track approach was being actively considered in key Spanish government circles.[13] The two-track strategy first appeared in the negotiations themselves in talks in Algeria in November 1987 between the Spanish representative, Julen Elgorriaga, and ETA's spokesman, Antxon Etxebeste.

The two-track approach offers a way around the unwillingness or inability of Spanish officials to negotiate "political" issues directly with terrorists. In ETA's view, for violence to end, certain political questions (such as the Basque right of self-determination, or the relationship of Navarra to the Basque Autonomous Community) must be addressed. Although the Spanish government is willing to discuss "nonpolitical" issues such as amnesty for ETA members, or police practices, Madrid will not negotiate political questions directly with ETA. Not only would most Spanish political leaders be opposed to such negotiations, but many Basques would object as well. The Basque leaders who opted to work through the democratic parliamentary system would feel betrayed by any substantial deal struck directly with ETA on which they were not consulted. The solution to this problem lies in the two-track approach, or the use of two negotiating channels. One track can be used for Madrid to talk directly to ETA about technical issues, while the political issues can be addressed in a forum where

ETA is not physically present, but where its interests are safe-guarded. Numbering these tracks "one" and "two" does not mean they have to proceed in sequence; in fact, it is presumed that they will overlap in time to some degree, and that negotiations on both sets of issues will be going on at the same time.

The potential for success of the two-track approach lies in the separation of the negotiations into two venues, two agendas, and two negotiating bodies. Such a division makes it possible for parties in conflict to negotiate with one another without actually appearing to do so. One negotiation arena is set aside for issues that can plausibly be characterized as narrowly technical, and for which institutional mechanisms and procedures already exist. Amnesty for convicted insurgents would be an example of one such issue. Since constitutional and statutory arrangements already sanction the discussion of this kind of issue, governments can engage in direct negotiations with insurgents without jeopardizing their own legitimacy. The other track can then be set aside for so-called political negotiations, or for the discussion of issues that cannot be encompassed within existing institutions. These issues challenge the legitimacy of existing constitutional arrangements, so they must be discussed among the widest possible array of political groups, including parties and other interested groups. Significantly, however, the insurgents themselves are not present at these "second track" negotiations. Since their presence would call into question the legitimacy of the state, the insurgents are represented at these talks by intermediaries who enjoy the complete confidence of the rebels but who are also regarded as legitimate participants in civil society.

Track One negotiations will deal with issues of public order, law enforcement, security, and the administration of justice, or in other words, issues that can be characterized as technical or non-political. The Spanish government would be represented in these talks by representatives of the affected ministries, particularly justice (because the prison system will be involved) and interior (to discuss the role of the national police and the Guardia Civil). However, ETA has made it clear that they also want to be present persons who can speak for, and make commitments for, the country's political leadership. In other words, ETA wants Madrid to recognize that violence in the Basque Country is not a police question but a political one. In view of the sensitivity of these discussions, most observers agree that they should be held at a site outside Spain, but still relatively accessible. Algeria was a suitable location; but there seems little interest in returning there and the Algerian government has officially withdrawn its offer to mediate the dispute. Other European countries, such as Belgium, might also be suggested. In June 1989, Venezuelan president Carlos Andrés Pérez offered his good offices as an intermediary and his country as a possible venue for resumed negotiations. Press coverage is sure to be intense; but the participants will doubtless try to conduct the talks in semi-secrecy.

The first major issue to be discussed in Track One is amnesty. If previous discussions on this topic are any guide, ETA will press for an amnesty declaration by King Juan Carlos that is immediate, unconditional, and total. That is, they will want amnesty automatically for all ETA members, whether in prison serving sentences or awaiting trial (estimated in mid-1989 at about five hundred individuals), at large in Spain or in exile in France or elsewhere. They will also demand that amnesty be extended to all ETA members regardless of the nature of their alleged crimes. Finally, they will insist that ETA members not be required to do anything special to obtain this pardon, either beforehand or subsequently.

The Spanish, on the other hand, will seek to make amnesty conditional and partial. Amnesty will be handed out on a case-by-case basis; ETA members must request it and will probably be required to sign some sort of statement affirming their intention to live within the laws of Spain; and not all crimes would be covered by the pardon. For example, many Spanish leaders would not be willing to pardon ETA members (about 150 persons) convicted of so-called blood crimes. For these cases, however, some sort of "covered amnesty" or "*amnistía encubierta*" might be granted; and the prisoners might be released from prison on the condition that they leave Spain for a long period.

The second half of Track One negotiations will involve measures to ensure the complete cessation of all acts of violence in Spain related to ETA's struggle. A number of details will need to be worked out here. For example, will the agreement restrain acts of police violence (e.g., torture in prisons or in local police stations) just as it prohibits armed attacks by ETA? Exactly what kinds of acts are "off limits"? Does the agreement prevent ETA from collecting funds or from carrying on propaganda activities? What happens if provocative acts occur while these and Track Two negotiations are being held? Given the hatred built up over the years between ETA and the Spanish police and Guardia Civil, violent incidents are likely to erupt more or less spontaneously. Will they be allowed to interrupt the negotiations process, or will the participants agree that there is some sort of "threshold" of violence that must be crossed for talks to be suspended? Another sensitive question involves ETA's weapons. Some Spanish officials have declared that ETA must turn over to the police all its weapons as a guarantee not to undertake further armed attacks. Apart from the obvious difficulty of policing such a step, it seems highly unlikely that ETA would ever agree to disarming, at least during the early stages of negotiations. And finally, who or what agency will act as the guarantor of these provisions? In ETA's January 28, 1988, truce communiqué, Algeria was proposed to guarantee the process; but Madrid quickly rejected such a suggestion with a declaration that these issues were an internal Spanish matter and the intervention of other governments would not be welcome.

The naming of the negotiating team for Track Two may be formalized during Track One talks, but it seems likely that there will already be substantial agreement on who will participate in Track Two discussions before any negotiations on Track One issues are held. The key to the success of Track Two negotiations (and, indeed, of the two-track approach in general) is ETA's willingness to let the more controversial political issues be settled in a forum where they are not actually present. The formula that makes this possible is the participation of representatives of the Basque National Liberation Movement (Movimiento de Liberación Nacional Vasco, or MLNV), an organization that includes the political coalition, Herri Batasuna.[14] Since ETA presumably has complete confidence in the HB leaders, and since HB is a legitimate political party that customarily wins between 15 and 20 percent of the vote in elections in the Basque Country, Madrid can claim that the sensitive political issues are not being discussed with a so-called terrorist group, but rather with a bona fide representative of a sizable segment of the Basque population.

Other participants in Track Two negotiations would depend

on the exact agenda and on the nature of subsequent ratification of what is agreed upon. At some point, other Basque political parties and the Basque government must be involved; and eventually the Basque parliament must be asked to ratify the accord. The role of the Basque parliament would prove difficult to resolve since Herri Batasuna and ETA do not accept its legitimacy in any regard, and the Navarrese certainly do not accept its authority over them. Nevertheless, for all the other Basque parties, it is essential that their parliament be centrally involved in the negotiations, especially when the time comes to produce workable solutions to the various other political issues. If the status of Navarra is to be discussed, Navarrese representatives must be present, and the Navarrese parliament and the people of Navarra must be amply consulted. Madrid may be represented by government officials or by representatives of the governing party, the PSOE. Most interested parties will probably insist that the talks be held in the Basque Country to symbolize that Basque issues are being settled locally by local authorities. These meetings cannot be kept secret, but the press should be excluded and informed periodically through briefings about the course of negotiations.

The agenda of Track Two negotiations will be difficult to work out as it will treat some of the most supremely sensitive questions in Basque-Spanish relations. ETA has announced many times that the sole basis for negotiations must be the KAS Alternative (see table 9.2). As we have seen, item number one of the KAS Alternative, amnesty, is to be dealt with in Track One negotiations. Since number two, party legalization, is already accomplished; since number four is vague and ambiguous; and since number five already exists at least partially, Track Two negotiations will probably boil down to three major issues: the withdrawal of Spanish law enforcement authorities from the Basque Country; the status of Navarra; and the right of the Basque people to self-determination. It remains to be seen exactly how a formula can be drawn up that will satisfy all interested parties on these three sensitive issues; but by separating them into a second track and by involving negotiating parties other than ETA in their solution, the two-track approach offers a feasible solution to the non-negotiable character of political questions.

NOTES

Introduction: Insurgency and Negotiations

1. Written by Erskine Childers the night before his execution for having fought with the rebels in the Irish Civil War, November 24, 1922. Quoted in Frank Pakenham (Lord Longford), *Peace by Ordeal: The Negotiation of the Anglo-Irish Treaty, 1921* (London: Sidgwick and Jackson, 1972), p. 271.

2. Robert Clark, "The Legitimacy of Ethnonationalist Insurgency: Evidence of Popular Support for the Basque Separatist Organization Euzkadi ta Askatasuna (ETA)." Symposium on Political Violence, University of Massachusetts at Amherst, 1987.

Chapter One: Interested Parties and Factions

1. For the following formulation, I am indebted to my colleague at the University of Maryland, Baltimore County, Chris Hewitt. See also, Andrew Mack, "Why Big Nations Lose Small Wars: The Politics of Asymmetric Conflict," *World Politics*, XXVII, 2 (January 1975), pp. 175–200.

2. Gurutz Jáuregui Bereciartu, *Ideología y estrategia política de ETA: Análisis de su evolución entre 1959 y 1968* (Madrid: Siglo Veintiuno, 1981). Pedro Ibarra Guell, *La Evolución Estratégica de ETA (1963–1987)* (San Sebastián: Kriselu, 1987).

3. It would take us far afield to review the history of ETA or of Basque nationalism. However, interested readers can consult the following: Stanley Payne, *Basque Nationalism* (Reno: University of Nevada Press, 1975); Robert Clark, *The Basques: The Franco Years and Beyond* (Reno: University of Nevada Press, 1980); Robert Clark, *The Basque Insurgents: ETA, 1952–1980* (Madison: University of Wisconsin Press, 1984); and John Sullivan, *ETA and Basque Nationalism: The Fight for Euskadi, 1890–1986* (London and New York: Routledge, 1988).

4. Ibarra, *La Evolución*, p. 108.

5. For more on ETA's organizational structure, see Clark, *The Basque Insurgents*, chapter 9. Also, *TVI Profile*, 8, 2, pp. 9–11.

6. *Euskadi Anuario 1988* (San Sebastián: *Egin*, 1988), pp. 172–174.

7. Robert Clark, "Spain's Autonomous Communities: A Case Study in Ethnic Power Sharing," *European Studies Journal*, II, 1 (1985), pp. 1–16. Robert Clark, "The Question of Regional Autonomy in Spain's Democratic Transition," in Robert Clark and Michael Haltzel, eds., *Spain in the 1980s: The Democratic Transition and a New International Role* (Cambridge, Mass.: Ballinger, 1987), chapter 9.

8. The literature on parties and voting behavior in the Basque Country is extensive. Most of it is reviewed in Francisco J. Llera Ramo, *Continuidad y Cambio en el Sistema de Partidos Vascos: 1977–1987* (Madrid: Centro de Estudios Constitucionales, 1988). For a different perspective, see Luís Nuñez, *Euskadi Sur Electoral* (San Sebastián: Ediciones Vascas, 1980). See also, Robert Clark, " 'Rejectionist' Voting as an Indicator of Ethnic Nationalism: The Case of Spain's Basque Provinces," *Ethnic and Racial Studies*, 10, 4 (October 1987), pp. 427–447.

9. Ibarra, *La Evolución*, pp. 111–112.

10. *Euskadi Anuario 1983* (San Sebastián: *Egin*, 1983), p. 159.

11. Juan Félix Eriz, *Yo He Sido Mediador de E.T.A.* (Madrid: ARNAO Ediciones, 1986).

12. Andrea Bonime-Blanc, *Spain's Transition to Democracy: The Politics of Constitution-making* (Boulder and London: Westview, 1987). See also, Clark and Haltzel, *Spain in the 1980s*.

13. See *Deia* (Bilbao), 2 November 1986, for an organizational diagram of the Ministry of Interior.

14. José Luís Morales, Teresa Toda, and Miren Imaz, *La trama del G.A.L.* (Madrid: Editorial Revolución, 1988), p. 19.

15. Clark, *The Basque Insurgents*, chapter 5.

16. The standard work on the Spanish party system is Richard Gunther, Giacomo Sani, and Goldie Shabad, *Spain after Franco: The Making of a Competitive Party System* (Berkeley: University of California Press, 1988).

17. Tasio Erkizia and others, *Euskadi: La Renuncia del PSOE* (Bilbao: Txalaparta Argitaldaria, 1988).

18. Robert Clark, "Spain and the Basques," in Frederick Shiels, ed., *Ethnic Separatism and World Politics* (Lanham, Md.: University Press of America, 1984), pp. 71–104. See also, Clark, *The Basque Insurgents*, pp. 233–235.

Chapter Two: Spanish Antiterrorist Policy

1. This framework draws heavily from *The Impact of Government Behavior on Frequency, Type and Targets of Terrorist Group Activity* (McLean, Va.: Defense Systems, Inc., December 15, 1982), esp. chapter three. See also, Christopher Hewitt, *The Effectiveness of Antiterrorist Policies* (Lanham, Md.: University Press of America, 1984).

2. Robert Clark, *The Basque Insurgents: ETA, 1952–1980* (Madison: University of Wisconsin Press, 1984), pp. 244–256.

3. Miguel Castells Arteche, *Radiografía de un Modelo Represivo* (San Sebastián: Ediciones Vascas, 1982), esp. table B.

4. Clark, *The Basque Insurgents*, p. 256.

5. Robert Clark, "Spain and the Basques," in Frederick L. Shiels, ed., *Ethnic Separatism and World Politics* (Lanham, Md.: University Press of America, 1984), esp. pp. 88–89.

6. Clark, *The Basque Insurgents*, pp. 256–271.

7. *Ibid.*, pp. 247–248.

8. Clark, *The Basque Insurgents*, pp. 256–257. Castells, *Radiografía*, pp. 145–146. There is a list of antiterrorist measures enacted to 1980 in Antonio Beristain, "Los Terrorismos en el País Vasco y en España," in Fernando Reinares, et al., *Violencia y Política en Euskadi* (Bilbao: Desclee de Brouwer, 1984), pp. 175–177.

9. *Deia* (Bilbao), 30 October 1980. Tom Burns, "Spain's Deputies Approve Stiff Antiterrorist Laws," *Washington Post*, 31 October 1980.

10. *Report of an Amnesty International Mission to Spain, 3–28 October 1979* (London: Amnesty International, November 1980), p. 20.

11. Castells, *Radiografía*, table A, p. 34, and table B, p. 35.

12. Clark, "Spain and the Basques," pp. 89–91.

13. *Deia*, 15, 18, and 24 March; 2, 8, and 22 April 1981. Also, Castells, *Radiografía*, pp. 147–149.

14. Castells, *ibid.*, pp. 149–150. *Deia*, 24 March 1981.

15. Castells, *ibid.*, p. 31.

16. *Euskadi Anuario 1988* (San Sebastián: Egin, 1988), p. 173.

17. *Deia*, 12 October 1981.

18. *El País* (Madrid), 27 October 1982.

19. *Deia*, 13 February 1982.

20. *El País*, 27 October 1982.

21. *Deia*, 24 and 28 March 1981. Tom Burns, "Spain Calls on Army To Fight Violence in Basque Country," *Washington Post*, 25 March 1981.

22. *Deia*, 26, 29, and 31 March; 2 April, and 25 September 1981. *El Diario Vasco* (San Sebastián), 26 September 1981.

23. *Deia*, 26 March 1981.

24. *Deia*, 20 and 21 April 1982.

25. Clark, "Spain and the Basques," pp. 92–93.

26. *Deia*, 28 January 1983.

27. *El País*, 3 November 1983.

28. *Deia*, 25 October 1983.

29. *Deia*, 22 February 1984.

30. Tom Burns, "Spanish Socialists Offer Tough Laws Against Terrorism," *Washington Post*, 25 November 1983.

31. *Deia*, 16 April 1983.

32. *Deia*, 27 February 1983.

33. *Deia*, 15 April 1983.

34. *Deia*, 26 June, 12 and 16 July, 1984.

35. *Tiempo*, 5 November 1984.

36. *Deia*, 27 October 1983; 23 October 1984. *El País*, 28 and 29 October 1984.

37. *Deia*, 4 and 6 April 1984.

38. *Spain: The Question of Torture* (London: Amnesty International, 1985), p. 7.

39. *Ibid.*, p. 22. See also the minister's denial of Amnesty International's report before the Congress of Deputies in *Deia*, 8 June 1984.

40. *Deia*, 5 March; 19 and 20 May 1983.

41. The entire text of Plan ZEN is printed in *Euskadi 1983* (San Sebastián: Anuario EGIN, 1983), pp. 106–126. See also *Tiempo*, 23 May 1983.

42. *Egin* (San Sebastián), 3 May 1983.

43. *Deia*, 8 October 1983.

44. *Deia*, 25 October 1983.

45. *Deia*, 4 November 1983.

46. Javier Garcia, *Los GAL, al descubierto* (Madrid: El País-Aguilar, 1988). José Luís Morales, Teresa Toda, and Miren Imaz, *La trama del G.A.L.* (Madrid: Editorial Revolución, 1988).

47. *Deia*, 31 December 1983.

48. *Deia*, 22 March 1984.

49. *Deia*, 7 April 1984.

50. *Deia*, 10 February 1986, has a list of all the GAL killings from its beginnings until September 1985. See also *Deia*, 14 August 1984.

51. Clark, "Spain and the Basques," p. 93.

52. *Euskadi Anuario 1983* (San Sebastián: *Egin*, 1983), p. 19.

53. *El País* (international edition), 6 August 1984.

54. *Deia*, 10 and 12 January 1983.

55. Tom Burns, "Socialist Ties Easing Animosity between Spain, France," *Washington Post*, 15 January 1983. *El País*, 12 June 1983.

56. *El País* (international edition), 6 August 1984.

57. *Deia*, 25 October and 12 November 1983.

58. *Deia*, 23 October and 15 November 1983.

59. *Deia*, 16 and 22 November 1983.

60. *Deia*, 14 August 1984. *Euskadi Anuario 1988*, p. 174.

61. While Lujambio was convicted and sentenced to fifty-four years in prison, the other two—Martínez Beiztegi and García Ramírez—were found not guilty by Spanish courts and released. See *El País* (international edition), 22 and 29 April 1985.

62. *Euskadi Anuario 1984* (San Sebastián: *Egin*, 1984), p. 166.

63. The complete text of the law is contained in *Spain: The Question of Torture* (London: Amnesty International, 1985), pp. 32–43. See also *Deia*, 21 November 1987, for a brief history of the law.

64. *Deia*, 27 October and 4 November 1983. *Cambio 16* (Madrid), no. 685, 14 January 1985, pp. 33–35. *Washington Post*, 25 November 1983.

65. *Deia*, 3 May 1985.

66. *El País* (international edition), 21 December 1987. *Deia*, 18 December 1987.

67. *Deia*, 13 January 1987. Also *Euskadi Anuario 1988*, p. 163.

68. *Euskadi Anuario 1988, ibid.*, p. 173.

69. *Deia*, 25 July 1987.

70. *Deia*, 10 February 1986. *El País*, 9 April 1984.

71. *Deia*, 2 June 1984.

72. *Deia*, 6 January and 5 March 1984.

73. *Deia*, 15 January 1984.

74. Edward Cody, "Police Accused in Basque Killing Probe," *Washington Post*, 22 January 1989.

75. *Tiempo*, 18 July 1987, p. 25.

76. Michael Dobbs, "Mitterand, Chirac Defuse Potential Row over Terrorism Issue," *Washington Post*, 5 April 1986.

77. Morales, Toda, and Imaz, *La trama*, pp. 15–16.

78. *Deia*, 18 July 1987. See also *The Economist*, 9 August 1986; Michael Dobbs, "French Antiterror Role Fuels Backlash in Spain," *Washington Post*, 27 August 1986; Edward Schumacher, "Suddenly, a Haven for Basques Is Full of Hazards," *New York Times*, 9 September 1986.

79. *Deia*, 6 November 1986.

80. *Euskadi 1988*, p. 174. *El País* (international edition), 25 February 1985.

81. *Deia*, 1 February and 12 December 1985. *El País* (international edition), 11 February 1985.

82. *Deia*, 21 November 1987.

83. *El País*, 14, 21, and 23 November 1987.

84. *The Economist*, 28 November 1987.

85. *Deia*, 13 May 1988.

86. *Euskadi 1988*, p. 173.

87. See *El País* and *Deia* throughout October, as well as *The Economist*, 10 October 1987; and Edward Cody, "France, Spain Cooperate in Crackdown on Basque Suspects," *Washington Post*, 10 October 1987.

88. *El País*, 28 December 1987.

89. *Deia*, 22 October 1987. *El País*, 10 November 1987.

90. *Euskadi 1988*, p. 175.

91. *Deia*, 22 October 1987.

Chapter Three: Early Attempts to Negotiate

1. This account is based on the article by Jesús Ynfante, "Hace diez años Marcelino Oreja tambien 'conversó' con ETA," *Deia* (Bilbao), 23 November 1985.

2. *El País* (Madrid), 21 July 1985.

3. The following is based on my analysis in *The Basque Insurgents: ETA, 1952–1980* (Madison: University of Wisconsin Press, 1984), pp. 90–103 and 252–253. See also, John Sullivan, *ETA and Basque Nationalism: The Fight for Euskadi, 1890–1986* (London and New York: Routledge, 1988), chapters 3–6.

4. Interview with Juan María Bandrés, San Sebastián, 2 August 1988. See also, Sullivan, pp. 139, 150–170.

5. Sullivan, *ETA and Basque Nationalism*, p. 169.

6. Anonymous interview.

7. Interview with Juan María Bandrés, San Sebastián, 2 August 1988.

8. Patxo Unzueta, "Las tentativas anteriores," *El País* (international edition), 27 August 1984. This article is reproduced in Patxo Unzueta, *Sociedad vasca y política nacionalista* (Madrid: Ediciones El País, 1987), pp. 189–191.

9. "El deshielo de ETA," *La Actualidad Española* (Madrid), no. 1313, 28 February–6 March 1977, pp. 14–19.

10. *El País*, 21 July 1985.

11. Pedro Ibarra Guell, *La Evolución Estratégica de ETA (1963–1987)* (San Sebastián: Kriselu, 1987), pp. 111–112.

12. Clark, *The Basque Insurgents*, pp. 106–110, 252–255.

13. *Deia*, 1 February 1978.

14. Ibarra, *La Evolución*, p. 120.

15. *Deia*, 5 February 1978.

16. *Deia*, 22 and 23 March, 1 April 1978.

17. José María Portell, *Los Hombres de ETA* (Barcelona: DOPESA, 1974).

18. The following is based on interviews with Gorka Aguirre, Bilbao, 26 July 1988; and with Xabier Arzalluz, Bilbao, 26 July 1988. See also, *El Diario Vasco* (San Sebastián), 1 April 1989; and Unzueta, "Las tentativas." Also interesting is the book by Juan Félix Eriz, *Yo He Sido Mediador de E.T.A.* (Madrid: Ediciones ARNAO, 1986), esp. pp. 243–260. The reader should know that Eriz is a very controversial figure in Basque politics, and his book, which is his account of several negotiation attempts, is a document of disputed veracity. However, I have relied on its contents partly because it does not contradict much of what I learned elsewhere, but also because its truthfulness has been vouched for by persons in whose judgment I have confidence. My efforts to obtain an interview with Eriz himself were unsuccessful.

19. Sullivan, *ETA and Basque Nationalism*, pp. 176, 196–197.

20. Eugenio Ibarzabal, "Comenzó la negociación," *Deia*, 25 April 1982. This article has been reproduced in abridged form in Joseba Goñi Alzueta, *Negociar* (Getxo: Colectivo Herria 2000 Eliza, 1983), pp. 391–393.

21. *El Diario Vasco*, 1 April 1989. See also Unzueta, "Las tentativas."

22. *El País*, 29 June 1978.

23. *Negociar*, pp. 393–396.

24. Ibarzabal, "Comenzó." See also J. C. Urrutxurtu, "En cuatro ocasiones quiso negociar Txiki Benegas," *Deia*, 10 November 1983.

25. *El País*, 28 June 1978. Ibarzabal, *ibid.*

26. *Deia*, 22 December 1978. *Cambio 16* (Madrid), no. 369, 31 December 1978.

27. *Deia*, 11 November 1986.

28. *El País*, 6 July 1978.

29. *El Diario Vasco*, 28 December 1978.

30. *Deia*, 22 May 1980.

31. *Deia*, 9 February 1979.

32. Robert Clark, " 'Rejectionist' Voting as an Indicator of Ethnic Nationalism: The Case of Spain's Basque Provinces," *Ethnic and Racial Studies*, 10, 4 (October 1987), pp. 427–446.

33. *Deia*, 3 and 4 August, 26 October 1979. See also Clark, *The Basque Insurgents*, pp. 113–114.

34. Clark, *The Basque Insurgents*, pp. 115–116.

35. *Deia*, 24 February 1980.

36. *Deia*, 4 July 1980.

37. *Deia*, 16 and 18 March, 17 May, and 4 July 1980.

38. *Deia*, 2 July 1980.

Chapter Four: "Social Reintegration"

1. Interview with Juan María Bandrés, San Sebastián, 2 August 1988.

2. John Sullivan, *ETA and Basque Nationalism: The Fight for Euskadi, 1890–1986* (London: Routledge, 1988), pp. 242–243.

3. Robert Clark, *The Basque Insurgents: ETA, 1952–1980* (Madison: University of Wisconsin Press, 1984), pp. 118–119.

4. The following analysis is based on contemporary press reports, including Eugenio Ibarzabal, "ETA (p-m): El debate no ha comenzado aún," *Deia* (Bilbao), 7 February 1982.

5. See Juan José Rosón's own statement, "Reflexiones sobre Euskadi," in Fernando Reinares *et al.*, *Violencia y Política en Euskadi* (Bilbao: Desclee de Brouwer, 1984), esp. pp. 108–109.

6. The text of the communiqué is in *Deia*, 18 February 1981.

7. *Deia*, 1 March 1981. There were attacks, including the kidnapping of industrialist Luis Suñer, attributed to ETA (p-m); but the organization maintained that this did not constitute a break in the truce, since no blood was shed. See Patxo Unzueta, *Sociedad vasca y política nacionalista* (Madrid: Ediciones El País, 1987), p. 178.

8. This discussion is taken from a long article written by a presumed ETA (p-m) member under the pseudonym "Oilarite," published under the title "ETA (p-m): La Tregua y Otras Precisiones," *Deia*, 3 February 1982. For a slightly different wording of the demands in the cease-fire statement, see Unzueta, *Sociedad vasca*, p. 168.

9. *Deia*, 3 March 1981.

10. *Deia*, 22 January 1983.

11. *Euskadi*, no. 201, 1 August 1985, p. 7. See also *El País* (Madrid), 25 August 1985.

12. This account is based on the daily press during the last ten days of August, particularly *Deia*, 25 August 1985, which contains a chronology of the case, as well as Arzalluz's account of the meetings with ETA (p-m). See also, Unzueta, *Sociedad vasca*, pp. 135–137.

13. *Deia*, 20 August 1985.

14. *Deia*, 21 August 1985.

15. *Deia*, 22 August 1985.

16. *Deia*, 23 and 24 August 1985.

17. Unzueta, *Sociedad vasca*, p. 137.

18. *Ibid.*, pp. 167–168.

19. *Washington Post*, 17 August 1981. See also Jane Monahan, "Spain Enjoys Calm Amid Uncertainty," *Wall Street Journal*, 3 September 1981. Also *Deia*, 13 September 1981.

20. *Deia*, 22 January 1982.

21. Eugenio Ibarzabal, "VIII Asamblea: Una escisión más en ETA," *Deia*, 28 February 1982, based on a press conference with ETA (p-m) members.

22. At the February 22 press conference called by the pro-truce faction, the only decoration on the walls of the meeting room was a huge photo of Pertur. See *Deia*, 23 February 1982.

23. *Deia*, 5 February 1982.

24. *Deia*, 7 February 1982.

25. *Deia*, 18 February 1982. On that same day, ETA (m) announced that it was renewing its violent attacks as well.

26. Patxo Unzueta, *Los Nietos de la Ira: Nacionalismo y violencia en el País Vasco* (Madrid: Editorial El País, 1988), pp. 195–196.

27. *Deia*, 23 February 1982.

28. *Deia*, 30 and 31 July, 2 and 3 September 1982.

29. Interview with Juan María Bandrés, San Sebastián, 2 August 1988. However, many Spanish observers believed Rosón to be one of the leaders of the transition to democracy, and probably Spain's best interior minister of the post-Franco period. See the obituary written about him in *El País* (international edition), 25 August 1986.

30. Interview with Juan María Bandrés, San Sebastián, 2 August 1988.

31. Ibarzabal, "El debate."

32. *Deia*, 12 March 1981.

33. *Deia*, 29 December 1981.

34. *Deia*, 1 November and 30 July 1982.

35. *Deia*, 31 July 1982.

36. *Deia*, 3 August 1982.

37. *Deia*, 4 and 10 August 1982.

38. *Deia*, 1 September 1982.

39. *Deia*, 9, 11, and 12 September 1982.

40. *Deia*, 29 and 30 September, and 1 October 1982.

41. *Deia*, 5 October 1982.

42. *Deia*, 1 November 1982.

43. *Deia*, 14 January 1983. See also *Deia*, 29 October 1983, for another such incident.

44. *Deia*, 15 May 1983.

45. *Deia*, 22 January 1983.

46. *Deia*, 15 January 1985.

47. Unzueta, *Sociedad Vasca*, pp. 179–180.

48. *Deia*, 31 October 1982. See also Unzueta, *Los Nietos*, pp. 69–70.

49. Ramon Zallo in Joseba Goñi Alzueta *et al.*, *Negociar* (Guecho: Colectivo Herria 2000 Eliza, 1983), pp. 357–358.

50. Patxo Unzueta, "El diálogo y la negociación con ETA," *El País*, 31 August 1987.

51. Interview with Juan María Bandrés, San Sebastián, 2 August 1988.

Chapter Five: New Actors, Initiatives, Failures

1. *Deia* (Bilbao), 18 February 1982.

2. *Cambio 16* (Madrid), 26 April 1982.

3. This was the title of an article by Eugenio Ibarzabal in *Deia*, on 18 April 1982, which is the basis for this paragraph.

4. Pedro Ibarra Guell, *La Evolución Estratégica de ETA, 1963–1987* (San Sebastián: Kriselu, 1987), pp. 140–141.

5. *Deia*, 22 April 1982.

6. *Cambio 16*, 3 May 1982. *Deia*, 23 April 1982.

7. *Deia*, 23 April 1982.

8. *Deia*, 27 May 1982.

9. *Deia*, 17 July 1982.

10. *Deia*, 21 April 1982.

11. *Cambio 16*, 3 May 1982.

12. *Tiempo* (Madrid), 25 October 1982.

13. *Tiempo*, 25 October 1982.

14. *Cambio 16*, 25 October 1982.

15. *Deia*, 16 September 1982.

16. *Deia*, 21 September 1982.

17. *Deia*, 21 October 1982.

18. *Deia*, 20 October 1982.

19. *Deia*, 1 November 1982.

20. *Deia*, 4 November 1982.

21. *Deia*, 10 November 1983.

22. *Deia*, 7 November 1982.

23. *Deia*, 7 November 1982.

24. *Deia*, 14 November 1982.

25. *Deia*, 14 November 1982.

26. *El País* (international edition), 13 December 1982.

27. *Deia*, 7 December 1982.

28. *Deia*, 8 December 1982.

29. *El País* (Madrid), 13 December 1982.

30. *Deia*, 23 December 1982.

31. *Deia*, 30 December 1982.

32. The following is based on numerous press reports from the period January–March 1983, many of which will be cited separately. For a summary account of these events, see Joseba Goñi Alzueta, ed., *Negociar* (Guecho: Colectivo Herria 2000 Eliza, 1983), pp. 415–428.

33. *Deia*, 7 January 1983.

34. *Deia*, 8 and 12 January 1983.

35. *Deia* and *El País*, 14 January 1983.

36. *Deia*, 14 January 1983.

37. *Deia*, 17 January 1983.

38. *Deia*, 18 January 1983.

39. *Deia*, 19 January 1983.

40. *Deia*, 21 January 1983.

41. *Deia*, 30 January 1983.

42. *Deia*, 1 February 1983.

43. *Deia*, 4 February 1983.

44. *Deia*, 8 February 1983.

45. *El País*, 20 February 1983.

46. Gurutz Jáuregui Bereciartu, "Violencia en Euskadi: Una Cuestión de Voluntad Política," in Fernando Reinares, ed., *Violencia y Política en Euskadi* (Bilbao: Desclee de Brouwer, 1984), p. 204.

47. *El País*, 20 February 1983.

48. *Deia*, 24 April 1983.

49. *Deia*, 10 November 1983.

50. *Deia*, 2 January 1983.

51. *Deia*, 11 and 12 March 1983. *El País*, 14 March 1983.

52. *Deia*, 24 April 1983. Emphasis in the original.

53. *Deia*, 26 and 27 April 1983.

54. *Deia*, 2 June 1983.

55. Tom Burns, "Basque Terrorists Kill Kidnaped Army Officer," *Washington Post*, 20 October 1983.

56. *Deia*, 5 November 1983.

57. *Deia*, 10 and 11 November 1983.

58. *El País*, 13 November 1983.

Chapter Six: New Negotiation Initiatives

1. Carlos Etxeberri, "1984, el año mas duro en la historia de ETA," *Deia* (Bilbao), 14 August 1984. Carlos Etxeberri, "Obligar a ETA a negociar," *Deia*, 27 February 1985.

2. *Cambio 16* (Madrid), 11 May 1984.

3. Patxo Unzueta, *Sociedad Vasca y Política Nacionalista* (Madrid: Ediciones El País, 1987), pp. 204–205.

4. *Deia*, 8 July 1984.

5. *El País* (Madrid), 21 July 1985.

6. *El País* (international edition), 27 August 1984. *Deia*, 24 August 1984.

7. *Deia*, 25 August 1984. *Tiempo* (Madrid), 3 September 1984. Several of my respondents in the Basque Country reported that the Spanish government uses *Tiempo* occasionally to leak sensitive information to the public.

8. *Deia*, 24 and 25 August 1984. *Tiempo*, 3 September 1984.

9. *Tiempo*, 3 September 1984.

10. *Deia*, 27 August 1984.

11. *El País*, 21 July 1985.

12. *Tiempo*, 19 November 1984.

13. *Tiempo*, 3 December 1984.

14. Jane Walker, "Spain Said To Conduct Secret Talks with Basques," *Washington Post*, 15 November 1984. *El País* (international edition), 19 November 1984. *Deia*, 15 and 17 November 1984.

15. *El Diario Vasco* (San Sebastián), 9 March 1987.

16. The Brouard assassination is discussed briefly in John Sullivan, *ETA and Basque Nationalism: The Fight for Euskadi, 1890–1986* (London and New York: Routledge, 1988), p. 257. The standard work on the GAL, Javier Garcia, *Los GAL al Descubierto: La trama de la "guerra sucia" contra ETA* (Bilbao: Ediciones El País, 1988), devotes an entire chapter to the killing, pp. 97–109. See also, Tom Burns, "Spanish General Wounded after Basque Leader's Assassination," *Washington Post*, 22 November 1984. Also, *Deia*, 21 November 1984, and *El País* (international edition), 26 November 1984. For an interpretation of the Brouard killing, see *Cambio 16*, 21 January 1985.

17. *El País* (international edition), 3 December 1984. *Deia*, 30 November 1984.

18. *Deia*, 17 November 1985.

19. Juan Félix Eriz, *Yo He Sido Mediador de ETA* (Madrid: Arnao Ediciones, 1986), pp. 265–276. Eriz's claims were amply covered in the press, especially *Deia*, 6 and 8 January, and 2 and 4 May 1986. Eriz's claims were explicitly denied by Spanish government officials, but substantiated by at least one other participant in the meetings. Persons I interviewed in 1988 seemed inclined to treat his claims as certainly possible, and very likely true. My attempts to secure an interview with Eriz in 1988 were unsuccessful.

20. *Deia*, 6 February 1985.

21. *El Correo Español - El Pueblo Vasco* (Bilbao), 10 February 1985.

22. *Deia*, 26 May and 1 June 1985.

23. *El País*, 16 June 1985.

24. *El País*, 16 June 1985.

25. This analysis is based on the following: *El País*, 21 July 1985; *Deia*, 27 July 1985; *Tiempo*, 29 July 1985; and *Euzkadi* (Bilbao), 1 August 1985.

26. *Deia*, 12 December 1985; 29 April 1986.

27. *Deia*, 28 August 1985.

28. *Deia*, 6 August and 4 September 1985.

29. *Deia*, 10 September 1985. *El País* (international edition), 16 September 1985.

30. *Deia*, 17 September 1985.

31. *Deia*, 12 November 1985.

32. *Deia*, 14, 15, and 17 November 1985. *El País* (international edition), 18 November 1985.

33. *Deia*, 26 November and 12 December 1985; 29 April 1986. *El País* (international edition), 2 December 1985.

34. Justo de la Cueva, *La Escisión del PNV* (Bilbao: Txalaparta, 1988).

35. *Deia*, 21 January 1985.

36. The text of the accord is printed in *Deia*, 20 January 1985.

37. *Deia*, 21 January 1985.

38. *El País* (international edition), 11 March 1985.

39. The text of the statement is in *Deia*, 14 March 1985. See also *Deia*, 15 March 1985, for excerpts from the parliamentary debate.

40. *Deia*, 14, 15, 16, and 28 March 1985. *El País* (international edition), 18 March 1985.

41. Interview with Iñaki Anasagasti, Washington, D.C., 14 March 1987. *Deia*, 7 April 1983.

42. Joseba Zulaika, "Terror, Totem, and Taboo: Reporting on a Report." Mimeographed report prepared for the Guggenheim Foundation's Seminar on "Terrorism: Research and Public Policy," cosponsored by the School of American Research, Santa Fe, New Mexico, 12–16 October 1987.

43. *Tiempo*, 19 October 1987.

44. *Deia*, 1 June 1985.

45. *El País*, 13 November 1985.

46. The entire text of the final report is in a special edition of *Deia* that is not dated, but which appeared shortly after 5 March 1986.

47. Unless noted otherwise, the following discussion is based on an interview with Joseba Azkarraga, Vitoria, 14 July 1988.

48. *Deia*, 4 August 1982.

49. *Deia*, 10 April 1984.

50. Interview with Joseba Zubia, Washington, D.C., 15 July 1989.

51. *Deia*, 18 July 1987.

52. *Deia*, 5 and 6 February 1984.

53. *El País* (international edition), 29 January 1985 and 21 October 1985. *Deia*, 18 and 19 October 1989.

54. *Deia*, 11 September 1986. *El País*, 14 September 1986.

55. *Deia*, 15 July 1988.

Chapter Seven: "Algerian Connection" Phase One

1. *Deia* (Bilbao), 28 April 1986.

2. *El País* (Madrid), 13 November 1985.

3. Pedro Ibarra Guell, *La Evolución Estratégica de ETA, 1963–1987* (San Sebastián: Kriselu, 1987), pp. 99–100.

4. *Deia*, 8 April 1986.

5. *El País* (international edition), 14 April 1986.

6. This conversation is reported in Patxo Unzueta, *Los Nietos de la Ira: Nacionalismo y Violencia en el País Vasco* (Madrid: Ediciones El País, 1988), pp. 196–197.

7. Patxo Unzueta, "Laberintos del Terror," *El País*, 27 September 1986. Reprinted in *Sociedad Vasca y Política Nacionalista* (Madrid: Ediciones El País, 1987), pp. 219–220. It should be noted that Unzueta's book was sharply criticized by the Basque left for exactly this kind of "defeatist" analysis. See the article by Luis Núñez in *Egin* (San Sebastián), 19 April 1988.

8. *El País* (international edition), 14 April 1986.

9. *El País*, 31 January 1988. *Deia*, 21 February 1988.

10. Interview with Gorka Aguirre, Bilbao, 26 July 1988.

11. Interview with Gorka Aguirre, Bilbao, 26 July 1988.

12. *Deia*, 26 April 1986.

13. *Deia*, 29 April 1986.

14. *Deia*, 29 April 1986.

15. *Deia*, 28 and 29 April 1986.

16. *Deia*, 29 April 1986.

17. *Deia*, 28 April 1986.

18. *Deia*, 29 April 1986. *El País* (international edition), 17 October 1988.

19. *Deia*, 29 April 1986.

20. *Deia*, 30 April 1986.

21. *Deia*, 16 May 1986. *El País* (international edition), 19 May 1986.

22. *Deia*, 25 and 27 June 1986.

23. Interview with Xabier Arzalluz, Bilbao, 13 July 1988.

24. *Deia*, 8 August 1986. *El País*, 10 August 1986. *El Diario Vasco* (San Sebastián), 21 February 1988.

25. Interview with Iñaki Esnaola, San Sebastián, 3 August 1988.

26. Interview with Gorka Aguirre, Bilbao, 26 July 1988. *Deia*, 8 August 1986. *El País*, 31 January 1988.

27. Interview with Iñaki Esnaola, San Sebastián, 3 August 1988.

28. *El País*, 10 August 1986. *Tiempo* (Madrid), 21 September 1987. *Deia*, 12 July 1986.

29. *Tiempo*, 21 September 1987.

30. *Deia*, 6 August 1986.

31. *El País* (international edition), 21 July 1986.

32. Interview with Iñaki Esnaola, San Sebastián, 3 August 1988. *El País*, 20 July 1986.

33. *El País*, 3 August 1986. In the summer of 1986 there were fourteen ETA members living in former French or Portuguese colonies in West Africa, including Cape Verde, Togo, and Gabon.

34. Interview with Iñaki Esnaola, San Sebastián, 3 August 1988. *El País*, 20 July 1986.

35. But confirmed in an interview with Iñaki Esnaola, San Sebastián, 3 August 1988. *Deia*, 5 and 19 August 1986.

36. *El Diario Vasco*, 21 February 1988. *El País* (international edition), 4 August 1986. Interview with Iñaki Esnaola, San Sebastián, 3 August 1988.

37. *Deia*, 3 August 1986.

38. *Deia*, 6 August 1986.

39. *Deia*, 7 August 1986.

40. *Deia*, 8 and 9 August 1986.

41. *Deia*, 26 August 1987.

42. *Deia*, 11 August 1986. *El País*, 10 August 1986. *El País* (international edition), 11 and 18 August 1986.

43. *Deia*, 13 August 1986. *El País* (international edition), 18 August 1986.

44. *Deia*, 12 August 1986.

45. *Deia*, 19 August 1986.

46. *El País*, 15 March 1987.

47. *Deia*, 8 March 1987.

48. *El País*, 4 March 1987.

49. *El País*, 15 March 1987.

50. *El País*, 7 September 1986.

51. *El País* (international edition), 15 September 1986. These reports directly contradict the claim that Iturbe had traveled to Algeria in secret and that the Spanish government did not know of his presence in that country for several months.

52. Interviews with Gorka Aguirre, Bilbao, 26 July 1988; Xabier Arzalluz, Bilbao, 26 July 1988; and Iñaki Esnaola, San Sebastián, 3 August 1988.

53. Interview with Gorka Aguirre, Bilbao, 26 July 1988.

54. According to Xabier Arzalluz, Barrionuevo was the instigator of negotiations once Iturbe arrived in Algeria. Interview, Bilbao, 13 July 1988. See also, *El País* (international edition), 22 September 1986.

55. *El Diario Vasco*, 21 February 1988.

56. *Tiempo*, 21 September 1987.

57. *El Diario Vasco*, 21 February 1988. *Deia*, 22 November 1986.

58. José Luis Morales, Teresa Toda, and Miren Imaz, *La Trama del G.A.L.* (Madrid: Editorial Revolución, 1988), p. 19. See also, *El País*, 3 March 1985; and *El País* (international edition), 21 April 1986.

59. Anonymous interview. The quote is from the ETA communiqué of September 1987, as reported in *El País*, 6 September 1987.

60. *Egin*, 26 November 1986. Excerpts from the interview are cited in

Justo de la Cueva, *La Escisión del PNV* (Bilbao: Editorial Txalaparta, 1988), pp. 442–443.

61. *Tiempo*, 21 September 1987.

62. While the ETA communiqué of September 1987 does not mention this meeting, it was confirmed to me in an anonymous interview by one of the participants.

63. *El Diario Vasco*, 21 February 1988. *El País*, 31 August 1987. ETA's version of the meetings is contained in the September 1987 communiqué.

64. Miguel Castells Arteche, *Radiografía de un Modelo Represivo* (San Sebastián: Ediciones Vascas, 1982), p. 95.

65. *Deia*, 24 May 1985.

66. *Deia*, 11 September 1987.

67. Anonymous interview.

68. *Deia*, 28 February 1987.

69. *Deia*, 4 March 1987.

70. *El País*, 4 March 1987.

71. *El Diario Vasco*, 9 March 1987.

72. *El Diario Vasco*, 9 March 1987.

Chapter Eight: "Algerian Connection" Phase Two

1. *Deia* (Bilbao), 23 March 1987. *Tiempo* (Madrid), 14 December 1987.

2. The document is included as an appendix in Patxo Unzueta, *Los Nietos de la Ira: Nacionalismo y Violencia en el País Vasco* (Madrid: Ediciones El País, 1988), pp. 237–246.

3. Interview with Joseba Azkarraga, Vitoria, 14 July 1988.

4. *Deia*, 29 and 31 March 1987; 13 May 1987. *El País* (international edition), 6 April 1987.

5. *Deia*, 7 May, 13 and 16 August 1986.

6. *Deia*, 12 July 1987. *El País* (international edition), 3 and 10 August 1987.

7. *Deia*, 11 and 12 August 1987. *El País* (international edition), 17 August 1987. *El País*, 29 August 1987.

8. See the ETA communiqué in *El País*, 6 September 1987. Also, *Deia*, 2 and 4 September 1987.

9. *El País*, 31 August 1987. *Deia*, 30 August 1987.

10. *Deia*, 23 and 25 August 1987. *El País*, 31 August 1987.

11. *Deia*, 25 August 1987.

12. *Deia*, 26 August 1987. *El País* (international edition), 31 August 1987. *El País*, 29, 30, and 31 August 1987.

13. *Deia*, 27 August 1987.

14. *Deia*, 31 August 1987.

15. The communiqué was widely published the next day. The following is based on the version that appeared in *El País*, 6 September 1987. See also, *Deia*, 6 September 1987, and *El País* (international edition), 7 September 1987.

16. *El País*, 7 September 1987. *Deia*, 8 September 1987.

17. *El País*, 10 September 1987.

18. *Deia*, 17 September 1987.

19. The wording is from the ETA truce communiqué of January 27, 1988, published in *Egin*, 29 January 1988.

20. *Deia*, 1 and 2 October 1987.

21. *El País*, 7 October 1987. *Deia*, 14 and 31 October, 1 November 1987.

22. *Deia*, 27 November 1987.

23. *Deia*, 21 October 1987. *Tiempo*, 14 December 1987.

24. *Deia*, 7 October 1987.

25. *Deia*, 11 October 1987.

26. *Deia*, 31 October 1987. *El País* (international edition), 2 November 1987.

27. *Deia*, 1 November 1987.

28. *El País*, 1 November 1987.

29. Interview with Iñaki Esnaola, San Sebastián, 3 August 1988.

30. *Deia*, 8 November 1987.

31. ETA's version of the talks is contained in the organization's January 1988 communiqué, published in *Egin*, 29 January 1988. See also, *Deia*, 13 November 1987, and *El País*, 14 November 1987.

32. *Egin*, 29 January 1988.

33. *El Diario Vasco* (San Sebastián), 7 February 1988.

34. *El País*, 15 November 1987.

35. *Deia*, 21 April 1982.

36. Ana Miranda, "El Acuerdo Interno del Pueblo Vasco: La Unica Vía de Pacificación de Euskadi," in Fernando Reinares, ed., *Violencia y Política en Euskadi* (Bilbao: Desclee de Brouwer, 1984), pp. 234–235.

37. Interview with Xabier Arzalluz, Bilbao, 26 July 1988. See also, *Cambio 16* (Madrid), 16 November 1987.

38. *Deia*, 5 September 1987. *El País*, 10 September 1987.

39. *El País*, 5 October 1987.

40. *El País*, 21 October 1987.

41. *Deia*, 12 October 1987.

42. *El País*, 23 October 1987.

43. *Deia*, 25 October 1987.

44. The complete text of the accord is in *El País* (international edition), 9 November 1987.

45. *El País*, 2 November 1987.

46. *Deia*, 5 November 1987.

47. *El País*, 2 November 1987. *Deia*, 3 November 1987.

48. *Deia*, 10 November 1987.

49. *Deia*, 16 November 1987.

50. *El País*, 12 November 1987.

51. *Deia*, 3 December 1987.

52. *Deia*, 15 and 18 December 1987.

53. *Deia*, 21 and 22 December 1987.

54. *Deia*, 23 December 1987.

55. *El País* (international edition), 29 December 1987.

56. See *Deia*, 30 December 1987, for the full text of the second draft.

57. *Deia*, 4 January 1988.

58. *Deia*, 11 January 1988.

59. *Deia*, 12 January 1988.

60. The full text of the final draft was published by the Basque government, and also was widely available in the Basque press, including *Deia* and *El Diario Vasco* of 13 January 1988. See also *Deia*, 13 January 1988, for a complete chronology of events leading up to the signing.

61. *El Diario Vasco*, 20 January 1988.

62. See ETA's truce communiqué in *Egin*, 29 January 1988.

63. Unzueta, *Los Nietos*, pp. 224–226.

64. *El Diario Vasco*, 20 January 1988.

65. *Deia*, 12 February 1988.

66. *El País*, 14 May 1988.

67. *Deia*, 30 July 1988.

68. *Deia*, 19 December 1987. *El País*, 18 December 1987.

69. This version of the Vera mission, confirmed substantially by interviews with persons who asked to remain anonymous, is contained in the ETA truce proposal as published in *Egin*, 29 January 1988. See also, *Deia* and *El País*, 23 January 1988.

70. *El País*, 18 December 1987.

71. *El País*, 9 January 1988. *El País* (international edition), 4 January 1988.

72. *Deia*, 21 January 1988.

73. *El País*, 5 February 1988.

74. *Egin*, 29 January 1988.

75. Interview with Iñaki Esnaola, San Sebastián, 3 August 1988.

76. Interviews with Iñaki Esnaola, San Sebastián, 3 August 1988; and Gorka Aguirre, Bilbao, 26 July 1988.

77. The London weekly *The Economist*, for example, reported erroneously that "ETA has . . . for the first time offered to halt the violence without obtaining a prior commitment from the Madrid government to enter into 'political negotiations'." *The Economist*, 6 February 1988.

78. *Deia*, 30 January 1988.

79. *El País*, 30 January 1988. *El Diario Vasco*, 30 January 1988.

80. *El Diario Vasco*, 2 February 1988.

81. See, for example, *El Diario Vasco*, 1 February 1988, and *Deia*, 31 January 1988.

82. *El Diario Vasco*, 31 January 1988.

83. See also the articles in *El País*, 31 January 1988, including Fernando Savater, "El precio de la sangre," and Patxo Unzueta, "ETA cambia el discurso."

84. *Deia*, 3 February 1988.

85. *Deia*, 4 February 1988.

86. *El País*, 5 February 1988.

87. The two-track approach was repeated in an *El País* article, "ETA, ante el final del tunel," by Victorino R. de Azúa, on 7 February 1988. The article was allegedly based on discussions with "a politician responsible for the antiterrorist struggle."

88. *El País*, 6 February 1988.

89. *El Diario Vasco*, 7 February 1988.

90. *El País*, 12 February 1988.

91. *Deia*, 13 February 1988.

92. *Deia*, 15 and 16 February 1988. The communiqué was analyzed in *El País* on 16 February 1988.

93. *El País*, 16 February 1988.

94. *Deia*, 19 February 1988.

95. *El País*, 21 February 1988. *El Diario Vasco*, 22 February 1988.

96. Anonymous interview.

97. *Deia*, 24 February 1988.

98. The text of the communiqué is in Justo de la Cueva, *La Escisión del PNV* (Bilbao: Txalaparta, 1988), pp. 458–459.

99. Interview with Xabier Arzalluz, Bilbao, 13 July 1988.

100. Interviews with Xabier Arzalluz, Bilbao, 13 July 1988, and Gorka Aguirre, Bilbao, 26 July 1988. See also, *Diario 16* (Madrid), 16 August 1988.

101. The text of the interview is contained in Unzueta, *Los Nietos*, pp. 247–251.

102. *El País* (international edition), 31 October 1988.

103. *El País* (international edition), 7 November 1988.

Chapter Nine: Obstacles to Peace

1. *El Diario Vasco* (San Sebastián), 5 and 13 April 1989.

2. This has been discussed by Pedro Ibarra Guell, in *La Evolución Estratégica de ETA, 1963–1987* (San Sebastián: Kriselu, 1987), pp. 180–183.

3. Based on a public opinion survey, the results of which were published in *Deia* (Bilbao), 17 October 1987. Many other such surveys reveal much the same findings. See, for example, *Euskadi 1988* (San Sebastián: EGIN, 1988), p. 157, for the results of three similar polls in late 1987 and early 1988.

4. The reader interested in these cultural factors is urged to consult Joseba Zulaika's provocative study, *Basque Violence: Metaphor and Sacrament* (Reno: University of Nevada Press, 1988).

5. This section is adapted from Robert Clark, "Obstacles to Negotiating a Ceasefire with Insurgents: The ETA Case," *TVI Report*, 7, 1 (1986), pp. 1–12.

6. Interview with Xabier Arzalluz, Bilbao, 26 July 1988.

7. Ibarra Guell, *La Evolución*. See above, chapter one, for more discussion on this subject.

8. Interview with Gorka Aguirre, Bilbao, 26 July 1988.

9. Patxo Unzueta, "El diálogo y la negociación con ETA," *El País* (Madrid), 31 August 1987.

10. *Tiempo* (Madrid), 3 September 1984. *Deia*, 30 August 1984.

11. Patxo Unzueta, *Sociedad Vasca y Política Nacionalista* (Madrid: Ediciones El País, 1987), p. 133.

12. *Tiempo* (Madrid), 21 September 1987. An interview with Iñaki Esnaola, San Sebastián, 3 August 1988, confirmed this basic sentiment, although not necessarily the exact quote.

13. Interview with Joseba Azkarraga, Vitoria, 14 July 1988. Also, *Deia*, 23 August 1987.

14. Ibarra Guell, *La Evolución*, pp. 142–144.

GLOSSARY

AP, Alianza Popular (Popular Alliance). Conservative Spanish political party created in 1976 by Manuel Fraga Iribarne. Strongly opposed to concessions to ethnic nationalists and to negotiations with ETA. Joined with other parties in 1980s to create Coalición Popular.

Basque A.C., Basque Autonomous Community (known officially in Spanish as the Comunidad Autónoma del País Vasco). The autonomous government established in three Basque provinces (Alava, Vizcaya, Guipúzcoa) in 1980 under the terms of the 1978 Spanish constitution and the Basque Autonomy Statute of 1979. ETA does not accept the legitimacy of this government since, among other reasons, it does not include the province of Navarra.

BVE, Batallón Vasco-Español (Basque-Spanish Battalion). A right-wing antiterrorist organization created in the late 1970s to conduct violent attacks against Basques in general, and against ETA in particular, primarily in France. Apparently ceased to exist in the early 1980s.

CC. AA., Comandos Autónomos (Autonomous Cells). Small faction that split off from ETA in late 1970s. Especially violent and unpredictable. Activities much reduced during 1980s.

CDS, Centro Democrático Social (Social Democratic Center). Center-right Spanish political party created in the early 1980s by Adolfo Suárez to replace the defunct UCD. Conservative on many issues, but tended to take a moderate position toward ethnic nationalist claims and toward concessions to ETA, especially in the area of amnesty.

CiU, Convergència i Unió (Convergence and Union). Moderate Catalan nationalist political party. Occupies an ideological space approximately the same as the PNV.

CP, Coalición Popular (People's Coalition). Conservative Spanish political coalition that replaced (and absorbed) AP in the mid-1980s.

EA, Eusko Alkartasuna (Basque Solidarity). Political party formed in 1986 by former Basque President Carlos Garaikoetxea after he left the PNV. Ideologically similar to the PNV, but tends to be somewhat more intransigent on questions of Basque self-rule.

EE, Euzkadiko Ezkerra (Basque Left). Coalition of Basque nationalist political parties formed in 1977. The coalition combines Basque nationalism with a Marxist ideological tendency. At one time closely linked to ETA (p-m). Originally rejected the legitimacy of the autonomous arrangement negotiated with the Basques in 1979, but has come to support autonomy. Its leaders were instrumental in amnesty negotiations in the early 1980s.

ETA, Euzkadi ta Askatasuna (Basque Homeland and Freedom). Insurgent organization founded in 1959 to conduct struggle for the independence of Euskadi.

ETA (m), ETA (militar), (military wing of ETA). Faction of ETA that developed out of its Frente Militar in 1973 and 1974. Formed its own organization in 1974. Remains today as the only viable wing of ETA.

ETA (p-m), ETA (político-militar), (political-military wing of ETA). Faction of ETA left after the split in 1974; (p-m) itself split in 1982. The séptimos wing eventually dissolved itself and most of its members were amnestied. The octavos wing in theory remains alive; but its few members are all in Cuba, and it has in effect ceased to be a factor in the insurgency.

GAL, Grupos Antiterroristas de Liberación (Antiterrorist Liberation Groups). Secret right-wing antiterrorist organization created in 1983. Responsible for killing about twenty-seven Basques between 1983 and 1986. Not heard from after 1986, but may have been responsible for attack in 1989 that killed one HB leader and wounded another.

HB, Herri Batasuna (Popular Unity). A coalition of Basque nationalist political parties formed in 1978. Rejects the legitimacy of the existing autonomy arrangement and advocates negotiating the KAS Alternative with ETA. HB is a part of the MLNV, and its leaders have offered many times to serve as intermediaries to get negotiations started.

IU, Izquierda Unida (United Left). Splinter faction of the Spanish Communist Party. Began to show electoral strength in 1986.

KAS, Koordinadora Abertzale Sozialista (Patriotic Socialist Coordinating Committee). An umbrella organization of pro-ETA groups formed in 1975. Set of five demands published in 1979, known as the KAS Alternative, have been the focal point of negotiations since that time.

MLNV, Movimiento de Liberación Nacional Vasca (Basque National Liberation Movement). An umbrella organization of diverse Basque left parties and other groups that advocate the independence of Euskadi. Includes Herri Batasuna. It has been suggested by ETA that the MLNV could serve as a negotiating party representing the insurgents.

PCE, Partido Comunista de España (Spanish Communist Party). One of the historic communist parties of Europe and an advocate of Eurocommunism in the 1970s. Opposed to concessions to ETA, but supported a federal solution to the problem of Basque self-rule. Suffered sharp decline in elections throughout the post-Franco period.

PDP, Partido Demócrata Popular (Popular Democrat Party). Moderately conservative Spanish political party. Joined with AP to form Coalición Popular in 1980s.

PL, Partido Liberal (Liberal Party). One of many moderately liberal political parties formed in Spain in the late 1970s. Merged with other parties and eventually lost separate identity.

PNV, Partido Nacionalista Vasco (Basque Nationalist Party). Moderate Basque nationalist party created in the 1890s. Party has dominated Basque political life since the Spanish Civil War. Basque president has always been from this party. Party split in 1986 by the withdrawal of Carlos Garaikoetxea and the creation of EA. The PNV favors negotiations with ETA conducted by, or through, Basque elected institutions —that is, the Basque parliament and government.

PSOE, Partido Socialista Obrero Español (Spanish Socialist Workers' Party). One of the historic Spanish political parties whose origins go back to the nineteenth century. Formerly took a strongly Marxist ideological position, but renounced Marxism in the 1980s and won the 1982, 1986, and 1989 Spanish parliamentary elections. Has moved toward the right of the ideological spectrum, and strongly opposes any concessions to ETA except those involving amnesty for individual members.

PP, Partido Popular (People's Party). The conservative Spanish political party that replaced AP and CP on the right of the ideological spectrum in the late 1980s.

UCD, Unión de Centro Democrático (Union of the Democratic Center). Moderate center-right Spanish political party formed by Adolfo Suárez in 1977. Was the governing party in Spain from 1977 to 1982. Dissolved after losing to the PSOE in 1982 elections.

AAA. *See* Apostolic Anticommunist Alliance

Action-repression spiral theory, 8–10, 231

Aguinagalde, Lucio, 180

Aguirre, Xabier, 100, 169

Aizpeolea, Luis, 217

Aizpurua, Itziar, 79

Aizpurua, Mertxe, 54

Alberdi Martiarena, Juan Carlos, 71

Aldecoa, Iñaki, 121, 169

Algeria: deportation of ETA members, 31, 71, 189–190; Spanish relations with, 27, 32; as training base, 31–32, 177; *See also* Algerian negotiations

Algerian Democratic Movement, 32, 178

Algerian negotiations, 21, 31, 165–166; Algerian objectives, 14, 31–32, 177–178; and death of Iturbe, 185–186, 187; ETA communiqués, 192–195, 214–217; and ETA violence, 190, 202, 212, 217, 219–220, 221, 223; Etxebeste-Ballestero talks, 190–192, 195–196, 197; Etxebeste-Elgorriaga talks, 198–202, 212, 219, 235; and Iturbe deportation, 31, 165, 177–179, 180–181, 182, 183–185; Iturbe role in, 180–182, 183–184, 193, 195;

Spanish government attitudes toward, 175–176, 189–190, 191–192, 197–198, 216, 238; truce proposal, 212–220, 221, 223–224

Alianza Popular. *See* Partido Popular

Alvarez Santacristina, José Luis, "Txelis," 197

Amedo, José, 67

Amezketa, Koldo, 100, 101

Amnesty, 1, 3, 24, 36, 41; Algerian negotiations, 184, 191, 195, 199–200, 202; *amnistía encubierta,* 200, 237; and antiterrorist pacts, 205, 208, 209–210; and collaboration, 57, 109–110, 133–134; ETA demands, 8, 78, 122, 140, 237; ETA (p-m) demands, 91, 92, 97; KAS Alternative, 82, 120, 166; *mesa para la paz,* 128; in six-stage negotiation calendar, 147; Spanish political parties' attitudes, 29, 122, 209; in two-track negotiation strategy, 149, 219, 234, 235, 236. *See also* Social reintegration programs

Amnesty International, 14, 32–33, 38, 43, 56

Ansola, Pello Larrañaga, "Peio el viejo," 60, 62, 172, 175

Antiterrorist legislation, 35, 69–70, 97, 206; and human rights violations, 41, 49–50; Plan ZEN,

Antiterrorist legislation (cont'd)
57, 136; under PSOE, 28, 53, 57,
64–65, 133–134; under UCD,
37–38, 40–42, 47–49, 89
Antiterrorist Liberation Groups
(GAL). See Grupos Antiterroristas de Libaración
Antiterrorist pacts, 70, 194, 200,
202–212, 215
Antxon (Eugenio Etxebeste), 143,
148, 220; and Algerian negotiations, 184, 193, 213, 214,
221; arrest of, 62–63, 69, 141,
172; Ballestero talks, 190–192,
195–196, 197; Elgorriaga talks,
198–202, 212, 219, 235
ANV. See Basque National Action
AP. See Partido Popular
Apala (Miguel Angel Apalategui),
75, 76–77, 79, 85, 86
Apalategui, Miguel Angel, "Apala,"
75, 76–77, 79, 85, 86
Apostolic Anticommunist Alliance (AAA), 77
Arakama, Iñaki, 185
Aramburu Garmendia, Juan
Ramón, "Juanra," 69, 149–150,
151, 172
Arana y Goiri, Sabino de, 19
Ardanza, José Antonio, 5, 28, 154,
155, 174; and antiterrorist pacts,
203, 204, 205, 207, 208–211; and
CAV internal crisis, 18, 19, 151–
152; and negotiation attempts,
166–167, 168, 173, 192, 235
Argala (José Miguel Beñarán Or-
deñana), 75, 81–82, 84, 85, 86;
death of, 5, 43, 87, 88, 186
Argote, Jorge, 180–181, 193
Arias Navarro, Carlos, 38
Armed forces. See Law enforce-
ment, Basque goals for; Spanish
government
Arregi, Joseba, 49, 96, 183
Arregui, Joseba, 212
Arrest rates, 42–43, 44, 45, 49, 53–

54, 64, 65; decreases in, 38–39,
70. See also French anti-ETA
policies
Arrospide, Santiago, "Santi Potros,"
71, 187, 196, 198, 205
Artapalo (Francisco Múgica Gar-
mendia), 149–150, 169, 187,
196–197, 220
Artexte, Joseba, 63
Arzalluz, Xabier, 59, 89, 98–102,
149, 151; and antiterrorist pacts,
204, 205, 209, 210; and interna-
tional experts study, 155–156;
and negotiation attempts, 169,
176
ASK, 21
Assassinations. See ETA violence;
Guerra sucia
Aulestia, Joseba, "Zotza," 113
Aulestia, Kepa, 149, 157, 204, 210
Auzmendi, Martin, 204
Azkarraga, Joseba, 5, 55, 134,
189, 206; social reintegration
program, 140, 158–163
Azua, Jon, 204
Azurmendi, José Félix, 54

Ballesteros, Manuel, 51, 58, 136,
140; and Algerian negotiations,
183, 190–192, 193, 195–196,
197, 215; and negotiation attempts, 108, 134, 135
Bandrés, Juan María, 5, 53, 65; and
cease-fires, 94, 95, 98–100, 102,
149; and negotiation attempts,
79, 92, 126–127, 129, 149, 233;
Rosón amnesty negotiations,
103, 106, 107–115, 124, 133, 162,
233
Barquero, José Manuel, 204
Barrionuevo, José, 26, 140, 150;
and Algerian negotiations, 179,
183–184, 195; and antiterrorist
policies, 52–53, 61, 134; and
human rights violations, 55, 56,
57; and Iturbe imprisonment,

171, 173, 174; and negotiation attempts, 126, 141–142, 143, 149, 151; and social reintegration programs, 113, 159

Basque Autonomous Community (CAV), 17–18, 57, 152; as essential to negotiations, 20, 142, 153, 185, 192, 205–206; Garaikoetxea resignation, 151–152; Herri Batasuna rejection of, 18, 19, 21, 128–129, 153, 208; internal conflicts, 151–152, 185; and international relations, 153; KAS Alternative, discussion of, 149; and negotiation attempts, 92, 126–132, 169, 176, 189; PSE agreement, 152–153, 156–157, 168; and social reintegration programs, 167; and Spanish government, 28, 151–152, 185, 206–207; ten-point program (1985), 152, 154–155, 156–157. See also Basque autonomy statute; Basque political parties; Basque self-determination; Law enforcement, Basque goals for; Navarrese integration

Basque autonomy statute, 17–18, 94; and antiterrorist pacts, 205, 207, 209, 210; and Basque political parties, 19, 20, 149, 170; CAV attitude towards, 167, 176; ETA demands, 82, 91, 97, 166; and Navarrese integration, 148; Spanish government attitudes toward, 199; ten-point agreement (1985), 153, 154. See also Basque Autonomous Community (CAV); Basque self-determination

Basque Homeland and Freedom. See ETA

Basque language. See Euskera

Basque Left (EE). See Euzkadiko Ezkerra; Koordinadora Abertzale Sozialista

Basque media, 12, 22, 53–54, 64, 229–230

Basque National Action (ANV), 120. See also Basque political parties

Basque National Liberation Movement (MLNV). See Movimiento de Liberación Nacional Vasco

Basque Nationalist Party (PNV). See Partido Nacionalista Vasco

Basque political parties, 12, 18–22, 122, 128, 168; antiterrorist pacts, 70, 194, 200, 202–212; and antiterrorist policy, 57, 65; and autonomy statute, 19, 20, 149, 170; and democratic transition, 78, 79; ETA demands for legalization, 78, 82, 147, 167, 239; and political negotiations, 213; restrictions on, 53–54, 58, 64; seven-point agreement (1984), 152–153. See also Basque Autonomous Community (CAV); individual parties

Basque Popular Socialist Party (EHAS; HASI), 21, 79, 84, 86–87, 98. See also Basque political parties

Basque Pro-Amnesty Committees. See Gestoras Pro-Amnistía

Basque Revolutionary Party (EIA). See Euskal Iraultzale Alderdia

Basque self-determination, 80, 101, 128, 148, 239; and Algerian negotiations, 184, 191, 199, 202; and antiterrorist pacts, 205, 206, 209, 210; CAV attitude towards, 153, 154, 167; ETA (p-m) demands (1980), 91, 97, 98; KAS Alternative, 82, 83, 120, 166; Spanish government attitudes toward, 27, 29. See also Basque Autonomous Community (CAV); Political negotiations

Basque Socialist Party (PSE). See Partido Socialista de Euskadi

Basque Solidarity (EA). *See* Eusko Alkartasuna
Batallón Vasco-Español (BVE), 14, 33, 39, 58, 66
Beihl, Eugen, 84
Belgium, 14, 176
Belloch, José María, 77–78
Benarán Ordenana, José Miguel, "Argala," 75, 81–82, 84, 85, 86; death of, 5, 43, 87, 88, 186
Ben Bella, Ahmed, 178
Benegas, Txiki, 60; and antiterrorist pacts, 202–203, 204, 205, 206, 207, 209, 210–211; Herri Batasuna negotiations, 124, 125, 127, 129–130, 131; and negotiation attempts, 84, 86–87, 88, 122, 132, 136–137, 142
Benyedid, Chadli, 178
Berezi Comandos, 77, 86
Bergara, Josu, 204
Betancur Cuartas, Belisario, 143
Bongo, Omar, 178
Brouard, Santiago, "Santi," 121, 143. *See also* Brouard killing
Brouard killing, 5, 144–145, 186; and antiterrorist policies, 52, 59, 64; and *guerra sucia,* 52, 66, 144, 229; and negotiation attempts, 140, 146
Burgos trial (1968), 9, 76
BVE. *See* Batallón Vasco-Español

Cabanillas, Pio, 107
Calvo Sotelo, Leopoldo, 25, 36, 50, 51, 93, 107
Carrero Blanco, Luís, 9
Castells, Miguel, 39, 43, 54, 65, 143
Catholic church leaders, 13, 22–23
CAV. *See* Comunidad Autónoma Vasca
CDS. *See* Centro Democrático Social
Cease-fires, 1–2, 4–5, 78, 96, 98, 173; and Algerian negotiations,

213–214, 215, 216, 219; and democratic transition, 79, 84; as ETA goal, 4, 8, 115; ETA offers, 169, 194; ETA (p-m) declarations, 79, 93, 96–98, 99–102, 103–104, 105–106, 109, 149; ETA technical truces, 150–151, 176–177; and Guardia Civil coup, 96–97; and KAS Alternative, 81, 82, 83; and negotiation attempts, 128, 129, 216, 226, 230–233, 237–238. *See also* ETA (político-militar) VII; Negotiation attempts
Central Intelligence Agency (CIA), 156
Centro Democrático Social (CDS), 13, 29, 203, 204, 205, 211
Chalandon, Albin, 172
Cherid, Jean Pierre, 66–67
Cheysson, Claude, 61
Chirac, Jacques, 68, 200, 205
Claveria, Carlos, 169
Coalición Popular. *See* Partido Popular
Cogolludo Vallejo, Santiago, 113
Colombia, 143
Comandos Autónomos (Autonomous Cells), 16, 159
Comunidad Autónoma Vasca (CAV). *See* Basque Autonomous Community
Conesa, Roberto, 42
Congress of Deputies. *See* Spanish parliament
Control Risk, Inc., 156
Convergéncia i Unió (CiU), 203
Corcuera, José Luís, 26, 220
Counterterrorism groups. *See* Guerra sucia
Crespo, Juan José, 49
Cuba, 11, 16, 32
Cueva, Justo de la, 54

Deferre, Gaston, 61
Democratic transition, 17, 24, 73–

74, 76, 77, 78; and cease-fires,
79, 84; and KAS Alternative, 80–
81; and negotiation attempts,
77–78, 81–82, 187–188, 199
Deportees, 12, 14, 16–17, 31, 32.
See also French deportation
policies; Social reintegration
programs
D'Estaing, Valéry Giscard, 46
Diaz Arcocha, Carlos, 154
Domínguez, Michel, 67

EA. See Eusko Alkartasuna
Echegaray, José Luís, 78
Echevarria, Antonio, 74
EE. See Euzkadiko Ezkerra
EHAS. See Basque Popular Social-
ist Party
EIA. See Euskal Iraultzale Alderdia
Electoral participation, 8, 12, 79,
94; vs. armed struggle, 15, 75,
76, 77. See also Basque Au-
tonomous Community; Basque
political parties
Elgorriaga, Julen, 197, 215, 216,
217–218, 220; Etxebeste talks,
198–202, 212, 219, 235
Elizari, Fermin, 73
Eriz, Juan Félix, 12, 22, 84, 85, 86;
Operation Wellington, 145–147,
151
Erkizia, Tasio, 204
Ertzainza, 18
ESB. See Partido Socialista de
Euskadi
Esnaola, Iñaki, 148, 173, 176; and
Algerian negotiations, 214; and
negotiation attempts, 125, 128–
129, 140–141, 169, 182, 186,
235
Esnaola, Tomás, 110–111
ETA, 5, 8, 38; as illegitimate, 20,
185, 205–206, 208; schisms
within, 10–11, 15, 75–77, 79,
81. See also Amnesty; Cease-
fires; ETA violence; ETA (mili-

tar); ETA (político-militar);
ETA (político-militar) VII; ETA
(político-militar) VIII; Negotiation attempts; ETA headings
under other subjects
ETA violence, 15, 40, 92, 121, 126,
133, 238; and Algerian negotiations, 190, 202, 212, 217, 219–
220, 221, 223; and antiterrorist
pacts, 209; and antiterrorist
policy, 40, 50, 51, 53, 58, 64, 136;
as attempts to force negotiations,
124–125, 139, 150, 190, 233;
and Bergara meeting, 169–170;
CAV responses to, 153–155; and
electoral participation issue, 79;
and ETA (p-m) cease-fire declaration, 94–95, 96, 98; and French
antiterrorist policies, 61, 106;
and Guardia Civil coup attempt,
47, 118; and guerra sucia, 58, 62,
136; and Iturbe imprisonment,
171, 174; and mesa para la paz,
130–131; and 1982 elections,
123; and Pertur faction, 76; PNV
attitude towards, 176; and prisoner transfer negotiations, 91;
six-stage negotiation calendar,
147; and social reintegration programs, 106, 159, 160, 162–163;
theoretical defenses, 8–9, 105,
119. See also Cease-fires
ETA (militar), 10, 12, 15, 75, 106;
and CAV, 19; and cease-fires,
98; and democratic transition,
79; and GRUPO 16 meeting,
140; and HB, 120; ideology of,
11, 105; and KAS, 21, 22; and
negotiation attempts, 78, 81–82,
84, 125, 145; negotiation offer
(1982), 118–119, 120; organizational structure of, 16; and social
reintegration programs, 113–114,
162–163. See also ETA violence
ETA (político-militar), 11, 12,
15–16, 54; and Basque politi-

ETA (político-militar) (cont'd)
cal parties, 19, 20, 21, 81, 94;
cease-fire declaration, 93, 96–
98, 99–102, 103–104, 105–106,
109, 149; electoral participation,
79, 81, 94; and negotiation attempts, 78, 84, 85, 90–92. See
also ETA (político-militar) VII;
Eusko Alkartasuna (EA)
ETA (político-militar) VII (Pertur
faction), 75–77, 78, 104, 105–
106, 134, 167–168; dissolution
of, 10, 20, 93, 100, 101, 102, 106,
107, 109, 111–112, 115; ETA
(político-militar) VIII, 100, 101,
102, 105; and Herri Batasuna
negotiations, 125; and Martín
Barrio killing, 136; and social
reintegration programs, 111, 112,
113, 114, 158–159
Etxabe, Jon, 84, 85, 86
Etxebarrieta, Xabi, 9
Etxebeste, Eugenio, "Antxon," 143,
148, 220; and Algerian negotiations, 184, 193, 213, 214,
221; arrest of, 62–63, 69, 141,
172; Ballestero talks, 190–192,
195–196, 197; Elgorriaga talks,
198–202, 212, 219, 235
Etxenike, Pedro Miguel, 135
European Community, 33, 206
Euskal Iraultzale Alderdia (EIA),
21, 77, 79, 81, 82, 94, 95, 96. See
also Basque political parties
Euskera (Basque language), 80, 82,
114, 148
Eusko Alkartasuna (EA), 12, 20, 24,
151, 189; and antiterrorist pacts,
70, 200, 203, 204, 206, 207, 209,
210, 211, 212. See also Basque
political parties
Euzkadiko Ezkerra (EE), 12, 19–
20, 77, 89, 94; and antiterrorist
pacts, 203; and CAV ten-point
statement, 155; and cease-fires,
103, 104, 105–106; and international experts' study, 157; and
negotiation attempts, 79, 92, 94,
95, 126–127, 129, 141; on political negotiations, 149; and social
reintegration program, 108, 112,
114. See also Basque political
parties
Euzkadi ta Askatasuna. See ETA

Fando, Christianne, 174, 175, 177
Fernández Ordóñez, Francisco, 190
Ferracuti, Franco, 156
Fraga, Manuel, 28, 29, 53, 93
France: Basques in, 16, 30–31, 112,
187; Spanish relations with, 27,
61, 122. See also French anti-
ETA policies; French deportation
policies; French extradition
policies; Guerra sucia
Franco, Francisco, 9, 10, 28, 37–38,
40, 64, 73; and GAL, 66
French anti-ETA policies, 14, 36,
37, 39–40, 46–47; and Algerian
negotiations, 217; and antiterrorist pacts, 205, 206; arrest
sweeps, 16, 62, 71, 139, 151, 205,
217; under Chirac, 68, 69; ETA
communiqué, 193; and ETA
negotiation offers, 168; French
public opinion, 205; and guerra
sucia, 31; Iturbe arrest, 171–172;
under Mitterrand, 51–52, 133; as
pressure for negotiations, 139–
140; and Spanish government
negotiations offers, 142; Spanish
pressure for, 61–62, 65, 89, 136,
197. See also French deportation policies; French extradition
policies
French deportation policies, 14,
16–17, 63; and Algerian negotiations, 200; and Etxebeste
leadership, 69, 199; and guerra
sucia, 31, 62, 64; Iturbe deportation, 172, 174–176; and Martín
Barrios killing, 106; as pressure

for negotiations, 139–140, 141; six-stage negotiation calendar, 147. *See also* French extradition policies

French extradition policies, 36, 40, 47, 139, 147, 172; under Chirac, 68, 69, 71; and *guerra sucia*, 31, 62, 63, 64, 68; under Mitterrand, 51, 52, 59–60, 68; and social reintegration programs, 161

Gabon, 174–175, 177, 178

GAL. *See* Grupos Antiterroristas de Libaración

GAR. *See* Rural Antiterrorist Groups

Garaikoetxea, Carlos, 5, 18, 20, 137, 142; and antiterrorist pacts, 207, 209, 210, 211; *mesa para la paz*, 117, 126–132, 136, 167; resignation of, 151, 152

Garalde, Isidoro María, "Mamarru," 69, 139

Garayalde, Javier, 78

Garcia Andoain, Genaro, 168–169, 173, 174, 177, 179–180

Garcia Damborenea, Ricardo, 129

García Ramírez, Juan Carlos, 63

Geneva Convention of 1951, 65

GEO. *See* Special Operations Group

Gestoras Pro-Amnistía, 13, 22, 55, 65, 78, 160

Gil Albert, José María, 110

Goiburu Mendizabal, Juan Miguel, 102, 140, 167–168

Goikoetxea, José Ramón, 65–66

González, Felipe, 5, 25, 155, 199; and Algerian negotiations, 191–192, 197–198, 199; antiterrorist measures under, 37, 52, 53, 70, 117; and antiterrorist pacts, 203, 204–205, 206; denials of negotiations, 123–124, 177; and French antiterrorist policy, 61, 68, 200; and human rights violations, 55, 56; and Iturbe imprisonment, 173, 176; *mesa para la paz*, 128; and negotiation attempts, 86, 88, 90, 108, 124–126, 142, 143; on political negotiations, 150

González Catarain, María Dolores, "Yoyes," 162–163, 179, 196

González Peñalba, Belen, 185

Gorostidi, Jokin, 79, 140–141, 143, 169

Great Britain, 156

GRUPO 16, 140

Grupos Antiterroristas de Libaración (GAL), 14, 33, 64, 136, 149, 150; and Brouard killing, 144, 229; disappearance of, 68, 69; and international experts' study, 157; six-stage negotiation calendar, 147; Spanish government involvement in, 59, 62, 66–68, 193

Guardia Civil. *See* Law enforcement, Basque goals for

Guardia Civil coup attempt, 24, 25, 118; and amnesty negotiations, 107, 108; and antiterrorist measures, 37, 47, 93; and cease-fire, 96–97, 101

Guerra, Alfonso, 150

Guerra sucia, 33, 36, 39, 58, 67, 147; Bandrés role in, 149; and Brouard killing, 52, 66; and ETA technical truce, 150; and French antiterrorist policies, 31, 62, 63, 64, 68; and international experts' study, 157; and Barrios killing, 58, 62, 136; and Portell killing, 43, 89; Spanish government involvement in, 27, 31, 59, 62, 66–68, 193

Guimon, Julen, 204, 210

Guzman, Juan Pedro, 171

HASI. *See* Basque Popular Socialist Party

HB. *See* Herri Batasuna

Hernandez Mancha, Antonio, 205
Herri Batasuna (HB), 12, 20–21, 25,
54, 149; and Algerian negotiations, 182, 191, 195, 213–214,
215, 218; and antiterrorist legislation, 65, 70; and antiterrorist
pacts, 202, 203, 206, 207, 208,
209, 210, 211; on Basque self-
determination, 148; CAV, rejection of, 18, 19, 21, 128–129, 153,
208; and CAV ten-point statement, 153, 155; and cease-fires,
98; electoral participation, 134,
141; and ETA, 120, 194, 238;
and GRUPO 16 meeting, 140;
on guerra sucia, 59; intermediary offers, 117, 120, 121, 124,
125–132, 150; and international
experts' study, 157; and Iturbe
deportation, 174; legalization
of, 167; and Navarrese autonomous community, 23–24; and
negotiation attempts, 84, 135,
136–137, 140–141, 153; PNV
meetings, 167, 168, 169–170,
173; and political negotiations,
142, 201, 213; popularity of, 89,
199; Spanish repression of, 58,
121; and two-track negotiation
strategy, 21, 142, 149, 235, 238
Horchem, Hans, 156
Human rights concerns, 3, 22,
36, 55–56, 65, 96; and Algerian
negotiations, 180; Amnesty
International investigations, 14,
32–33, 43, 49–50, 56, 66; and
antiterrorist legislation, 41, 49–
50; decrease in interest, 38–39;
and French extradition policy,
52, 60; and international experts'
study, 157; and negotiations,
130; Rosón role, 107; Spanish
courts role, 27; and Spanish
intelligence agencies, 26, 122;
Spanish parliament role, 25, 91

Ibarguren, Carlos, "Nervios," 60,
62, 172, 175
Ibarra Guell, Pedro, 11, 22, 120
Ibarzabal, Eugenio, 111, 119, 132–
133, 134–135, 136, 156–157,
176
Ideology: action-repression spiral
theory, 8–10, 231; revolutionary
war thesis, 1, 7–8, 231; two-stage
theory of struggle, 11, 81, 231
Idígoras, Jon, 121, 134, 140–141,
167; and negotiation attempts,
120, 169, 218
Incontrolados, 39, 43. See also
Guerra sucia
Independent negotiators, 12, 22,
228–229
Industrialization, 9–10
Infante, Juan, 108, 113, 133–134
Insausti, Jesús, 148, 169
Institute for the Study of Conflict,
156
Interest groups, multiplicity of,
11–15, 226–227. See also indi-
vidual groups
International cooperation, 33, 200,
204, 206. See also France and
French headings
International experts' study, 152,
154–157, 166
International media, 14, 32
Iparretarrak (the Northerners), 16
Iraeta, Josu, 204
Iriarte, Eusebio, 73, 74
Italy, 57, 87, 109, 133, 134
Iturbe, Angel, 165, 171
Iturbe, Txomin, 43, 86, 151; and
Algerian negotiations, 179, 180–
182, 183–184, 193, 195; death of,
59, 185–186, 187, 196; deporta-
tion of, 31, 165, 174, 177–179;
imprisonment of, 52, 60, 69, 165,
166, 169, 170–174; and nego-
tiation attempts, 142, 144, 145,
147, 149, 150; and social reinte-

gration programs, 163, 181–182;
sympathy to negotiations, 139,
141, 167–168
IU. *See* Izquierda Unida
Izaguirre, Markel, 169
Izquierda Unida (IU), 13, 29, 203

Jaime, Antton, 100, 101
Janke, Peter, 156
JARRAI, 21
Jáuregui, Ramon, 135
Jáuregui Bereciartu, Gurutz, 132
Juan Carlos (king of Spain), 13,
237; and antiterrorist legislation,
38, 41, 64; defense of democracy,
24, 47, 77; ETA demonstrations
against, 95–96, 121; negotiation
offer (1975), 73–75
Juanra (Juan Ramón Aramburu
Garmendia), 69, 149–150, 151,
172

KAS. *See* Koordinadora Abertzale
Sozialista
KAS Alternative, 12, 37, 82–83, 89,
91, 119; and Algerian negotiations, 182, 183, 194, 195, 199,
216; CAV discussion of, 149;
and democratic transition, 80–
82; ETA insistence on, 143, 145,
194, 220, 231, 232; Herri Batasuna insistence on, 20, 120, 125,
128, 129, 130, 141, 148, 167,
170; 1986 revisions of, 166; and
six-stage negotiation calendar,
147; Spanish response to, 83,
136, 137, 166; and two-stage
theory of struggle, 11; and two-
track negotiation strategy, 239.
See also Political negotiations
Koordinadora Abertzale Sozialista
(KAS), 12, 21–22, 78–79, 82, 114;
and ETA, 120, 194; and negotiation attempts, 87, 214. *See also*
KAS Alternative

LAB. *See* Patriotic Workers Coun-
cil
Labor organizations, 10, 75
Lago Roman, Victor, 124, 125
LAIA. *See* Patriotic Revolutionary
Workers Party
LAK. *See* Patriotic Workers Com-
mittee
Lara, José Mari, 111
Larretxea, José María, 62, 136
Lasa, José Antonio, 58, 59
Lasa, Juan, 212
Lasa Mitxelena, Juan Lorenzo
Santiago, "Txikierdi," 69, 139
Law enforcement, Basque goals for,
18, 118, 119, 149, 167, 181, 238;
Algerian negotiations, 199, 202,
215, 216; ETA (p-m) demands,
91, 92, 97; KAS Alternative,
82; Madrid antiterrorist pact,
204; *mesa para la paz,* 128; and
six-stage negotiation calendar,
148; and two-track negotiation
strategy, 114, 239. *See also* Span-
ish government law enforcement
policy
Leaute, Jacques, 156
Lemoiz nuclear plant, 47, 50, 95,
97, 98
Linaza, Tomás, 51
LOAPA (Organic Law for the Harmonization of the Autonomy
Process), 101. *See also* Basque
self-determination
Lopetegi, Mikel, 70
Lopez, Iñaki, 197
Lopez, Txema, 68
Lujambio, Francisco, 63

Madrid antiterrorist pact, 70, 194,
200, 202–207
Mamarru (Isidoro María Garalde),
69, 139
Manzanas, Melitón, 9
Marco Tobar, Alfredo, 204, 210

Marey, Segundo, 59
Martín Barrios, Alberto, killing of:
    and antiterrorist policies, 53, 58,
    61, 64; and French antiterrorist
    policies, 61–62, 106; and *guerra
    sucia*, 58, 62, 136; and negotia-
    tion attempts, 133; and social
    reintegration programs, 159
Martínez Beiztegi, José Manuel, 63
Martínez Suárez, Pedro, 183
Martínez Torres, Jesús, 26, 180,
    191, 193
Martín Villa, Rodolfo, 26, 95; and
    antiterrorist policies, 40, 42, 89;
    and negotiation attempts, 83, 84,
    85, 86, 88
Martorell, Joaquin Domingo, 140
Marxism, 15
Mass organizations, 8, 10
Mayor Oreja, Jaime, 155
Mendizabal, Eustakio, 9
Mesa para la paz, 117, 126–132,
    136, 167
Milis. *See* ETA (militar)
Military. *See* Law enforcement,
    Basque goals for; Spanish govern-
    ment
Miranda, Ana, 202
Mitterrand, François, 51–52, 61,
    68, 200
MLNV. *See* Movimiento de Libera-
    ción Nacional Vasco
Monforte, Andoni, 100, 101
Moran, Fernando, 61
Moreno Bergareche, Eduardo,
    "Pertur," 5, 10, 75–77, 78
Movimiento de Liberación Na-
    cional Vasco (MLNV), 193–194,
    215, 216, 238
Múgica Garmendia, Francisco,
    "Artapalo," 149–150, 169, 187,
    196–197, 220
Munoa, Jesús Mari, 78

National Liberation Front (Algeria),
    178

Navarrese integration, 91, 92, 98,
    128, 167, 239; Algerian negotia-
    tions, 184, 191, 199, 202; and
    antiterrorist pacts, 205, 208,
    209; KAS Alternative, 120, 140–
    141, 166; Navarrese attitude,
    13, 23–24; six-stage negotia-
    tion calendar, 147, 148. *See also*
    Political negotiations
Negotiation attempts, 1–2, 224–
    226; Ballesteros attempt (PSOE),
    134–135; Barrionuevo offer,
    141–142, 149; Basque political
    parties' attitudes toward, 20;
    benefits of, 2–3; conversation
    strategy, 188–189; and demo-
    cratic transition, 77–78, 81–82,
    187–188, 199; and ETA legiti-
    macy, 2, 83, 87, 183, 188; French
    interest in, 139, 141; Garcia An-
    doain talks, 168–169, 173, 174,
    177, 179–180; GRUPO 16 meet-
    ing, 140; HB intermediary offers,
    120, 121, 124, 125–132, 150; HB-
    PNV meetings, 167, 168, 169–
    170, 173; internal conflicts over,
    10, 76, 77, 79, 94; and Iturbe
    imprisonment, 165, 166, 169,
    170–171, 173, 176; *mesa para
    la paz*, 117, 126–132, 136, 167;
    obstacles to, 226–239; Onainda
    offer (1984), 141; Operation
    Wellington, 145–148; six-stage
    calendar, 144; two-track strategy,
    149, 201, 216, 219; under UCD,
    83–87, 90, 91, 93, 119. *See also*
    Cease-fires; Algerian negotia-
    tions; negotiation attempts
    headings under other subjects;
    Social reintegration program
Nervios (Carlos Ibarguren), 60, 62,
    172, 175
North Atlantic Treaty Organiza-
    tion (NATO), 199
Núñez, Luis, 181, 182

Octavos. See ETA (político-militar) VIII

Olarra, Luis, 67

Oliberi, Iñaki, 204, 210, 211

Onaindia, Mario, 79, 95, 155; and Bandrés-Rosón amnesty negotiations, 94, 107, 110; and negotiation attempts, 92, 114, 126–127, 132, 141, 233

Onederra, Ramón, 59

Operation Wellington, 145–148

Oreja, Marcelino, 74

Ormaza, Josu, 63

Otaegi, Angel, 21

Otero Novas, José Manuel, 78, 79

Pagoaga Gallastegui, José Manuel, "Peixoto," 78, 113

Paredes Manot, Jon, 21

Partido Comunista de España (PCE), 13, 29

Partido Demócrata Popular (PDP), 203

Partido Liberal (PL), 203

Partido Nacionalista Vasco (PNV), 8, 9, 12, 95, 157, 199; and antiterrorist pacts, 203, 204, 206–207, 208, 210, 211; and cease-fires, 98, 99, 100, 149; and democratic transition, 82; on *guerra sucia,* 59; HB meetings, 167, 168, 169–170, 173; and negotiation attempts, 89, 92, 99, 127, 129, 148, 169–170, 176; and PSE, 18, 19, 28, 152–153, 156, 168, 185, 205. *See also* Basque political parties

Partido Popular (PP), 13, 28–29, 155; and antiterrorist pacts, 203, 204, 207–208, 209, 210

Partido Socialista de Euskadi (PSE), 18, 19, 28, 84, 120; and PNV, 18, 19, 28, 152–153, 156, 168, 185, 205

Partido Socialista Obrero Español (PSOE), 13, 25, 28, 95, 122;

and Algerian negotiations, 201–202, 213; antiterrorist measures under, 28, 37, 52, 53, 57, 64–65, 117, 122, 133–134, 136; and antiterrorist pacts, 208, 209; and negotiation attempts, 124–126, 127, 134, 135; refusals to negotiate, 123–124. *See also* Negotiation attempts; Partido Socialista de Euskadi (PSE); Spanish government

Pascua, Charles, 171

Patriotic Revolutionary Workers Party (LAIA), 21

Patriotic Socialist Coordinating Council (KAS). *See* Koordinadora Abertzale Sozialista

Patriotic Workers Committee (LAK), 21

Patriotic Workers Council (LAB), 21

PCE. *See* Partido Comunista de España

PDP. *See* Partido Demócrata Popular

Peio el viejo (Pello Larrañaga Ansola), 60, 62, 172, 175

Peixoto (José Manuel Pagoaga Gallastegui), 78, 113

Pérez, Carlos Andrés, 237

Pérez Arenaza, Javier, 59

Pérez Revilla, Tomás, 59

Pertur (Eduardo Moreno Bergareche), 5, 10, 75–77, 78, 94, 186

Pikabea, José Ignacio, 71

PL. *See* Partido Liberal

Plan ZEN, 57, 136

PNV. *See* Partido Nacionalista Vasco

Police. *See* Law enforcement, Basque goals for

Poli-milis. *See* ETA (político-militar)

Political negotiations: and Algerian negotiations, 200–201, 202, 213, 216; and antiterrorist pacts,

Political negotiations (*cont'd*) 203–204, 208, 212; CAV rejection of, 152, 156–157, 213; EE attitude towards, 149; ETA insistence on, 142, 150, 194, 232; and international experts' study, 157; lack of success, 3–4; Spanish government attitudes toward, 13, 27, 114, 184, 189, 192, 197, 200–201, 213; and Spanish political parties, 13, 29. *See also* KAS Alternative; Two-track negotiation strategy

Popular support for ETA, 2, 9–10, 95, 122, 142

Popular Unity. *See* Herri Batasuna (HB)

Porres, Juan, 204

Portell, José María, 84, 86. *See also* Portell killing

Portell killing, 5, 22, 43, 85–86, 146; and antiterrorist policies, 36, 40, 227; and negotiation attempts, 80, 87, 186, 227, 229

PP. *See* Partido Popular

Prat, José, 146, 147

Prisoners, 8, 12, 36; transfers of, 90–91, 103, 118–119, 125, 159. *See also* Amnesty; Arrest rates; Human rights concerns

Pro-Amnesty Committees. *See* Gestoras Pro-Amnistía

Pro-Human Rights Association of the Basque Country, 55

"Propaganda of the deed," 7

PSE. *See* Partido Socialista de Euskadi

PSOE. *See* Partido Socialista Obrero Español

Retolaza, Luis María, 169, 173, 174

Revilla, Emiliano, 219–221

"Revolutionary tax," 3, 67, 98, 122, 147

Revolutionary war thesis, 1, 7–8, 231

Rose, Clive, 156

Rosón, Juan José, 26, 51, 88, 92, 121; Bandrés amnesty negotiations, 103, 106, 107–115, 124, 133, 162, 233; human rights, 49, 107

Rosón, Luís, 144

Ruíz Jiménez, Joaquin, 159

Ruíz Pinedo, Iñaki, 167

Rupérez, Javier, 91

Rural Antiterrorist Groups (GAR), 42

Ryan, José María, 47, 95–96

Saenz de Santa María, José Antonio, 142

Sainz González, José, 83

Sanchez Erauskin, Javier, 53–54

Sancristobal, Julián, 26, 183, 193, 195

Santi (Santiago Brouard), 121, 143

Santi Potros (Santiago Arrospide), 71, 187, 196, 198, 205

Selective amnesty. *See* Social reintegration programs

Self-determination. *See* Basque self-determination

Séptimos. See ETA (político-militar) VII

Six-stage negotiation calendar, 144, 147–148

Socialist International, 60

Social reintegration programs, 15, 55, 70, 149, 153; and antiterrorist pacts, 204, 208; Azkarraga negotiations, 140, 158–163; Bandrés-Rosón negotiations, 93–94, 98, 103, 106, 107–115, 162; CAV support for, 167; ETA reactions, 110–111, 112–113, 181–182; and ETA violence, 106, 159, 160; PSOE attitudes, 124; Spanish courts role in, 27; and Spanish government negotiation offers, 142–143, 197

Solana, Javier, 123, 192, 197, 216

Solaun, Mikel, 162
Solchaga, Carlos, 88
Sotillos, Eduardo, 135, 144
Spanish-Basque Battalion (BVE).
   See Batallón Vasco-Español
Spanish Civil War, 10
Spanish court system, 27–28, 41
Spanish government, 13, 24–28;
   intelligence activities, 26, 42,
   58, 122, 144, 145–148, 150, 151;
   and Iturbe imprisonment/depor-
   tation, 170–171, 174, 175–176,
   178–179; KAS Alternative, response to, 83; parliament, 13, 25,
   91; refusals to negotiate, 88–92,
   121, 123, 149. *See also* Amnesty;
   Antiterrorist legislation; Democratic transition; Guardia Civil
   coup attempt; Law enforcement;
   negotiation attempts headings
   under other subjects; Spanish
   government law enforcement
   policy; Spanish political parties
Spanish government law enforcement policy, 27, 36, 58, 142, 154;
   under Franco, 9, 39, 40; Plan
   ZEN, 56–57; under PSOE, 52,
   122, 197; under UCD, 42, 50–51
Spanish media, 13, 14, 30, 229–
   230; legal restrictions on, 35–36,
   48, 53
Spanish political parties, 13, 25,
   28–30, 122; antiterrorist pacts,
   70, 194, 200, 202–212. *See also*
   Spanish government
Spanish socialist party, Basque
   wing (PSE). *See* Partido Socialista de Euskadi
Spanish Socialist Workers Party
   (PSOE). *See* Partido Socialista
   Obrero Español
Special Operations Group (GEO),
   42
Suárez, Adolfo, 25, 29, 36, 58, 74;
   and antiterrorist pacts, 203; and
   democratic transition, 78, 79;

and negotiation attempts, 77, 78,
   81, 85, 86, 88–89, 90, 95

Torture. *See* Human rights concerns
Trevi Group, 33
Truces. *See* Cease-fires
Two-stage theory of struggle, 11,
   81, 231
Two-track negotiation strategy,
   21, 142, 149, 234, 235–239; and
   Algerian negotiations, 216, 219,
   233; GRUPO 16 agreement,
   140; origination of, 114–115,
   201–202. *See also* Political negotiations
Txelis (José Luis Alvarez Santacristina), 197
Txikierdi (Juan Lorenzo Santiago
   Lasa Mitxelena), 69, 139

UCD. *See* Unión del Centro
   Democrático
Unión del Centro Democrático
   (UCD), 13, 23, 24–25, 26, 95;
   antiterrorist policy under, 36–
   38, 40–42, 47–49, 89; decline
   of, 90, 118, 119; negotiation at-
   tempts under, 83–87, 90, 91, 93,
   119. *See also* Spanish govern-
   ment; Spanish political parties
Unión del Pueblo Navarro (UPN),
   23
Union of Socialist Parties (France),
   61
United Left (UI). *See* Izquierda
   Unida
United States, 156
Unzueta, Patxo, 102, 168
UPN. *See* Unión del Pueblo
   Navarro
Uriarte, Teo, 79
Urruticoechea Bengoechea, José
   Antonio, 196

Venezuela, 237

Vera, Rafael, 26, 55, 56–57, 135, 136, 142; and Algerian negotiations, 180, 190, 191, 212–213, 215; and French policy, 61; and negotiation attempts, 142, 189, 235

Violence. *See* ETA violence; *Guerra sucia*

Vitoria antiterrorist pact, 207–212

Vizcaya, Marcos, 53

Waldo (José Javier Zabaleta Elosegui), 197

Working class: ETA goals, 10, 75, 80, 82, 83, 167; PSOE mobilization, 122

World Cup soccer matches, 118, 121

Ybarra, Javier, 79

Yoyes (María Dolores González Catarain), 162–163, 179, 196

Zabala, José Ignacio, 58, 59

Zabaleta Elosegui, José Javier, "Waldo," 197

Zabalza, Mikel, 66

Ziluaga, Txomin, 98, 121, 157, 174; and negotiation attempts, 120, 167, 169

Zona Especial del Norte, 57

Zotza (Joseba Aulestia), 113